Taking Action!

2nd Edition

About IPSEA

IPSEA was established in 1983 and provides free advice to parents of children with special educational needs. Through its telephone advice lines and its networks of volunteers covering England, Wales and Northern Ireland*, IPSEA offers a range of support to parents, including:

- advice on the rights of children and young people with special educational needs and their parents

- free independent second professional opinions on children's special educational needs

- free advice and support for parents appealing to the Special Educational Needs Tribunal

For further information write to:

IPSEA, 4 Ancient House Mews, Woodbridge, Suffolk IP12 1DH

IPSEA is a registered Charity (No 327691) and a Limited Company (No 2198066), and relies on grants and donations for all of its work.

*Note: this guide does not apply to Scotland or Northern Ireland

Taking Action!

Your child's right to special education

A guide for parents, teachers, advocates and advice workers

John Wright and David Ruebain

2nd Edition

The Questions Publishing Company Ltd
Birmingham
MM

First published in 2000 by
The Questions Publishing Company Ltd
27 Frederick Street, Birmingham B1 3HH

© 2000 John Wright and David Ruebain

Edited by Brian Asbury
Designed by Al Stewart
Cover design by James Davies

ISBN: 1-84190-010-9

Acknowledgements

Part 3, *Appealing to the Special Educational Needs Tribunal*, was written by
Sally Capper.

Thanks to David Phillips for help with proof-reading the law, and to Sally
Capper for her comments on the text.

Extracts from the Education Act 1996, The Education (Special Educational
Needs) Regulations 1994, and The Special Educational Needs Tribunal
Regulations 1995 are reproduced with the permission of the Controller
of Her Majesty's Stationery Office.

Dedication

This book was written to help parents and carers who are struggling to get the special educational provision their children are legally entitled to. It is dedicated to them and to their children.

Contents

Notes on the text

The 'he's and 'she's

In English law, everyone is a 'he', therefore where we quote from special education law all children, parents and professionals will be male. Elsewhere in our text we have interchanged gender in order to avoid the risk of stereotyping and for the sake of variety. For the record, in IPSEA's case work the majority of children with special educational needs are boys and the majority of parents taking on the responsibility for sorting out problems with LEAs are their mothers.

Citations

The cases which are referred to in this book all include what are known as their citations. These are the letters and numbers that appear after the name of each case, which are used by lawyers to trace the judgments. When writing to a Local Education Authority or school, you do not usually need to quote the citation of the case, as well as the name, but sometimes it is useful to do so if you would like their lawyers to read the judgment. It is also useful for you to give the full case name, including the citation, to any solicitors who become involved on your behalf.

Part 1

First, find your problem

First, find your problem . . . or one which sounds similar, from the 40 problems set out below.

Then, turn to the case number in Part 2, where we suggest steps you can take to deal with it.

If your child has special educational needs but no statement . . .

These are some of the problems you might face when your child has special educational needs, but has not been assessed by the Local Education Authority and does not have a statement of special educational needs.

1. "The LEA say they have no responsibility for under 2s."

2. "The LEA say they won't assess our child until she starts school."

3. "The school won't accept our child has special educational needs."

4. "We believe our son has serious learning difficulties, but the school won't ask the educational psychologist to see him."

5. "Our daughter isn't getting the help at school which her Individual Education Plan says she should get."

6. "I've asked for my daughter to be withdrawn from the class to receive help, but the school won't agree to it."

7. "The school want the LEA to assess my child, but I don't."

8. "The head wants our daughter to be moved to a special

2

school while the LEA do an assessment and before a statement is issued."

9. "The LEA refuse to assess my nephew – they say his problem is caused by his lack of English, not special needs, and that he has not been through the school-based stages."

10. "The LEA won't assess our son because they say 'his needs are not severe and complex and he isn't one of the 2%'."

11. "The school asked the LEA to assess my son, but nothing has happened."

When an LEA assessment is under way . . .

These are some of the problems you might face while your LEA are assessing your child under the 1996 Education Act.

12. "The assessment has just started but I suspect that the LEA are not going to keep to the deadlines."

13. "The assessment is delayed and the LEA blame the Health Authority for not sending in their advice report on time."

14. "We have been given confusing information on the educational psychologist's power to do an examination without our permission, and on our right to be present at an examination."

15. "We are not happy with the way the assessment is going and would like to stop it."

When the assessment is finished but there's no statement . . .

This is a common problem parents face when the assessment is finished.

16. "The LEA say the school can meet our child's needs from their own resources, so there's no need for a statement. The school says they can't."

When the assessment is finished and you are sent the proposed statement . . .

These are some of the problems you might face when you receive the proposed statement and copies of the professional advice.

17. "The psychologist told us verbally what provision our son needs, but said nothing about provision in the written advice."

18. "The local school has made it plain they don't want our son and the LEA Officer says it's best not to force them. But that's the school we want for him."

19. "The proposed statement is fine, but the head says there'll be no help till the statement is finalised."

20. "The proposed statement is full of hints that our son should go to a special school, which is going to make it hard to ask for a place in our local school."

21. "Part 2 of the statement does not describe our daughter's needs in any detail at all."

22. "Part 3 of the statement does not give any detail of the provision our son is to get and it leaves the decision up to the school."

23. "We have been told we can't express a preference for an independent school, but that's exactly what we believe is needed."

24. "Speech therapy is listed in Part 2 as one of our daughter's special educational needs, but the provision is written under Part 6 as a 'non-educational provision'."

25. "The speech therapist's advice says our son's need for speech therapy is educational, not medical, but the

statement lists it under Parts 5 and 6 as 'non-educational'."

26. "We want a school in the neighbouring LEA, but they've told our LEA that it's full."

27. "We disagree with the description of our son's needs in Part 2."

28. "We do not understand what kind of help, or how much, our child is going to get, because Part 3 is so vaguely written."

When the LEA send the final statement . . .

These are some of the problems you might face when the LEA finalise the statement .

29. "The LEA have refused our request for a place in our local mainstream school. Instead, they want to bus our daughter 52 miles a day."

30. "The statement names an LEA special school when we know that they cannot make the provision our daughter needs. This can only be made at a specialist independent school."

Your child already has a statement of special educational needs . . .

These are some of the problems you might face even though your child has a statement .

31. "We have lost our appeal to the Tribunal to have speech therapy moved to Part 3 of our son's statement – what else can we do?"

32. "My son is not getting the provision which Part 3 of his statement says he should get."

33. "The LEA have proposed an amendment to the statement

saying that the first five hours of our son's help are to be paid for by the school. The school say they can't afford it."

34. "Our son refuses to go to school. We asked the LEA for a fresh assessment. They refused and sent an Attendance Order."

35. "Our daughter has been excluded from her special school. What now?"

36. "We moved 6 months ago but the new LEA still haven't given our son the provision the old LEA's statement says he should have."

37. "Our daughter is coming up to secondary transfer, and we are worried because no decision on her next school has been made."

38. "It's time for our son's statement review. How can we best influence the outcome of the review?"

39. "After six years in a special school we want our son to have a chance in a mainstream school – but the LEA disagree."

40. "Our son is coming up to 16 and the LEA say he must leave school and that his statement will lapse then – but what about his needs?"

If your problem is not here . . .

Sorry . . . turn to the list of Helpline organisations in part 7 for advice. Also see the index on page 325.

Part 2

The cases

Case 1

66 Our daughter was born with spina bifida and, although she has just turned one year old, both the family doctor and our social worker have advised us to find out what help might be available from the LEA. But when we met with an Education Welfare Officer to discuss Clara's needs, we were told that the LEA had no responsibility towards children under 2 and that we were wasting our time by going to them. 99

The first step

The EWO was wrong. LEAs have a duty towards children with special educational needs from birth. Your first step should be to write to the Special Needs Officer asking for the LEA's published information about their special educational provision and asking for a meeting with the Officer to discuss what help they can offer Clara. Your letter could start like this:

Dear Sir or Madam,

I am writing as the parent of a child with special educational needs to ask for the information on special education provision which I understand every LEA has a legal duty to publish. Also, I would like to arrange a meeting with you, after I have had a chance to read through your published information, to discuss with you the particular needs of my daughter, Clara, who is 18 months old ... (then give some details about Clara, including the fact that the doctor and the social worker have suggested that you contact the LEA).

Yours sincerely

Ask your social worker to come with you to the meeting with the Special Needs Officer.

If that doesn't work

If you are not happy with the information you receive from the LEA, or if the meeting with the Officer gets you nowhere, you will have to decide whether or not to ask the LEA to do an assessment of Clara's special educational needs.

But before doing this you should contact one of the Helpline organisations listed in part 7 to discuss the pros and cons of having Clara assessed, and possibly 'statemented'. Also, see the PS below.

An assessment of a child under 2 can take whatever form the LEA decides, and so can the statement (if they issue one). However, the Code of Practice sets out a bare minimum of information which LEA statements on children under 2 should contain.

2

Case

1

What the law says

The Education (School Information) Regulations 1998 say:

'Information to be published by authorities:

14. The authority's detailed arrangements and policies in respect of –

a)   the identification and assessment of children with special educational needs and the involvement of parents in that process . . .
c)   special educational provision provided otherwise than at school . . .

16. The arrangements for parents who consider that their child may have special educational needs to obtain further advice and further information.'

Section 331 of the 1996 Education Act says:

2

**Case
1**

'(1) Where a local education authority are of the opinion that a child in their area who is under the age of two falls, or probably falls, within subsection (2) –

(a) they may, with the consent of his parent, make an assessment of the child's educational needs, and
(b) they shall make such an assessment if requested to do so by his parent.

(2) A child falls within this subsection if –

(a) he has special educational needs, and
(b) it is necessary for the authority to determine the special educational provision which any learning difficulty he may have calls for.

(3) An assessment under this section shall be made in such manner as the authority consider appropriate.

(4) After making an assessment under this section, the authority –

(a) may make a statement of the child's special educational needs, and
(b) may maintain that statement, in such manner as they consider appropriate.'

What the Code of Practice says

'If a decision is made to issue a statement (on a child under 2) . . . it should include:

● all available information about the child, with a clear specification of the child's special educational needs

● a record of the views of the parents and any relevant professionals

- a clear account of the services being offered, including the contribution of the education service and the educational objectives to be secured, and the contribution of any statutory and voluntary agencies, and

- a description of the arrangements for monitoring and review.'

(Paragraph 5:6)

2

Case

1

PostScript

The law gives LEAs the right to decide whether or not to assess individual children, but they must make each decision on the basis of the needs of the individual child concerned. The law does not allow LEAs to operate a policy which rules out assessment for whole groups of children – for example, for all children not yet old enough to attend a school.

If you suspect at any time that your LEA are making a decision on the wrong basis, get advice from one of the Helpline organisations listed in part 7. You do not need to know anything about the law to get the feeling that something is not quite fair, or reasonable. When you get that feeling, it costs nothing to get further advice. See also the PS for Case 10.

Case 2

66 Our son, Ashraf, is three and a half years old. He has Down's Syndrome and has been attending a nursery school, without specialist support, for around six months. The head of the nursery told us that they can't provide any additional help and suggested that we ask the LEA for an assessment under the 1996 Education Act. However, the educational psychologist says that the Authority's policy is to wait until children start school before doing special educational needs assessments. But we were hoping an assessment would lead to Ashraf being given extra support for his learning, now, in the nursery. 99

The first step

The decision to assess a child is made by the Education Office of the LEA, not by an individual educational psychologist, although the LEA may seek his or her views before making their decision. You should write directly to the Chief Education Officer, asking for an assessment. Your letter could start like this:

Dear Sir or Madam,

I am writing as the parent of a child with special educational needs to ask for an assessment under section 329 of the 1996 Education Act. My child's name is Ashraf . . . and his date of birth is . . . My reasons for wanting an assessment are . . .

The LEA must reply to your letter within six weeks. They must agree to your request for an assessment, unless they believe that an assessment is not 'necessary'. This decision must be made with reference to Ashraf's special educational needs, not his age nor any policy which the LEA may have with regard to children not yet on the roll of a school.

If that doesn't work

If the LEA refuse to do an assessment, you will have the right to appeal to the Special Educational Needs Tribunal (see part 3 of this book for advice on this). You will need evidence that Ashraf has special educational needs which the nursery cannot meet from its own resources. Speak to the head of the nursery, who may be able to provide evidence and may also agree to appear as a witness for you at an appeal. If in doubt, speak to someone from one of the Helpline organisations listed in part 7.

What the law says

Section 329 of the 1996 Education Act says:

'(1) Where –

(a) the parent of a child for whom a local education authority are responsible but for whom no statement is maintained under section 324 asks the authority to arrange for an assessment to be made in respect of the child under section 323,

(b) no such assessment has been made within the period of six months ending with the date on which the request is made, and

(c) it is necessary for the authority to make an assessment under that section,

– the authority shall comply with the request.

(2) If in any case where subsection (1)(a) and (b) applies the authority determine not to comply with the request –

(a) they shall give notice of that fact and of the effect of paragraph (b) below to the child's parent, and

(b) the parent may appeal to the Tribunal against the determination.'

2

Case 2

Regulation 11 of the Education (Special Educational Needs) Regulations 1994 says:

'(3) Where under sections 328(2) or 329(1) a parent asks the authority to arrange for an assessment to be made under section 323 they shall within 6 weeks of the date of receipt of the request give notice to the child's parent –

(a) under section 323(4) of their decision to make an assessment, or

(b) under section 328(3)(a) or 329(2)(a) respectively of their decision not to comply with the request and of the parent's right to appeal to the Tribunal against the determination.'

What the Code of Practice says

'In deciding whether to make a statutory assessment, the critical question for LEAs will be whether there is convincing evidence that, despite the school, with the help of external specialists, taking relevant and purposeful action to meet the child's learning difficulties, those difficulties remain or have not been remedied sufficiently and may require the LEA to determine the child's special educational provision.'

(Paragraph 3:49)

Post Script

A statement of special educational needs is a two-edged sword.

On the one hand, a statement may be the only way that you can get your child the help he or she needs. You have the right to be consulted about the way your child's needs are described in a statement and, at the end of the day, the statement should guarantee that the help needed will in fact be given. If you are not happy with the statement, you can appeal to the Tribunal and, as a result, may get the statement rewritten.

On the other hand, some parents worry about their child being stigmatised by having a statement. And, if you end up with a statement which names a school which you think will not meet your child's needs, or may even perhaps be damaging for your child, you will have real problems deciding what to do if your appeal to the Tribunal fails.

So, it is important to think through the pros and cons of having a statement before asking your LEA to assess your child. It might help to discuss the situation with someone from one of the Helpline organisations listed in part 7.

2

Case 2

2

Case 3

Case 3

66 Our son is 7 and is making very little progress with his reading and number work. His teacher last year tried to give him extra help, but the teacher this year doesn't seem that worried. She says Will is just lazy and a 'daydreamer' and that if he made more effort to listen he would start to learn. She offered to send a note home on days when he tries hard, so that we can reward him. But we tried this with his teacher last year. How far behind does he have to fall before the school does something? 99

The first step

You have already taken the first step, by sharing your worries with Will's teacher. Now you need to ask the headteacher for a meeting, together with Will's class teacher and the school's special educational needs coordinator (SENCO). Ask if Will's class teacher from last year can also be there.

At the meeting, you should:

- Explain how Will has been having difficulties for a number of years. Take in some of his old school reports.
- Explain what Will is like at home and why you think his problem is not 'laziness'. Describe the ways you have tried to encourage him in the past which have not worked.
- Ask for Will to be placed on the school's special educational needs register and for his class teacher to give him extra help or support.
- Ask for targets to be set for his progress, and ask for a date to be fixed to review his progress.

If that doesn't work

If you get nowhere at the meeting, you should write to the school governors, who are responsible for the work of the school. Your letter could begin like this:

To: The Chair of the Governing Body,

Dear Sir or Madam,

I am writing to you as the parent of Will . . . who is in class X at Y School. I believe that Will has special educational needs and that he should be on the register at the school and receiving support at one of the school-based stages. I have discussed this with my son's class teacher, and with the headteacher, without satisfaction.

I understand that the governors have a duty in law to 'use their best endeavours' to see that children with special educational needs have their needs met. My reasons for believing that Will has special educational needs are . . .

2

Case 3

(Set out your reasons and include copies of any reports on Will which back you up)

If you need help wording this letter, talk to one of the Helpline organisations listed in part 7. While you are waiting for a reply, ask your family doctor to check Will's hearing. Many children have problems in their early years at school because of 'glue ear'. This may be Will's problem. Your doctor will explain what it is and how it can be treated.

What the law says

The 1996 Education Act says:

'The governing body . . . shall . . . use their best endeavours . . . to secure that, if any registered pupil has special educational needs, the special educational provision which his learning difficulty calls for is made.'

(Section 317 (1)(a))

'The Secretary of State shall issue . . . a code of practice giving practical guidance in respect of the discharge by local education authorities and the governing bodies . . . of their functions under this Part of the Act. It shall be the duty of local education authorities, and such governing bodies . . . to have regard to the provisions of the code.'

(Section 313 (1) & (2))

Case 3

What the Code of Practice says

'The needs of all pupils who may have special educational needs . . . must be addressed.'

(Paragraph 1:2)

'All children with special educational needs should be identified and assessed as early as possible and as quickly as is consistent with thoroughness.'

(Paragraph 1:3)

'Schools should keep a register of all children with special educational needs.'

(Paragraph 2:25)

'The child's parent should always be informed of the action which the school proposes to take.'

(Paragraph 2:81)

PostScript

Try to be calm and polite in your dealings with the school. This is for three reasons:

First, whatever happens, Will is going to have to continue with the same class teacher and you are going to have to continue to talk to her and the head, whether they agree with you or not.

Second, there are a number of organisations which exist to help parents in your position. Many of them are listed in part 7 of this book. Rather than getting angry, use them.

Third, as a last resort, if at the end of the day you believe that Will has special educational needs which the school, for whatever reason, are not meeting, you will be able to ask the local educational authority for an assessment. The LEA will then ask the school what they are doing about Will's needs.

2

**Case
3**

Case 4

66 We've just had the review of my daughter's progress under her individual education plan. Josie is 9 and has problems with her reading and writing and spelling. Both her class teacher and the special needs coordinator agree that the targets set in her individual education plan have not been met, and this was its second review. I asked them to get an educational psychologist to see Josie to advise on a more specialised programme that might lead to some improvement. But the special needs coordinator says outside specialists can't be called in unless a child is on stage 3, the last stage before an LEA assessment. She also said that the LEA are so short of psychologists that by the time Josie is seen it would be time for the next school review anyway. 99

The first step

If everyone agrees that the targets in Josie's individual education plan have not been met, one of three things must be wrong: either she has not been getting the help, or she has not been getting enough of it, or it is the wrong kind of help.

The first step is to ask the headteacher to arrange a meeting between herself, yourself, Josie's class teacher and the special education needs coordinator. At the meeting you should ask these questions:

- Exactly how much help has Josie received under her individual education plan since it was adopted?
- What does the school think is the reason for Josie not meeting her progress targets for the second review period running?
- Will the school now ask for an educational psychologist's advice on Josie's difficulties? If not, why not?

You may need to remind the staff that the Code of Practice says outside specialist advice can be requested at any time, not just when a child is on stage 3. If the headteacher repeats the comment about there not being enough educational psychologists to go around, remind her that the governors have a duty to use their 'best endeavours' to meet Josie's needs. The very least the school can do is to put in a request for a psychologist to visit Josie.

2

Case 4

If that doesn't work

Write to the headteacher, this time asking for your questions to be answered in writing. Your letter could start like this:

Dear Mr/Mrs/Ms . . . ,

Thank you for arranging the meeting last week to discuss Josie's repeated failure to meet the targets set out in her individual education plan. I am sorry to say that I was disappointed with your answers to the questions I put at the meeting and am writing now to repeat these questions and ask you to put your answers in writing, in order that I can take further action, in Josie's best interests . . .

When you get the head's reply, send it, together with a copy of your letter, to the school governors, reminding them of their responsibilities to use their 'best endeavours' to ensure that Josie's special educational needs are provided for by the school.

If none of this is successful, you should consider asking the LEA for a formal assessment under the 1996 Education Act. See case 2 on page 12 for an example of a letter asking for an LEA assessment and the PS to case 1 and case 10 for a discussion of the pros and cons of assessment. You can get advice on asking for an assessment from one of the Helpline organisations listed in part 7.

2

**Case
4**

What the law says

Section 317(1)(a) of the 1996 Education Act says:

'The governing body . . . shall . . . use their best endeavours, in exercising their functions in relation to the school, to secure that, if any registered pupil has special educational needs, the special educational provision which his learning difficulty calls for is made.'

What the Code of Practice says

'The needs of all pupils who may have special educational needs . . . must be addressed.'

(Paragraph 1:2)

'Schools should always consult specialists when they take action on behalf of a child at stage 3. But the involvement of specialists need not be confined to stage 3. Outside specialists can play an important part in the identification of special educational needs and in advising schools on effective provision which can prevent the development of more significant needs.'

(Paragraph 2:60)

PostScript

To make sure your child is making progress, you need to check whether the objectives set out in her individual education plan are being achieved. If they are not, there could be something wrong either with the school's view of your child's needs or with the type or amount of provision being made to meet them.

At stage 1, plans to meet a child's needs have to be recorded. Ask for a copy to keep at home for reference. At stages 2 and 3, individual education plans should contain a lot of detail about provision and targets. Always make sure you get a copy to keep at home.

Whenever you are at all concerned by anything you are told, ask for it to be put in writing. Also, keep a copy of any letter you send.

2

**Case
4**

Case 5

❝ We were having chat with our 12 year old daughter about her school work and how she was getting on with her friends and teachers, that sort of thing, when she staggered us by saying that she has not seen her special support teacher since the beginning of term – around eight weeks ago. Shirley has an individual education plan and under it is supposed to get two one-hour sessions of special teaching a week. We have had no information at all from the school about this change. Perhaps Shirley doesn't need the help any more? ❞

The first step

It is very unlikely that the help was dropped because Shirley did not need it. If that were the case, her progress would have been reported to you at a review meeting. It is more likely that the teacher has left suddenly, or is ill, and the school has neglected to make alternative arrangements. The first step, then, is to find out exactly what has happened.

You should ask the headteacher for a meeting, together with the special education needs coordinator (SENCO). At this meeting you should:

- tell them Shirley's account of what has happened and ask for confirmation that she has had no special help for eight weeks;
- ask what the school plans to do in order to ensure that Shirley receives the help she is entitled to under her individual education plan from this point on;
- ask what the school intends to do to help Shirley catch up with the help she has missed over the last term.

You should make the headteacher aware that you know that the governors of the school have a legal duty to 'use their best endeavours' to meet Shirley's needs, and ask whether the governors have been made aware of the situation, which presumably has affected other children as well as Shirley.

If that doesn't work

At the meeting you will almost certainly receive an apology for what has happened. But you may not get a promise of immediate help for Shirley or extra help to make up for what she has missed over the last term.

In which case, you might consider writing direct to the chair of the school governors, pointing out their failure to fulfil their duty towards Shirley and asking formally for immediate action to resume her special help and for some extra help in the short term. Your letter could begin like this:

> To: The Chair of the Governing Body,
>
> Dear Sir or Madam,
>
> I am writing as the parent of a pupil at your school, Shirley . . . , who is registered as having special educational needs. I have only recently discovered that for the last eight weeks Shirley has not been receiving the special provision set out in her individual education plan. This is because the teacher who is supposed to work with her has left. I have discussed the situation with the headteacher, but she is unable to give me a date when Shirley's help will be resumed and is unable assure me that additional provision will be made available to Shirley in the short term to help overcome the effects of the help which has been lost to her.
>
> I am writing to ask you to take action which will fulfil your legal duty to 'use your best endeavours' to ensure that Shirley's needs (and the needs of other children who may be similarly affected) are met . . .

If this gets you nowhere, you could make a formal complaint

2

to the Secretary of State on the grounds that the governing body is failing to fulfil its duty under the 1996 Education Act and under the Code of Practice. But before doing this, you should discuss the situation with one of the Helpline organisations listed in part 7.

Case

5

What the law says

Section 317(1)(a) of the 1996 Education Act says:

'The governing body . . . shall . . . use their best endeavours, in exercising their functions in relation to the school, to secure that, if any registered pupil has special educational needs, the special educational provision which his learning difficulty calls for is made.'

What the Code of Practice says

'The needs of all pupils who may have special educational needs . . . must be addressed.'

(Paragraph 1:2)

Post Script

'Sorry' is not really good enough when a child has been denied the help she needs and to which she is legally entitled. So when you do have to complain to school, try to suggest something positive they can do which will actually help your child catch up on what she has missed.

This has benefits for your relationship with the school, as it offers a way for them to deal with a problem themselves, saving them the embarrassment of having a parent make a formal complaint to the Secretary of State. This might seem like a gentle form of blackmail . . . but everyone stands to gain from a friendly conclusion to a dispute between parents and school, particularly the child involved.

Case 6

66 Jasvinder is 8 and she was born with mild cerebral palsy. She has fine motor problems and needs coaching in using a ruler and protractor and with forming her letters and numbers. Her individual education plan for last term gave her support in the classroom for three lessons a week by a non-teaching assistant. But Jasvinder has not been happy with this because she is embarrassed in front of the other children to be receiving individual help. It has not helped matters that her mother tongue is Punjabi and she is not very good at English. To make it worse, there is a small group of children in her class who taunt her, saying 'Where's your baby minder?' and calling her racist names.

Jasvinder is making very little progress and I think if she could have her help in a withdrawal situation for a while, away from the class, she might thrive. I've mentioned this on a number of occasions at the school, but of course I am just her mother, so no-one listens to my views. 99

The first step

The Code of Practice says schools should take the views of parents and children seriously. And, if there is evidence that Jasvinder is failing to meet the targets set out in her individual education plan, they should already be questioning the arrangements for her help.

You should ask the headteacher for a meeting. Take someone with you who knows the points you want to make. At the meeting, explain:

- That you are very happy with the amount of help Jasvinder is receiving and with the efforts being made by her assistant, but . . .

- That you do not believe that the best use is being made of the assistant's time because Jasvinder is not able to benefit

Case

6

from being helped in the classroom as much as you believe she would by being helped in a one-to-one situation away from the classroom. You should remind the headteacher that the school's basic duty is to ensure that where a child has special educational needs, 'the special educational provision which (his or her) learning difficulty calls for is made'. In-class support does not seem, at present, to be the provision which Jasvinder's learning difficulties 'call for'.

- That you agree it is important for Jasvinder to overcome her embarrassment about being given extra help, but that it is more important for her to be making real progress towards the objectives set out for her in her individual education plan.

- That you are not asking for Jasvinder to be withdrawn as a solution to the abuse she is receiving from other children in the class, and that you would like to know what action the school takes to curb this kind of bullying between children.

If that doesn't work

If the meeting gets you nowhere, you should put your views and requests in writing and send them to the chair of the governors. For help with the wording of the letter, ring one of the Helpline organisations listed in part 7. If the governors ignore your request, you are going to need more detailed advice and support from one of the Helpline organisations.

What the law says

Section 317(1)(a) of the 1996 Education Act says:

'The governing body . . . shall . . . use their best endeavours, in exercising their functions in relation to the school, to secure that, if any registered pupil has special educational needs, the special educational provision which his learning difficulty calls for is made.'

What the Code of Practice says

'The knowledge, views and experience of parents are vital. Effective assessment and provision will be secured where there is the greatest possible degree of partnership between parents and their children and schools, LEAs and other agencies.'

(Paragraph 1:2)

'Consideration should be given to the ascertainable wishes and feelings of the child.'

(Paragraph 2:64)

'The identification and assessment of the special educational needs of children from minority ethnic groups, including children whose first language is not English or Welsh, requires very careful consideration ... Care should be taken to consider the child within the context of his or her home, language, culture and community . . . '

(Paragraph 2:18)

Post Script

Remember that the main duty which the law on special education places on school governors is 'to use their best endeavours' to ensure that children with special needs get the help they need.

At the end of the day, this is a stronger duty than the duty to follow the particulars of the Code. So, although it is important for parents to keep the school up to scratch on its adherence to the Code of Practice, in terms of taking account of parents' and children's views, Jasvinder's mother's most important argument is that the in-class support is failing to enable Jasvinder to meet the targets set out in her individual education plan. If there is clear evidence to show this, then on this basis alone, regardless of whether the school has followed the Code in detail, they should be prepared to re-examine the arrangements made for Jasvinder's help.

Case 7

    ❝ Lloyd has just turned 14 and has been getting into trouble at school for some time. He has a casual manner towards teachers which some of them find difficult to tolerate. Over the last year he has been given a series of punishments (detention, placed on report, temporary exclusion from school) which he considers petty and unjust. His respect for the teachers has taken a nose-dive and so has the school's tolerance of him.

    I was called to a meeting last week by the head and informed that Lloyd had been the subject of a 'stormy' house case conference and that a majority of his teachers wanted the LEA to do an assessment of Lloyd's special educational needs under section 323 of the 1996 Education Act. Apparently they believe that Lloyd has emotional and behavioural difficulties and that he should be in a special school. When I objected, on the grounds that Lloyd does not have special educational needs, he said that he would ask for an educational psychologist to visit and see him, to give an expert opinion. I don't want Lloyd seen by a psychologist. What can I do? **❞**

The first step

Parents cannot be forced to produce their children for examination by an educational psychologist unless an LEA assessment under section 323 of the 1996 Education Act is already under way.

Nor can teachers or headteachers decide that an LEA assessment should be carried out. They can make recommendations, but the decision is for the LEA to make.

So there are some things you need not worry about. However, it is clear that Lloyd and the school are not getting on and that won't help his education. You say that his attitude irritates 'some' of his teachers. Does that mean that there are other 'more positive' members of the teaching staff who might speak up for him? If so, I think you should have a word with one of them in confidence and ask their advice on what, if anything, can be done to overcome the problems between Lloyd and the other teachers.

It might also help if someone Lloyd trusts could have a heart to heart with him over his attitude to the school. For although the headteacher can't force the LEA to do an assessment, what he can do is exclude Lloyd from the school. It is important that Lloyd understands the risks if a solution to this problem cannot be found.

Case 7

Try for another meeting with the head and ask for the special education needs coordinator to be present and, if possible, one of the teachers Lloyd does get on with. You should consider asking if Lloyd can also be present.

At the meeting you should try to get answers to these questions:

- How does the school see Lloyd's problems? Is he, for example, listed on the school's register of students with special educational needs? Has the special needs co-ordinator any responsibility for him?
- What extra help so far has the school been able to give Lloyd?
- Is there anything in addition that they believe might help Lloyd cope with the school, and vice versa?
- What do they believe you, as parent, can do to help Lloyd and the school?

Following this meeting, you should have a clearer idea of whether it is going to be possible for the school and Lloyd to overcome their problems. You will also know whether the school has good enough grounds for asking the LEA to do an assessment. For example, if Lloyd is not on the school's register of special needs and has not received any special educational provision from the school to date, the LEA are unlikely to do an assessment under the 1996 Act.

If that doesn't work

If the head does decide to recommend an assessment, and the LEA agree, the LEA will write to you giving you 29 days to comment. You should write back straight away. Your letter could begin like this:

To: The Chief Education Officer

Dear Sir or Madam,

I am writing to object to your proposal to assess my son Lloyd under section 323 of the 1996 Education Act. I know that the school have difficulty with Lloyd's behaviour and I have discussed this fully with them, but I do not believe that his problems are caused by an emotional or behavioural difficulty. Therefore I do not accept that Lloyd should be assessed for special educational provision.

In my opinion, some of the teachers do not treat the older students with the respect that they should, and in Lloyd's case this has undermined his respect for them and for the school rules in general. However, there are some teachers who speak highly of Lloyd and he is a very cooperative and reasonable young man at home, helping with his younger brothers and sisters and generally taking responsibility for himself.

I am enclosing a letter which the leader of the youth club has written about Lloyd, in support of my objection . . .

If, having read your letter, the LEA decide to go ahead with an assessment, they have to give you notice in writing of their decision and the reasons for it. If you have not already made contact with one of the Helpline organisations, you should do so now. Their numbers are listed in part 7.

What the law says

Section 323 of the 1996 Education Act says:

2

Case 7

'Where a local education authority are of the opinion that a child for whom they are responsible . . . has special educational needs, and . . . it is necessary for the authority to determine the special education provision which any learning difficulty he may have calls for . . . they shall serve a notice on the child's parent informing him that they propose to make an assessment of the child's educational needs . . . and . . . of the parent's right to make representations, and submit written evidence, to the authority within such period (which shall not be less than 29 days beginning with the date on which the notice is served) as may be specified in the notice.'

What the Code of Practice says

'When making a referral for a statutory assessment, the school should state clearly the reasons for the referral and submit the following material:

i. information, including:

- the recorded views of parents and, where appropriate, children on the earlier stages of assessment and any action and support to date;
- evidence of health checks, for example relevant information on medical advice to the school;
- when appropriate, evidence relating to social services involvement.

ii. written individual education plans at stages 2 and 3 indicating the approaches adopted, the monitoring arrangements followed and the educational outcomes.

iii. reviews of each individual education plan indicating

decisions made as a result.

iv. evidence of the involvement and views of professionals with relevant specialist knowledge and expertise outside normal competence of the school.'

(Paragraph 3:8)

Case 7

PostScript

Some schools do use the threat of referring a pupil for special needs assessment as a way of dealing with a discipline problem. And sometimes they follow through on that threat. Although it may be possible for a parent to argue against an assessment, the LEA have the legal power to undertake an assessment of any child over the age of 2 if they believe it is necessary. Either way, that still leaves the problems between the school and the child to be tackled. It is obviously no solution if the head immediately excludes a child. A parent faced with this situation needs to do two things: consider whether a transfer of school might not be in their child's best interests; and, get immediate advice on their rights and their child's rights from one of the Helpline organisations listed in part 7.

Case 8

66 The headteacher of my daughter's primary school attended the latest review of her individual education plan and suggested that it would best for Ann if we agreed to an immediate transfer to a special unit, where she could be assessed for special education by the LEA. We have also asked the LEA to do an assessment, but we are not happy with Ann being moved to a special school for the assessment, as we always hoped that she would have her needs met in an ordinary school, whether statemented or not. What can we do? 99

The first step

If you have not already done so, you should let the headteacher know that you are not in agreement with his proposal for a transfer to a special school. The Code of Practice says that this should not happen except in emergency cases and unless professionals and parents agree.

The simplest thing to do is to write a short letter to the headteacher, putting your views on record. Your letter could begin like this:

Dear . . . ,

I am writing to you to put on record the fact that we do not agree to Ann being placed in a special school during her assessment for special educational provision. We understand that this cannot happen without our agreement as parents, and we are sending a copy of this letter to the local education authority so that they also know our views.

If that doesn't work

The real danger in this situation is not that you can be made to agree to Anne transferring to a special school for her assessment, but that the headteacher may exclude her, leaving

2

Case 8

her without a school altogether. If that happens, you should get advice immediately from one of the Helpline organisations in part 7.

Also, it is clear that the headteacher does not think that his school is suitable for Anne. This means that it is unlikely that his educational advice (the report he will send the LEA as part of her assessment) will recommend that she receives special education provision in his school. Although there is nothing you can do about the school's advice until the proposed statement is issued, it might be an idea to think about looking for another mainstream school which might be suitable.

What the Code of Practice says

'An emergency placement should be made only when the LEA, parents, school and any relevant professionals who will be involved in the statutory assessment are all agreed that the child's needs are such that action must be taken immediately and an emergency placement is the best way forward.'

(Paragraph 4:15)

Post Script

It is a good idea to know what options are available to you, as a parent, if you suspect that the headteacher of your child's school believes that she should be in a special school – and you don't. One option is to request a transfer to another local school. LEAs have to provide parents with information on all their schools and parents can visit schools and talk about the possibility of a transfer at any stage in their child's education. However, headteachers do discuss children transferring, so you should be open about Ann's needs and your reasons for looking around at different schools. See the Helpline organisations listed in part 7 for the numbers you can ring to get advice.

Case 9

❝ My nephew, Tin Wo, is making slow progress at school. Tin Wo is 9 and came from Hong Kong to live with us last year when his father died. He spends most of his time learning English as a second language. The school refuse to accept that he may have a learning difficulty other than his need to learn English. We phoned the LEA but they refused our request for an assessment, saying they agreed with the school and that Tin Wo had to go through the school-based stages before they would assess him. But we believe his language difficulties are hiding his special needs. His spoken Cantonese is limited and he can't read it. We believe that he would have learning difficulties, whatever language he was taught in. ❞

The first step

Your LEA seems to believe that Tin Wo's learning difficulties arise solely because the language in which he is being taught (English) is different from his 'home' language. On these grounds they can, quite legally, exclude him from special educational provision.

As a first step you should try to collect as much evidence as you can that Tin Wo's difficulties cannot be solely explained by language difference. This evidence could come, for example, from a Cantonese-speaking teacher who would know what level of language development to expect in a child of Tin Wo's age. This person may also be able to do some other assessment work with Tin Wo, observing his mani-pulative skills, trying out some maths, checking his general knowledge, etc. Ask the teacher to put his or her views in writing.

It might also help to ask your family doctor if he/she has any comments to make on Tin Wo's physical development and, if this seems helpful, again ask for it in writing.

The Code of Practice makes it clear that children do not have to pass though all of the school-based stages before they can be considered for statutory assessment.

Ring one of the Helpline organisations listed in part 7 for further advice on getting evidence on Tin Wo's learning difficulties. A second professional opinion may help.

Case 9

2

When you have as much information as you can collect, write (don't phone!) again to the LEA, asking for an assessment, and send them all of your evidence. Your letter could start off like this:

To: The Chief Education Officer

Dear Sir or Madam,

I am writing as the guardian of Cheung Tin Wo to request an assessment under section 323 of the 1996 Education Act. I make this request as is my right under section 329 of the same Act and I understand that you have a duty to reply to this letter within 6 weeks.

My reasons for asking for an assessment are . . .
. . . I have enclosed copies of letters and reports which support my opinion that Tin Wo has special educational needs which call for the LEA to undertake an assessment.

If that doesn't work

If the LEA refuse your written request, you will have the right to appeal to the Tribunal. Your argument would be based on the belief that Tin Wo has learning difficulties which have nothing to do with his mother-tongue language being different from the language of the school. The evidence you collected together in the hopes of persuading the LEA to do an assessment will be useful to you if you appeal, but you should contact one of the Helpline organisations listed in part 7 for further advice at this stage.

What the law says

The 1996 Education Act says:

2

**Case
9**

'A child is not to be taken as having a learning difficulty solely because the language (or form of the language) in which he is, or will be, taught is different from a language (or form of a language) which has at any time been spoken in his home.'

(Section 312(3))

'(1) Where a local education authority are of the opinion that a child for whom they are responsible falls, or probably falls, within subsection (2), they shall serve a notice on the child's parent informing him –

(a) that they propose to make an assessment of the child's educational needs . . .

(2) A child falls within this subsection if –

(a) he has special educational needs, and

(b) it is necessary for the authority to determine the special educational provision which any learning difficulty he may have calls for.'

(Section 323)

What the Code of Practice says

'These stages (school-based stages) will not usually be steps on the way to statutory assessment. Nor are they hurdles to be crossed before a statutory assessment can be made . . .'

(Paragraph 2:24)

'When a child is referred by a parental request for a statutory assessment, the LEA should . . . immediately contact the parents in order to investigate further the nature of their concern (and) ascertain the degree of their involvement and agreement with the special educational provision which has been made for their child at school . . .'

(Paragraph 3:20)

Case 9

'The identification and assessment of the special educational needs of children from minority ethnic groups, including children whose first language is not English or Welsh, requires very careful consideration . . . Care should be taken to consider the child within the context of his or her home, language, culture and community.'

(Paragraph 2:18)

Post Script

Do not forget that your own observations and thoughts about your own child's needs are important and should be taken into account by the LEA. It is relevant to compare the development of the child you are seeking an assessment for with that of other children you have brought up. Write down any observations which you think might be relevant. There is a checklist in the Code of Practice which might help you (see paragraph 3:100).

Remember that the law says that LEAs must act where there is a probability that a child has needs which require an assessment. As parent, you should only have to prove that the probability exists.

Case 10

66 The school told us they can't give George the help he needs so we asked the LEA to do an assessment. The LEA have written saying that George's needs are 'not severe and complex' and that he does not fall within the 2% of pupils who need statements. Surely the school knows better than the officer from the LEA whether George needs more help than they can give him? After all, they've been teaching him for four years now, whereas the officer hasn't even met him. 99

The first step

LEAs have a duty to assess a child if a parent requests it, unless they consider that an assessment is not 'necessary'. In practice, an assessment is not necessary if a child does not have special educational needs, or if it is clear that the school can make the provision required to meet his or her needs. When the LEA inform parents that they do not believe an assessment is necessary, they must also inform them of their right to appeal to the Special Educational Needs Tribunal. In addition, the Code of Practice says that LEAs should write to parents and school 'giving full reasons for their decision' not to assess a child. George's needs may not be 'severe and complex' and he may not be one of the 2% of children who have the greatest difficulties in our schools, but these reasons, on their own, do not justify the LEA deciding that they will not assess him. As well as seeking advice on appealing to the Tribunal, you should write back to the LEA and remind them what the Code says about giving full reasons and about the basis on which they should make decisions on whether to assess individual children. Your letter could start like this:

To: The Chief Education Officer

Dear Sir or Madam,

Your letter informing us of the decision not to assess

our son, George . . . , did not contain the information it should, according to the Code of Practice. It did not give 'full reasons' for your decision. Would you please write to us again, this time setting out your reasons in detail.

Case 10

Would you also please read that section of the Code of Practice which gives LEAs guidance on the criteria for deciding to make an assessment, that is paragraph 3:49. You will see that it makes no mention of a child's needs being 'severe or complex', nor that a child must be among the 2% of the most disabled children in our schools before an assessment can be done. Perhaps you are quoting from another section of the Code or from the 1996 Education Act or the Regulations? If so, we would be grateful if you would give us the references so that we can check for ourselves . . .

Our reasons for believing that you have a duty to assess George are . . .

If that doesn't work

If the LEA refuse to give reasons for not deciding to assess George, you will be able to point this out to the Tribunal. Your own case will need to focus on George's needs and the evidence from the school that, despite the help they have given, he is not making progress. Any reports that you have from the school and from reviews of his individual education plan may help you (see part 3 of this book).

What the law says

Section 323 of the 1996 Education Act says:

'(1) Where a local education authority are of the opinion that a child for whom they are responsible falls, or probably falls, within subsection (2), they shall serve a notice on the child's parent informing him –

(a) that they propose to make an assessment of the child's educational needs . . .

(2) A child falls within this subsection if –

(a) he has special educational needs, and

(b) it is necessary for the authority to determine the special educational provision which any learning difficulty he may have calls for.'

2

Case
10

What the Code of Practice says

'In deciding whether to make a statutory assessment, the critical question for LEAs will be whether there is convincing evidence that, despite the school, with the help of external specialists, taking relevant and purposeful action to meet the child's learning difficulties, those difficulties remain or have not been remedied sufficiently and may require the LEA to determine the child's special educational provision.'

(Paragraph 3:49)

Post Script

LEAs should make the decision on assessing a child on the basis of that individual child's needs and the provision which is available to him in his or her school, without the benefit of the extra resources which a statement can bring. Whenever you hear an LEA laying down general rules about when they assess children or make statements – such as 'we only assess the severely disabled, or the 2%, or children over 5, or children who have passed through all of the school-based stages' – you should immediately suspect that they are acting against the intentions of the law on special education. When you suspect this, you should get immediate advice from one of the Helpline organisations listed in part 7. See also the PS to case 1 on page 11.

Case 11

66 We have been waiting for six months for the LEA to start an assessment of our son Duane under the 1996 Education Act. The school says they sent in a referral to the LEA immediately after the last review of his individual education plan, but we have heard nothing and it is coming up to time for the next review. Duane is slipping further and further behind with his reading and writing and we are getting really desperate to get him some extra help. 99

The first step

Either the school, the LEA or both are at fault here. The LEA should have responded long before now to the school's referral of Duane for assessment, either by writing to you proposing an assessment, or by informing the school that they did not think an assessment was necessary – in which case, the school should have told you.

Your first job is to find out exactly what has happened. When a school makes a referral of a child for assessment they must, under the Code of Practice, send information on the child to the LEA. Ask the headteacher to give you the date when the referral and the information was sent to the LEA. Perhaps this did not happen as promptly as it should have.

The Code of Practice says that LEAs should consider requests for assessment 'as quickly as possible'. If you know when the head made the request, you can work out how long they have had to make a decision.

Ask for a meeting with the headteacher. Ask if he will ring the office directly, in your presence, and get a date from them by which a decision is going to be made.

If that doesn't work

Hopefully, the LEA will move quickly once the delay is pointed out to them. But if they don't – or if they actually refuse the school's request – you should write yourself as Duane's parent asking for an assessment. Your letter could start like this:

To: The Chief Education Officer

Dear Sir or Madam,

I am writing to request an assessment for my son Duane . . . under section 323 of the 1996 Education Act. I am making this request as is my right under section 329 of the same Act and I understand that you have a duty in law to reply to this letter within six weeks. However, as you know, Duane's school requested an assessment for him over six months ago, so you should already have the information you need to respond to my request.

Should you refuse my request, I shall appeal to the Tribunal.

My reasons for believing that Duane has special educational needs which require an assessment are . . .

What the law says

Regulation 11 of the Education (Special Educational Needs) Regulations 1994 says:

'(3) Where under sections 328(2) or 329(1) a parent asks the authority to arrange for an assessment to be made under section 323 they shall within 6 weeks of the date of receipt of the request give notice to the child's parent –

(a) under section 323(4) of their decision to make an assessment, or

(b) under section 328(3)(a) or 329(2)(a) respectively of their decision not to comply with the request and of the parent's right to appeal to the Tribunal against the determination.

2

Case 11

(4) An authority need not comply with the time limits referred to in paragraphs (1) to (3) if it is impractical to do so because –

(a) the authority have requested advice from the headteacher of a school during a period beginning one week before any date on which that school was closed for a continuous period of not less than 4 weeks from that date and ending one week before the date on which it re-opens;

(b) exceptional personal circumstances affect the child or his parent during the 6 week period referred to in paragraphs (1) to (3); or

(c) the child or his parent are absent from the area of the authority for a continuous period of not less than 4 weeks during the 6 week period referred to in paragraphs (1) to (3).'

What the Code of Practice says

'It is important that all requests for assessment are considered as quickly as possible, regardless of the source of the referral.'

(Paragraph 3:5)

Post Script

It is always safer to request an assessment yourself, as a parent, rather than leaving it to the school. If a school refers a child, there is no deadline on the LEA's reply. If a parent requests an assessment, however, the LEA must respond within 6 weeks, unless it is impractical for them to do so (see 'What the law says', above). Also, if the LEA turn down the school's referral, parents have no right to be given reasons and no right to appeal – whereas, if the LEA refuse a parent's request for assessment, you can appeal to the Tribunal.

It is always best for the parent and the headteacher to make separate requests at the same time. Then the LEA have all the information to hand from the school and should easily be able to meet the legal deadline for replying to the parent's request for assessment.

2

Case 11

An LEA's grounds for refusing an assessment are rarely that a child does not have special needs, but that the school already has the resources needed to meet those needs. What parents need to argue at an appeal, then, is that the school is not able to meet their child's needs. It is important to have evidence that progress is not being made, despite the help given by a school.

Case 12

66 We are about to ask for our son to be assessed for the first time by the LEA, but we've heard that they are not keeping to the legal time limits on assessments. What are the time limits, and what can we do if the LEA ignore them? 99

The first step

Here is a chart which shows the legal timetable for assessments:

You ask the LEA to assess your child or the LEA write proposing an assessment	*LEA have 6 weeks to decide whether or not to do an assessment*
LEA decide to assess your child	*LEA have 10 weeks to complete the assessment (that's 16 weeks so far)*
LEA complete assessment and decide if statement is needed	*LEA have 2 weeks to decide if statement is needed (that's 18 weeks so far)*
LEA invite parents' comments and decide whether to change statement before finalising it	*LEA have 8 weeks to consider parents' comments before finalising the statement (that's 26 weeks from assessment being requested)*

The first step is mark the date on your calendar two working days after you post your letter, first class, asking for the assessment. Then count forward six weeks, and write: 'LEA refuse, or assessment begins'. Then count forward another ten weeks and write 'Assessment should end'. Two weeks later write 'Proposed statement'. Then eight weeks after that write 'Statement finalised'.

This is the timetable the LEA should work to. Of course, you can't assume that they have done something just because the date comes round on the calendar. If you have not heard anything by the beginning of the week after one of your marked dates, you should telephone to find out what is happening. Get new dates from them for the following deadlines and adjust your calendar. (You will also have to change your calendar if the LEA move more quickly through some of the stages.)

If the deadlines are not met

LEAs do not have to keep to the first six-week deadline if it is impractical for them to do so because:

- they have requested advice from a headteacher in the period from one week before the school was about to close for four weeks (normally, the summer holiday) until one week before it was about to open again;
- there were exceptional personal circumstances affecting you or your child during the six weeks;
- you or your child were absent from the area for four weeks during the first six weeks.

LEAs do not have to keep to the ten-week deadline for assessment if it is impractical for them to do so because:

- the LEA decided they needed further advice on a child's needs, in an exceptional case;
- the LEA agreed to consider advice provided by the parents six weeks or more after the advice was requested;
- the LEA requested advice from a headteacher in the period from one week before the school was about to close for four weeks (normally, the summer holiday) until one week before it was about to open again;
- the health authority or the social services department have failed to provide their advice within the six-week deadline given them in law;
- there were exceptional personal circumstances affecting a parent or child during the ten weeks;
- a child or parent was absent from the area for four weeks during the first ten weeks;

- the child failed to keep an appointment for an examination or test.

2

Case

12

If your LEA fail to meet a deadline, you must give them the opportunity to explain. They must show that one of the situations listed above has occurred and that it has made the deadline impractical. If you are not happy with their explanation, you should contact one of the Helpline organisations listed in part 7 of this book for advice. You may need to make a formal complaint to the Secretary of State for Education on the grounds that the LEA are failing to fulfil their legal duty towards your child. See page 230 for advice on complaining to the Secretary of State.

What the law says

Regulation 11 of the Education (Special Educational Needs) Regulations 1994 says:

'(1) Where under section 323(1) the authority serve a notice on the child's parent informing him that they propose to make an assessment of the child's educational needs under section 323 they shall within 6 weeks of the date of service of the notice give notice to the child's parent –

(a) under section 323(4) of their decision to make an assessment, and of their reasons for making that decision, or

(b) under section 323(6) of their decision not to assess the educational needs of the child.

(3) Where under sections 328(2) or 329(1) a parent asks the authority to arrange for an assessment to be made under section 323 they shall within 6 weeks of the date of receipt of the request give notice to the child's parent –

(a) under section 323(4) of their decision to make an assessment, or

(b) under section 328(3) or 329(2)(a) respectively of their

decision not to comply with the request and of the parent's right to appeal to the Tribunal against the determination.

Case 12

(4) An authority need not comply with the time limits referred to in paragraphs (1) to (3) if it is impractical to do so because:

(a) the authority have requested advice from the headteacher of a school during a period beginning one week before any date on which that school was closed for a continuous period of not less that 4 weeks from that date and ending one week before the date on which it re-opens;
(b) exceptional personal circumstances affect the child or his parent during the 6 week period referred to in paragraphs (1) to (3); or
(c) the child or his parent are absent from the area of the authority for a continuous period of not less than 4 weeks during the 6 week period referred to in paragraphs (1) to (3).

(5) Subject to paragraph (6), where under section 323(4) an authority have given notice to the child's parent of their decision to make an assessment they shall complete that assessment within 10 weeks of the date on which such notice was given.

(6) An authority need not comply with the time limit referred to in paragraph (5) if it is impractical to do so because –

(a) in exceptional cases after receiving advice sought under regulation 6 it is necessary for the authority to seek further advice;
(b) the child's parent has indicated to the authority that he wishes to provide advice to the authority after the expiry of 6 weeks from the date on which a request for such advice under regulation 6(a) was received, and the authority have agreed to consider such advice before completing the assessment;
(c) the authority have requested advice from the headteacher

of a school under regulation 6(1)(b) during a period beginning one week before any date on which that school was closed for a continuous period of not less that 4 weeks from that date and ending one week before the date on which it re-opens;

(d) the authority have requested advice from a district health authority or a social services authority under regulation 6(1)(c) or (e) respectively and the district health authority or the social services authority have not complied with that request within 6 weeks from the date on which it was made;

(e) exceptional personal circumstances affect the child or his parent during the 10 week period referred to in paragraph (5);

(f) the child or his parent are absent from the area of the authority for a continuous period of not less than 4 weeks during the 10 week period referred to in paragraph (5);

(g) the child fails to keep an examination for an appointment or a test during the 10 week period referred to in paragraph (5).'

What the Code of Practice says

'It is important that all requests for assessment are considered as quickly as possible, regardless of the source of the referral.'

(Paragraph 3:5)

' . . . the LEA must take all parental requests seriously and take action immediately'.

(Paragraph 3:18)

Post Script

The deadlines do not prevent an LEA acting more quickly, if you feel that is needed. For example, if the school asks for an assessment and sends in the information required at the same time as you ask as a parent, then the LEA may be able to reach their decision well before the six weeks are up. If your child needs help urgently, press your LEA to act before the deadline dates are reached wherever possible.

The envelopes are important! For the purposes of the deadlines on assessments, the key dates are the ones on which letters and documents are posted, not when they are dated. So, it is important to keep the envelopes with letters. If a 2nd class stamp is used, documents are counted as having arrived four working days after the postmark on the envelope. If a 1st class stamp is used, documents are counted as arriving two working days after the postmark.

2

Case 12

Many parents find it useful to keep all documents relating to their child's special educational needs in a file, in date order. This certainly helps when you ring an organisation for advice.

Case 13

2

Case 13

❝The assessment of our son, Charles, has now taken almost three months. The special needs officer says that they are unable to complete it because both the health authority and the social services department have not yet sent in their advice. Who can I complain to in order to get things moving?❞

The first step

The first thing you must do is get the facts straight about who did what, when.

Both the social services department and the health authority should have been notified about the possibility of Charles being assessed at the time you asked for the assessment or the LEA proposed it. Then, when the LEA decided to go ahead with the assessment, both bodies would have been asked to send written advice on Charles.

The law allows health authorities and social service departments six weeks to send advice to LEAs. However, there are circumstances which may allow them to go over this deadline:

- if exceptional personal circumstances affect the child or his parent during the six-week period;
- if the child or her parent are absent from the area for a period of four weeks during the six-week period;
- if the child fails to keep an appointment for an examination or a test made by either the health authority or the social services department during the six-week period;
- if the health authority and the social services department had no information on the child before they received the initial notification from the LEA.

If none of these circumstances apply, or if you still believe that it was practicable for the deadline to be met, you should write to the special needs officer and ask for answers to these questions:

- On what date were the health authority and social services departments notified that the assessment had been requested or proposed?
- On what date did the LEA send in the requests for advice?
- What are the names and addresses of the people in the health authority and the social services department to whom the requests for advice were sent?

When you have this information, write directly to the people responsible and ask for an explanation of the delay. Also ask to be told a firm date by which they intend to send their advice to the LEA.

If that doesn't work

If these letters fail to get things moving, you will need expert advice from an organisation with experience of complaints against health authorities and social services departments. Your local Citizens Advice Bureau or Local Law Centre will be able to advise you whom to contact.

What the law says

Regulation 11 of the Education (Special Educational Needs) Regulations 1994 says:

'(7) Subject to paragraph (8), where an authority have requested advice from a district health authority or a social services authority under regulation 6(1)(c) or (e) respectively they shall comply with that request within 6 weeks of the date on which they receive it.

(8) A district health authority or a social services authority need not comply with the time limit referred to in paragraph (7) if it is impractical to do so because –

(a) exceptional personal circumstances affect the child or his parent during the 6 week period referred to in paragraph (7);

(b) the child or his parent are absent from the area of the authority for a continuous period of not less than 4 weeks during the 6 week period referred to in paragraph (7);

(c) the child fails to keep an appointment for an examination or a test made by the district health authority or a social services authority respectively during the 6 week period referred to in paragraph (7); or

(d) they have not before the date on which a copy of the notice has been served on them in accordance with regulation 5(1) or a notice has been served on them in accordance with regulation 5(3) produced or maintained any information or records relevant to the assessment of the child under section 323.'

What the Code of Practice says

'If the SSD (social services department) do not know the child and the family, and if they have no reason to suppose from evidence provided by the school or the LEA that they should seek further information, they should say so and need provide no further written advice.'

(Paragraph 3:117)

'LEAs should always strive to ensure that any delay arising from the exceptions is kept to a minimum. As soon as the conditions which have led to an exception no longer apply, the LEA should endeavour to complete the process as quickly as possible.'

(Paragraph 3:44)

PostScript

If there has been a delay, this is the best possible argument for your LEA pressing on as quickly as they can once the problem has been overcome. Ask to be given, in writing, the date on which the assessment will be completed and a proposed statement sent to you. Mark these new deadlines on a calendar and make sure the LEA stick to them.

2

Case 13

Case 14

❝ We are getting increasingly suspicious about special education. First, our social worker told us that under the Code of Practice the LEA would have to get our consent before Jamie could be seen by an educational psychologist. But his headteacher told us that we could be prosecuted if we refused to take Jamie for examination. The social worker told us that the Code of Practice advised against parents being present when children were examined. But the head said that in law we have an absolute right to be present. Now we are not sure whether to ask for an LEA assessment for Jamie. The more confused we get, the more worried and suspicious we are about the whole business. ❞

The first step

Your rights with regard to your child being examined are as follows:

- If an LEA does an assessment of Jamie under section 323 of the 1996 Education Act, you will be given a time and a date and a place to take him for psychological examination. If you fail to take him without a good reason, you *may* be prosecuted.

- However, it is only when LEAs are doing an assessment under section 323 that you can be prosecuted for failing to produce your child for examination.

- The Code of Practice is wrong when it says that LEAs should seek parents' consent to medical or psychological assessment (in paragraph 3:14 and again in paragraph 3:97). LEAs have a duty to assess children who may need a statement, whatever their parent's wishes. The law gives them the power to prosecute parents who do not cooperate.

- Parents have an absolute right in law to be present at any examination of their child which takes place as part of a section 323 assessment.

- The Code of Practice advises that sometimes a parent's presence can be off-putting for the child and cause her to behave differently than she otherwise would (paragraph 3:97). Therefore, the Code suggests, it might be best in some circumstances if parents are not present. However, the decision is for individual parents to make. If you believe that it is important for you to be present when your child is examined, then you have the legal right to insist on it.

2

Case 14

Unfortunately, professionals do sometimes give parents wrong information about special education assessment. If you are in this situation, you should ask for a meeting with the Special Needs Officer. Inform him/her of the wrong information you have been given and ask for confirmation of the correct position.

If that doesn't work

If the officer will not meet you, you should write a letter, enclosing photocopies of the relevant parts of the law which are being misrepresented by the authority's professionals. Your letter could say something along these lines:

To: The Special Needs Officer

Dear . . . ,

I am very concerned that parents whose children have special educational needs may be given wrong information about their rights in law by professionals employed by the authority, and I believe that this is a situation which requires some response from you as an officer for the authority.

Specifically, over the last two months I have been told that . . .

You should also contact one of the Helpline organisations listed in part 7 and speak to someone about the problems you are having with your LEA.

2

Case
14

What the law says

The 1996 Education Act says:

'The parent of a child examined under this paragraph may be present at the examination if he so desires.'

(Schedule 26 paragraph 4(2))

'Any parent who fails without reasonable excuse to comply with any requirements of a notice served on him under paragraph 4 above commits an offence if the notice relates to a child who is not over compulsory school age at the time stated in it as the time for holding the examination.'

(Schedule 26 paragraph 5(1))

What the Code of Practice says

'Parents should be informed of their right to be present with their child at any interview, test, medical or other assessment which is being conducted for the purpose of providing that advice and should be told of the time and place of appointments. Parents should be told that, whilst it is their right to be present, in certain circumstances it may be counterproductive: for instance, where a classroom observation is carried out as part of an assessment, a child will behave differently if his or her parent is present, which would negate the purpose of the observation.'

(Paragraph 3:97)

Post Script

Much of the information in the Code of Practice is an explanation of what the law says and means. But the Code is not the law itself. When there is a contradiction between what the Code says and what the law says on a particular point, you should be guided by the law.

Where the Code and the law say the same thing, quote directly from the law and not the Code. This is because LEAs have a stronger duty to obey the law than they do the Code.

2

Case 14

In general, it is best not to rely too much on what professionals such as educational psychologists (EPs) tell you about the law on special education and your LEA's duties. They do not always know that much about it. To be safe, if you are in doubt about what you have been told about your rights as a parent or your child's rights, speak to someone from one of the Helpline organisations listed in part 7 of this book.

Case 15

66 We've been tricked. Our son's headteacher advised us to ask the LEA to assess Lloyd in order to get some more help for him in the school. But his class teacher has just shown us a copy of the report that went in from the school which says his needs cannot be met in a mainstream school. If we had known that was going to happen, we wouldn't have asked for the assessment in the first place. Can we stop it? 99

The first step

No, you can't stop it going ahead, but there is no harm in asking! The Code of Practice tells LEAs to take parents' views into account and work in partnership with them as much as possible at all times. Ask the Special Needs Officer for a meeting and ask for the headteacher to be present also. You might want to contact one of the Helpline organisations (part 7) to see if they can arrange for someone to accompany you.

At the meeting, ask the headteacher these questions:

● Whenever we have discussed Lloyd's needs has it not been in terms of the support he can be given in an ordinary school?
● Isn't it the case that you have never once mentioned the possibility of Lloyd needing to go to a special school?
● When the idea of an LEA assessment of Lloyd was first mentioned, at his last stage 3 review meeting, everyone talked about it bringing more help for Lloyd into the school. Why are you now saying that Lloyd has to go to a special school?

Ask the officer this question:

● In view of the fact that I feel, as Lloyd's parent, that I have been misled as to the purpose of the assessment, will you call it off and look again at how Lloyd's needs could be met by the school without a statement?

If the officer claims that it is 'too late now to call it off', remind him that Section 323(6) gives LEAs the power to call off assessments 'at any time'.

If the officer argues that a lot of valuable information on Lloyd's needs has been gathered together and it is in his best interests that some action is taken on the basis of it, suggest that the new information on the help Lloyd should receive in school should be included in his individual education plan, in line with the recommendations in the Code.

Case 15

Make a note of all the answers you are given. Ask for confirmation in writing of what has been agreed.

If that doesn't work

If you get nowhere at the meeting, you should put all of your questions into a letter to the Chief Education Officer. Quote the section from the Code of Practice which encourages LEAs to work closely with parents (see 'What the Code of Practice says' below).

If this does not persuade the LEA to call off the assessment, you will have to wait until you receive the proposed statement. Along with this, you will get all of the professional reports on Lloyd, including the school's. Perhaps things will not be as bad as you fear. For example, the headteacher may have suggested a special school in his advice, but the LEA may ignore his opinion and propose extra help at his mainstream school anyway. In any event, if there is to be a statement, you will be able to argue for it to give extra support in the mainstream school.

2

Case 15

What the law says

Section 323 of the 1996 Education Act says:

'(6) Where, at any time after serving a notice under subsection (1), a local education authority decide not to assess the educational needs of the child concerned they shall give notice in writing to the child's parent of their decision.'

What the Code of Practice says

'The fundamental principles of the Code are . . . the knowledge, views and experience of parents are vital. Effective assessment and provision will be secured where there is the greatest possible degree of partnership between parents and their children and schools, LEAs and other agencies.'

(Paragraph 1:2)

PostScript

Whenever you have to go to a meeting where there may be a dispute over 'who said what', and tempers may get stretched, take someone with you who can keep cool ... and in particular, someone who can make careful notes of what is said. Always ask for decisions to be confirmed in writing after a meeting.

Case 16

2

❝ We have just received a letter from the LEA telling us that they do not intend to issue a statement for our daughter, following the assessment of her special educational needs. They have also sent us a document called 'A note in lieu of a statement' and copies of all of the advice collected during Sui Ling's assessment. This describes her special needs and says that she should have 'occasional non-teaching support as necessary to assist with her personal welfare'. But we do not understand who is going to provide this. The head said the school can't, because the welfare workers are too busy with other children. That's the reason why the school referred Sui Ling for assessment in the first place. ❞

The first step

You must appeal against the LEA's decision. You have two months to write the notice of appeal and get it to the Special Educational Needs Tribunal. Mark the date on a calendar, to remind you of the deadline, but do your notice of appeal as soon as possible. See part 3 of this guide for advice on appealing and speak to someone from one of the Helpline organisations listed in part 7.

Then, ask the named officer if he or she will arrange a meeting between the school, the LEA and yourself in order to discuss the note in lieu, as suggested in the Code of Practice (paragraph 4:19). If you can, take someone along to this meeting as support and to take notes on what might be said. One of the Helpline organisations may be able to arrange this for you.

What you should try to bring into the open at the meeting is the headteacher's opinion that the school cannot make the provision Sui Ling needs from its own resources. At the meeting, ask the headteacher:

2

Case

16

- What is the school's budget for special educational needs provision and what provision is made out of this budget?
- What help has the school been giving Sui Ling over the last year, and how much, roughly, has this cost?
- Are there any unspent funds under the special needs budget which the school can draw upon to make the provision specified in the 'note in lieu of a statement'?
- If not, where would the school get the resources for the extra help Sui Ling should get under the note in lieu? (e.g. from other children with special educational needs?)

Take careful note of the answers and (if it would help your case) ask the headteacher to put her views in writing for you. Send a copy to the LEA, with a letter asking them to reconsider their decision not to issue a statement.

If that doesn't work

If they agree, you will be able to withdraw your appeal. If not, you will have to go ahead with it. Perhaps the head will be prepared to appear as a witness on your side? Contact one of the Helpline organisations listed in part 7 for advice.

What the law says

Section 325 of the 1996 Education Act says:

'(1) If, after making an assessment . . . of the educational needs of any child for whom no statement is maintained . . . the local education authority do not propose to make such a statement, they shall give notice in writing of their decision . . .

(2) In such a case, the child's parent may appeal to the Tribunal . . .'

What the Code of Practice says

'The main ground on which an LEA may decide that they

must make a statement is when the LEA conclude that all the special education provision necessary to meet the child's needs cannot reasonably be provided within the resources normally available to mainstream schools in the area'

(Paragraph 4:2)

2

PostScript

Case 16

Headteachers are not used to being asked detailed questions about their school's budget by parents. If she refuses, it might help to remind her that the Tribunal has the power to order that this information is disclosed and order the head to appear. This might sound a bit threatening, but it is true. The Tribunal has similar powers to a court of law in terms of summoning witnesses and requiring relevant documents to be produced.

Case 17

66 We have always wanted our son, Jacob, to go to the local primary school, along with his sisters. But Jacob has been a slow developer and will need support from a specialist teacher if he is to make progress. His nursery teacher warned us that the LEA may not consider this an efficient use of resources and on those grounds might try to put Jacob in a special school. We spoke to the educational psychologist immediately after he had examined Jacob and he said: 'If Jacob were my boy, I'd be pushing for mainstream support rather than special school.' We have just got the proposed statement, and a copy of the psychological advice. We are surprised to see that it is noncommittal on the question of inclusion. We are now not sure what the psychologist thinks and we are beginning to suspect that he has been 'leaned on' by his employers. 99

The first step

Now that you have the proposed statement, you have the right to ask for a meeting with the officer responsible for the statement and any of the professionals who have contributed advice. The first step, then, is to ask for a meeting with the officer and the educational psychologist. Take someone along with you who can witness your discussion and take notes. Remind the officer of the LEA's duty to 'seek ... written advice', then ask the psychologist this question:

"The law says that written advice must include the professional's opinion on 'the provision which is appropriate for the child'. Your advice made no mention of the type of placement which you thought Jacob needed – mainstream or special school. What, in fact, are your views on this?"

If the psychologist says he is not allowed to give his view on what school a child should attend in his advice, remind him that he **is** allowed to say what type of school would be appropriate (including a mainstream or a special school) and tell him that this is what you want to know his opinion on. Explain that you are not asking him to name a specific school.

If the psychologist remains reluctant to share his views with you, remind him that the Code of Practice makes clear that professionals should discuss their views on inclusion openly with parents (paragraph 3:98).

2

Case 17

When (or if) the psychologist does give his opinion, ask the officer for an assurance that the advice will be expanded to include the opinion.

If that doesn't work

If the statement is finalised, naming a special school, then you will have to appeal to the Tribunal. In this case, you will be able to ask the Tribunal to summons the psychologist to attend and for him to be placed on oath. This might be your only option. Of course, you do need to be sure in your own mind that his professional opinion does in fact support what you will be arguing for. At this stage you should get in contact with one of the Helpline organisations for more detailed advice and support – see part 7.

What the law says

Section 6 of the Education (Special Educational Needs) Regulations 1994 says:

'(2) The advice . . . shall be written advice relating to –

(a) the educational, medical, psychological or other features of the case . . . which appear to be relevant to the child's educational needs (including his likely future needs);

(b) how those features could affect the child's educational needs; and

(c) the provision which is appropriate for the child in light of those features of the child's case, whether by way of special educational provision or non-educational provision, but not relating to any matter which is to be specified in a statement by virtue of Section 324(4)b.'

N.B. Section 324(4)b of the 1996 Education Act refers to 'the name of any school or institution'.

Case 17

What the Code of Practice says

'. . . discussions between advisers and parents about the child's needs and the adviser's written advice may include consideration of various options including the scope for mainstream education for the child and the type of school in which the child's needs might best be met, for example mainstream, special or residential . . . '

(Paragraph 3:98)

PostScript

If you want your child to attend a mainstream school, name an actual school – even if you would be happy with any mainstream school. This forces the LEA to consider that particular school and to justify not granting your preference by making specific reference to that school. This, in turn, can make it easier for you to counter their arguments. For more discussion on arguing for inclusion, see cases 18 and 20.

For comments on the role of educational psychologists, see the PS to case 14.

Case 18

❝ I've visited the local secondary school, which is the school we want our son, Toby, to attend. Toby has Down's Syndrome, and the school made it clear that they do not want him. At our meeting with the special needs officer to discuss the proposed statement, she said it would not be in Toby's best interests to force the school to take him, but we do believe he thrives best in a mainstream setting. And, anyway, the next nearest mainstream school is almost twenty miles away. ❞

The first step

The LEA is under a legal duty to place Toby in the school of your preference, provided that:

- it is suitable to his age, ability or aptitude and his special educational needs;
- his attendance will not affect the education of other children there;
- there is an efficient use of resources.

The LEA must consult the school you name as your preference, but the decision is made by the LEA, not the school. Once a school is named on a statement, it must accept your child.

Your first step is to study Toby's statement, in particular section 2 (which describes his needs) and section 3 (which sets out the provision necessary to meet his needs). If you believe that the provision necessary to meet his needs could be arranged at the local school, then go ahead and ask for it to be named on the statement.

You have the right to ask for meetings with any of the professionals who have provided written advice on Toby for the assessment. If any of these have recommended a mainstream place for Toby in their advice, but not been specific about the help Toby would need to make progress, you should ask for a meeting with them. Ask them face to face what kind of help – and how much – Toby would need to be supported in the mainstream school. Make careful note of their answers.

Case 18

If that doesn't work

If the LEA decide not to name the school of your preference on Toby's statement, the Code of Practice says that they should explain their decision in writing and consult you about any other school you would like him to attend. Remember, however, that once the LEA have finalised the statement, you only have two months to prepare and submit your notice of appeal to the Tribunal. So you should immediately get in touch with an organisation which can give you advice on appealing – see part 7.

Study the LEA's reasons for not allowing you the school of your preference. Basically, the onus is on them to prove that at least one of the three conditions listed above cannot be met in Toby's case. If you think a second professional opinion might help, now is the time to try and arrange it (see the Helpline organisations in part 7).

As soon as the LEA finalise the statement, send in your notice of appeal. You can always withdraw it if the LEA change their mind. See part 3 of this guide for advice on appealing.

What the law says

The 1996 Education Act says:

'(1) Every local education authority shall make arrangements for enabling a parent on whom a copy of a proposed statement has been served ... to express a preference as to the maintained or grant maintained special school at which he wishes education to be provided for his child and to give reasons for his preference.

(2) Any such preference must be expressed or made within the period of fifteen days beginning –

(a) with the date on which the written notice . . . was served on the parent, or
(b if a meeting has (or meetings have) been arranged . . . with the date fixed for that meeting (or the last of those meetings).

(3) Where a local authority make a statement in a case where the parent of the child concerned has expressed a preference . . . as to the school at which he wishes education to be provided for his child, they shall specify the name of that school in the statement unless –

(a) the school is unsuitable to the child's age, ability or aptitude or to his special educational needs, or
(b) the attendance of the child at the school would be incompatible with the provision of efficient education for the children with whom he would be educated or the efficient use of resources.

(4) A local education authority shall, before specifying the name of any maintained, grant-maintained or grant-maintained special school in a statement, consult the governing body of the school and, if the school is maintained by another local education authority, that authority.'

(Schedule 27(3))

'(b) If the name of a maintained, grant-maintained or grant-maintained special school is specified in the Statement, the governing body of the school shall admit the child to the school.'

(Section 324 (5)(b))

What the Code of Practice says

'Where the LEA decide that the final statement will not name the parents' first choice of school, the LEA should explain that decision in writing to the parents.'

(Paragraph 4:54)

Case

18

'The governing body of a school can **not** refuse to admit a child solely because he or she has special educational needs.'
(Paragraph 4:57 – emphasis in the Code)

'When the LEA decide not to name the parents' preferred school in a statement . . . they should consult the parents about any other schools they would like their child to attend.'

(Paragraph 4:59)

Post Script

If you feel that the headteacher of a school is less than enthusiastic about your child attending his school, remember that his prejudices will not necessarily be shared by all members of the school staff. For example, there may be teachers and other workers in the school who are also parents of children with special educational needs and who believe, as strongly as you do, in inclusive education.

Case 19

66 The LEA have sent us a proposed statement and we are very happy with the level of support specified in it and so is the headteacher of our son's school. However, he says that nothing will happen in practice until the statement is finalised. Is there anything we can do to speed things up, or at least ensure that the LEA do not drag their heels at this point? 99

The first step

In law the LEA have to finalise a statement eight weeks after it has been sent to parents in proposed form. They are allowed to go beyond this eight-week period if it is impractical for them to keep to the deadline because:

- exceptional personal circumstances have affected the child or parent during the eight weeks;
- the child and parent are absent from the area for four consecutive weeks during the eight-week period;
- parents ask to make representations about the content of the proposed statement after the expiry of the 15-day deadline for these;
- parents ask for a second meeting with an officer or a meeting with a professional who has submitted advice;
- the LEA are waiting for a reply from the Secretary of State to a request for a child to be placed in an independent school which is not on the DoE's approved list.

This does not mean that the LEA can automatically ignore the deadline of eight weeks if, for example, you ask for a second meeting with an officer. They must show that this second meeting has made it 'impractical' for the deadline to be met, which is not the same thing.

In your case, however, you do not need one meeting with an officer, let alone two, so you should write immediately saying that you do not want to make representations or meet with anyone, and ask for the statement to be finalised immediately.

If that doesn't work

2

Case

19

If this does not work, you will probably have to wait the full eight weeks before the LEA finalise the statement. In the meantime, however, you should check with the school that arrangements are in hand to get the extra support to your son as soon as the statement comes into force. For example, if an extra support teacher is to be employed, the plans for doing this should be under way now. Waiting until the statement is finalised before advertising or appointing someone will inevitably mean a further delay after the statement is finalised before the provision is made.

If the statement is not finalised by the ninth week, you should contact one of the Helpline organisations listed in part 7 of this guide for advice.

What the law says

Regulation 14 of the Education (Special Educational Needs) Regulations 1994 says:

'(3) Subject to paragraph (4), where an authority have served a copy of a proposed statement on the child's parent under paragraph 2 of schedule 27 to the Act they shall within 8 weeks of the date on which the proposed statement was served, serve a copy of the completed statement and a written notice on the child's parent under paragraph 6 of that schedule, or give notice to the child's parent that they have decided not to make a statement.

(4) The authority need not comply with the time limit referred to in paragraph (3) if it is impractical to do so because –

(a) exceptional personal circumstances affect the child or his parent during the 8 week period referred to in paragraph (3);

(b) the child or his parent are absent from the area of the authority for a continuous period of not less that 4 weeks during the 8 week period referred to in paragraph (3);

(c) the child's parent indicates that he wishes to make representations to the authority about the content of the statement under paragraph 4(1)(a) of schedule 27 to the Act after the expiry of the 15 day period for making such representations provided for in paragraph 4(4) of that schedule;

(d) a meeting between the child's parent and an officer of the authority has been held pursuant to paragraph 4(1)(b) of schedule 27 to the Act and the child's parent has required that another such meeting be arranged or under paragraph 4(2) of that schedule has required a meeting with the appropriate person under to be arranged; or

(e) the authority have sent a written request to the Secretary of State seeking his consent under section 347(5)(b) to the child being educated at an independent school which is not approved by him and such consent has not been received by the authority within two weeks of the date on which the request was sent.'

Case
19

Post Script

In this situation, as with others, the headteacher of your child's school is a potential ally. He or she will be as anxious as you to get extra support in place, not just for your son but for the staff as well. Heads cannot make decisions in relation to when statements will come into effect, or when the provision will be made for a child, but they can find out, and let parents know if delay is likely. If you have good reason to believe an LEA might be dragging their feet then you should seek advice from one of the Helpline organisations listed in part 7, rather than waiting until the actual deadline has been breached.

Case 20

66 We do not believe that the LEA have any intention of integrating Tom. Under Part 2 of his statement they have listed his needs, and it is clear to us that all of these could be met in an ordinary school. However, under Part 3 they use phrases like: 'requires a developmental curriculum', 'needs to work alongside pupils with a similar level of learning difficulty in small groups', 'programme to be delivered by teachers experienced in working with pupils with severe learning difficulties'. Even though this is a proposed statement, and there is no school named, we know that these phrases mean 'special school'. Is there anything we can do about it at this stage? 99

The first step

Write to the officer within 15 days, asking for a meeting to discuss the proposed statement. At this meeting, you should ask:

- Which of Tom's needs listed under Part 2 does the LEA think could *not* be provided for in a mainstream school?
- What specific investigations have been undertaken by the authority to discover whether Tom could receive the special education provision he needs in a mainstream school?
- Given that schedule 27(2)(b) says that a proposed statement must not refer to a type of school, will the officer amend the proposed statement to remove the coded references to 'special school'?

You should be ready to present as much argument and information as possible on the ways in which Tom's provision could be made in a mainstream school. If there is any support for inclusion in any of the professional advice which is attached to the proposed statement, then draw the officer's attention to it.

At the end of the meeting, leave the officer with a written note of the questions you have asked and ask him/her to confirm the answers to your questions in writing as soon as possible.

It may help if you have advice before the meeting – see the Helpline numbers in part 7 of this guide.

If that doesn't work

If the officer fails to answer your questions satisfactorily and seems determined to press ahead with the idea of a special school placement firmly in mind, then it might be necessary to ask for a meeting with one or more of the professionals who have prepared advice for the assessment. You could ask these questions:

- In their professional opinion, what arrangements would be needed for Tom to receive his special education provision in an ordinary mainstream school?
- In their professional opinion, are there any reasons why such arrangements could not be made?
- In their professional opinion, would it benefit Tom to have his needs met in a mainstream school?

You should contact one of the Helpline organisations listed in part 7 for advice before going to this meeting. It may help to have someone who can support you, if only by taking careful notes of the answers you get. This may help you later on when it comes to deciding which of the LEA's professionals, if any, might be good witnesses for you if you appeal to the Special Educational Needs Tribunal.

What the law says

The 1996 Education Act says:

'(1) Any person exercising any functions under this Part in respect of a child with special educational needs who should be educated in a school shall secure that, if the conditions mentioned in subsection (2) are satisfied, the child is educated in a school which is not a special school unless that is incompatible with the wishes of his parent.

(2) The conditions are that educating the child in a school which is not a special school is compatible with –

(a) his receiving the special educational provision which his learning difficulty calls for,
(b) the provision of efficient education for the children with whom he will be educated, and
(c) the efficient use of resources.'

(Section 316)

'(2) Before making a statement, a local education authority shall serve on the parent of the child concerned –

(a) a copy of the proposed statement, and
(b) a written notice explaining the arrangements under paragraph 3 below, the effect of paragraph 4 below and the right to appeal under section 326 of the Act and containing such other information as may be prescribed, but the copy of the proposed statement shall not specify any matter in pursuance of section 324(4) of this Act or any prescribed matter.'

(Schedule 27)

'(4) The statement shall –

(a) specify the type of school or other institution which the local education authority consider would be appropriate for the child,
(b) if they are not required under Schedule 27 to specify the name of any school in the statement, specify the name of any school or institution (whether in the United Kingdom or elsewhere) which they consider would be appropriate for the child and should be specified in the statement, and

80

(c) specify any provision for the child for which they make arrangements under section 319 and which they consider should be specified in the statement.'

(Section 324)

2

What the Code of Practice says

Case 20

'The LEA must draw up a proposed statement, completing all Parts except Part 4: the proposed statement must not contain any details relating to where the proposed special educational provision should be made.'

(Paragraph 4:37)

'. . . discussions between advisers and parents about the child's needs and the adviser's written advice may include consideration of various options including the scope for mainstream education for the child and the type of school in which the child's needs might best be met, for example mainstream, special or residential . . .'

(Paragraph 3:98)

Post Script

Remember that at the proposed statement stage the LEA are not supposed to make up their minds on placement until you have expressed your preference for a particular school. Then, the onus will be on the LEA to show why your preference cannot be met.

There are three reasons why you should take full advantage of your rights in law to ask for meetings with officers and professionals at the proposed statement stage:

First, changes can be made quickly at this stage, and the LEA officer will be anxious to compromise, provided you have strong evidence to back you up. In this way, the LEA can avoid Tribunal appeals which they are likely to lose.

The second reason is that you can collect a lot of information which can be of use to you if you have to go to appeal at the next stage. Make careful note of the questions you ask and the answers given. Ask for answers to be confirmed in writing after a meeting.

The third reason is that LEA officers are not always aware of the law on special education. You should remind the special needs officer that when you name a school as your preference, the onus will be on the LEA to show that it is not suitable.

2

Case 20

Case 21

66 We have just received our daughter's proposed statement and we are not happy with the way her needs have been described in Part 2. All it says is that Jenny is a friendly and attractive little girl (which we already knew!) with 'a general delay with her learning'. In fact she has a specific problem with reading and writing. In other areas her development is fine. 99

The first step

You have 15 days to write back and ask for a meeting with the special needs officer. Do this. Do not put your views in writing at this stage – simply ask for a meeting to discuss the proposed statement.

Before the meeting, read through all of the professional advice which you will have received along with the proposed statement. There are bound to be more specific descriptions of Jenny's learning difficulties than the one contained in Part 2 of the statement.

If you agree with the descriptions of Jenny's needs in the advice, then at your meeting with the officer ask that the proposed statement is amended in order to include the specific descriptions of her needs as they appear in the professional advice. Remind the officer that in law Part 2 of the statement must refer to the needs identified during Jenny's assessment.

If you disagree with the way Jenny's needs are described in the professional advice, you should consider getting a second professional opinion – see the Helpline numbers in Part 7 of this guide for the name of an organisation which may be able to help you with this. If the second opinion backs you up, send a copy of it to the LEA and ask for Part 2 of the statement to be amended in order to include more specific reference to

Jenny's needs as these have been identified by the second professional opinion.

When you ask the officer to amend the statement, give him/her a copy of what it is you want the statement to say under Part 2. Prepare this before the meeting. Leave a copy with the officer and keep one for yourself.

2

Case

21

If that doesn't work

If the LEA finalises the statement as it was originally proposed, and without amending it according to your request, then you will have to decide whether to appeal or not. Someone from one of the Helpline organisations can help you make this decision (see part 7 for telephone numbers).

What the law says

Section 324 of the Education Act 1996 says:

'(3) In particular, the statement shall –

(a) give details of the authority's assessment of the child's special educational needs.'

Regulation 13 of the Education (Special Educational Needs) Regulations 1994 says:

'A statement of a child's special educational needs made under section 324(1) shall be in a form substantially corresponding to that set out in Part B of the Schedule, shall contain the information therein specified, and shall be dated and authenticated by the signature of a duly authorised officer of the authority concerned.'

The Schedule to the 1994 Regulations says:

'Part B – Statement of Special Educational Needs.

Part 2: Here set out the child's special educational needs, in terms of the child's learning difficulties which call for special educational provision, as assessed by the authority.'

What the courts have said

Case
21

In a judgement known as *R vs The Secretary of State for Education and Science ex parte E [1992] 1 ELR 377*, the Court of Appeal ruled that Part 2 of a statement ('special educational needs') must set out all of a child's special educational needs identified during an assessment. In addition, Part 3 of a statement must specify the provision required to meet each of the needs identified in Part 2, whether that provision was to be made by the LEA or by the child's own school. For more information on this judgement, see part 5 of this guide.

What the Code of Practice says

'Part 2 of the statement should describe all the child's learning difficulties identified during the statutory assessment. It should also include a description of the child's functioning – what the child can and cannot do. The description in Part 2 should draw on and may refer to the professional advice attached in the appendices. Where the LEA adopt that advice in their description of the child's learning difficulties, they should say that they have done so but merely stating that they are adopting the advice in the appendices is not sufficient. The appendices may contain conflicting opinion or opinion open to interpretation, which the LEA must resolve, giving reasons for the conclusions they have reached.'

(Paragraph 4:27)

PostScript

It is important to get Part 2 of your child's statement right. This is because the LEA must specify, under Part 3, provision to meet each and every one of the needs identified in Part 2. If Part 2 fails to mention one of your child's needs, the child may not get the provision required to meet that need. If you are not happy with the provision for your child (set out under Part 3 of the statement) when it is finalised, then it is vital to check to make sure whether you need to appeal against Part 2 as well as Part 3 of the statement. Read case 22 immediately, and contact one of the Helpline organisations in part 7 if you need to discuss the situation with someone.

2

Case 21

Case 22

66 We are unhappy with the special education provision in Part 3 of our son's proposed statement. It is not specific enough. There is no indication of what kind of help he should get, nor how much. Also, the statement says that the school will decide on the help he needs – whereas we thought that the LEA made this decision when they decided what a statement should say. 99

The first step

You are right in thinking that when an LEA makes a statement, they are accepting that they – rather than anyone else, including the school – must make the decision on what a child's needs are and what provision is necessary to meet them (see *What the courts have said* below).

It seems that one of three things might have gone wrong here:

- Part 2 of the statement (special educational needs) does not set out all of Joe's needs. As a result, Part 3 can not specify the provision necessary to meet all of his needs. If this is the problem, read case 21 as well as this one.

- Part 2 sets out all of Joe's needs, but the provision in Part 3 does not match up with all the needs identified in Part 2.

- The provision in Part 3 has not been sufficiently specified.

You have 15 days to write asking for a meeting with an officer to discuss the proposed statement. Study all of the professional advice before meeting the officer. You may find that the educational advice and the psychological advice both contain full descriptions of Joe's needs and of the provision necessary to meet them. If so, when you go to the meeting with the officer, you should ask:

"Why have you ignored your own professional advice in writing the statement? Please amend the statement to include specific reference to the needs identified in the professional advice and to the provision which the advice says is necessary."

If the statement refers to the kind of provision Joe needs but fails to specify how much, you will need to draw the officer's attention to paragraph 4:28 of the Code of Practice and the judgement in 'L vs Clarke and Somerset County Council [1998] ELR 129' (see *What the courts have said* below).

Write down what *you* think Joe's statement should say in Parts 2 and 3 and leave a copy of this with the officer at the end of the meeting.

If you disagree with the way Joe's needs are described in the professional advice, you should consider getting a second professional opinion – see Helpline numbers in part 7 for the name of an organisation which may be able to help you with this. If the second opinion supports your views, copy it to the LEA with a letter asking for Parts 2 and 3 of the statement to be amended in order to include more specific reference to Joe's needs and the provision necessary to meet them, as these have been identified in the second professional opinion.

If the LEA's professional advice fails to say what provision Joe needs, then also read case 17 before meeting the officer.

If that doesn't work

If the LEA finalises the statement without amending it, then you will probably want to appeal. See part 3 of this book for advice on how to do so.

What the law says

The 1996 Education Act says:

'(1) A parent on whom a copy of a proposed statement has

been served under paragraph 2 above may –

(a) make representations (or further representations) to the local education authority about the content of the statement, and

(b) require the authority to arrange a meeting between him and an officer of the authority at which the statement can be discussed.'

(Schedule 27(4))

Case

22

'(3) In particular, the statement shall –

(b) specify the special educational provision to be made for the purpose of meeting those needs . . .'

(Section 324)

The schedule to part B of the Education (Special Educational Needs) Regulations 1994 says:

'Statement of Special Educational Needs.

Part 3 . . . Here specify the special educational provision which the authority consider appropriate to meet the needs specified in Part 2 and to meet the objectives specified in this Part, and in particular specify –

(a) any appropriate facilities and equipment, staffing arrangements and curriculum,

(b) any appropriate modifications to the application of the National Curriculum,

(c) any appropriate exclusions from the application of the National Curriculum, in detail, and the provision which it is proposed to substitute for any such exclusions in order to maintain a balanced and broadly based curriculum, and

(d) where residential accommodation is appropriate, that fact.'

What the courts have said

Case 22

In a judgement known as *R vs The Secretary of State for Education and Science ex parte E [1992] 1 ELR 377*, the High Court ruled that Part 2 of a statement ('special educational needs') must set out all of a child's special educational needs identified during an assessment. In addition, Part 3 of a statement must specify the provision required to meet each of the needs identified in Part 2, whether that provision was to be made by the LEA or by the child's own school.

A statement which says in Part 2, for example, 'Joe has a variety of special educational needs, but is a very happy child' has not been written in accordance with the judgement in 'Ex parte E' and therefore is legally challengeable. Similarly, a statement which says 'The special educational needs coordinator at Joe's school will decide on the level of support required to meet Joe's needs' has not been written in accordance with 'Ex parte E' and, again, is legally challengeable.

In a judgement known as *L vs Clarke and Somerset County Council [1998] ELR 129*, the court ruled on the duty of an LEA to be specific when writing part 3 of a statement of special educational needs:

"A requirement that the help to be given should be specified in the statement in terms of hours per week was not an absolute and universal precondition of the legality of any statement ... however ... in very many cases it will not be possible to fulfil the requirement to specify the special educational provision considered appropriate to meet the child's needs, including specification of staffing arrangements and curriculum, unless hours per week are set out."

What the Code of Practice says

'The provision set out in this sub-section should normally be specific, detailed and quantified (in terms, for example, of hours of ancillary or specialist teaching support) although there will be cases where some flexibility should be retained in order to meet the changing special educational needs of the child concerned.'

(Paragraph 4:28)

Post Script

One of the comments reported in 'Ex parte E' was that Part 2 of a statement was like a doctor's diagnoses of what was wrong with you, and Part 3 was like his prescription for the medicine which would put you right. Sometimes LEAs write both Parts 2 and 3 of their statements like diagnoses – writing long lists of a child's needs, but never getting around to saying what provision they intend to make to meet those needs.

Another way of thinking of Parts 2 and 3 of a statement is to imagine them as pieces of a jigsaw puzzle which must fit exactly together. For example, if Part 2 lists seven special educational needs, then Part 3 should refer to special educational provision to meet each and every one of these needs. These two Parts of the statement should lock together.

Case 23

" We have received the proposed statement and all the professional advice. We have been told that we can express a preference for an LEA school or a grant maintained school in our area or in another LEA area. However, we believe our son needs intensive special help of the kind which can only be provided in a specialist independent school for autistic pupils. But if we can't express a preference for an independent school, how are we going to be able to appeal when our preference is not met? **"**

The first step

The law says that you can only express a preference for a maintained (i.e. LEA) school, but this does not mean that you can not ask for a place at an independent school.

The difference is this:

When you 'express a preference' for an LEA school, the LEA has to comply with your request. If they don't, the onus is on them to prove why it is not possible.

However, when you ask for an independent school as part of your 'representations' on the proposed statement, the onus is on you to prove that none of the schools the LEA can offer can meet your child's needs – and that, therefore, they must place your child in the independent school.

Within 15 days of receiving the proposed statement, you must ask for a meeting with the special needs officer. At that meeting, explain why you do not believe that the schools the LEA can offer can meet your child's special educational needs. If you can convince them of this, then they will have to consider an independent school. But if you cannot persuade them, they are under no obligation to look at independent provision – and it does not matter that the independent school you have in mind is an excellent school and clearly better suited to your child's needs than the school the LEA has in mind. LEAs are not bound to offer a child with special needs 'the best' provision to meet their needs (see *What the courts have said*, below) – only what is necessary to meet their needs.

2

Case 23

It may be that the professional advice gives you the evidence you need to prove that your child's needs cannot be met by any school the LEA can offer him. If not, you might have to consider getting a second professional opinion – see the Helpline numbers listed in part 7 of this book for organisations which may be able to help you with this.

If that doesn't work

If you are unable to persuade the LEA at the proposed statement stage to name the independent school you want, then you will have to consider appealing to the Tribunal when the statement is finalised.

What the law says

Schedule 27 of the 1996 Education Act says:

'(3)(1) Every local education authority shall make arrangements for enabling a parent on whom a copy of a proposed statement has been served . . . to express a preference as to the maintained, grant-maintained or grant-maintained special school at which he wishes education to be provided for his child and to give reasons for his preference.

(4)(1) A parent on whom a copy of a proposed statement has been served . . . may –

(a) make representations (or further representations) to the local education authority about the content of the statement, and
(b) require the authority to arrange a meeting between him

and an officer of the authority at which the statement can be discussed.'

What the courts have said

In a judgement known as *R vs Surrey County Council Education Committee ex parte H (1985) 83 LGR 219*, the High Court ruled: "There is no question of Parliament having placed the local education authority under an obligation to provide a child with the best possible education . . . or to educate him or her to his or her maximum potential."

What the Code of Practice says

'When LEAs send parents a copy of the proposed statement, they must tell the parents that they have the right to make representations to the LEA in favour of a school outside the maintained sector and that, if they wish to make such representations, they should do so within 15 days of receiving the proposed statement. If the LEA do not agree to the parents' representations, they should inform the parents of their decision before naming any school in the final statement. Parents will then have the opportunity to express a preference for a maintained school under paragraph 3 of Schedule 27 if they wish to do so.'

(Paragraph 4:46)

'When LEAs send parents a copy of the proposed statement, they must also send a list of all LEA-maintained and grant-maintained schools within the area of the LEA which cater for children of the appropriate age. They may also send parents a list of all such schools in neighbouring areas. LEAs must inform parents of the names of all independent schools approved under section 347 of the Act and of all non-maintained special schools. The Department for Education and the Welsh Office Education Department will make comprehensive lists of such schools available to LEAs on a regular basis.'

(Paragraph 4:47)

'If the parents make representations in favour of a non-maintained special school or an independent school, an officer of the LEA should discuss with them why they believe that school should be named. If naming the school in question would provide the child with residential education, the LEA should discuss with the parents why they feel such provision is necessary to meet the child's special educational needs and, if appropriate, may choose to involve the social services department in discussing the child's wider needs with the family. If parents have not visited the school and wish to do so, an officer of the LEA should help arrange such a visit.'

(Paragraph 4:48)

2

Case 23

Post Script

Remember, the most important point you must prove is not that the independent school is better than the LEA school, but that the school offered by the LEA cannot meet your child's needs. It would help your case to have a report which backs your opinion from an independent professional who has met and assessed your child and visited the school in question.

It is very unlikely that the school itself, or the LEA, will object to an independent professional making a visit – but it has been known! If it happens to you, contact one of the Helpline organisations listed in part 7 for advice on dealing with the situation.

Case 24

" The LEA has sent us a proposed statement on Emily, our daughter, which lists speech therapy as one of her special educational needs under Part 2, but then lists the speech therapy provision for her under Part 6 as 'Non-educational provision.' Surely it should be included under Part 3 as 'special educational provision'?

We had a meeting with the officer to discuss the proposed statement but she was not convinced that there was any need to change it. She just kept telling us that we would be able to appeal to the Tribunal if we weren't happy. But surely parents shouldn't have to appeal to the Tribunal just to get the LEA to write a statement properly? "

The first step

You are right in saying that it should not be necessary to have to go through an appeal to the Special Educational Needs Tribunal just to get the LEA to write their statement in accordance with the law. However, even though it should not be necessary, it often is!

As your daughter's statement is still at the proposed stage, it might be worth raising the issue in writing with the Chief Education Officer. In your letter, set out the grounds for believing that the statement has not been properly written and ask for it to be amended. Your letter could say something like this:

To: The Chief Education Officer

Dear Sir or Madam,

We are writing to request that you amend the proposed statement of special educational needs on our daughter on the grounds that it is not written in accordance with the law. Emily's need for speech therapy is educational, not medical, and this is confirmed by the fact that the statement lists her need for therapy under Part 2, headed 'Special Educational Needs'.

As you will be aware, following the court ruling in the 'Ex parte E' case, Part 3 of a statement must contain a reference to provision to meet any need identified in Part 2. Would you please amend the statement to bring it in line with the law, removing the reference to speech therapy in Part 6 and specifying the speech therapy provision as 'Special Education Provision' in Part 3.

If you are not prepared to make the changes I have asked for, then would you please finalise the statement immediately and I will prepare my case for the Special Educational Needs Tribunal . . .

2

Case 24

If that doesn't work

If your letter to the Chief Education Officer gets no results then you must appeal to the Special Educational Needs Tribunal as soon as the statement is finalised. You have an excellent case, but see part 3 of this guide for advice on appealing to the Tribunal.

What the law says

Regulation 13 of the Education (Special Educational Needs) Regulations 1994 says:

'A statement of a child's special educational needs made under section 324(1) shall be in a form substantially corresponding to that set out in part B of the schedule, shall contain the information therein specified, and shall be dated and authenticated by the signature of a duly authorised officer of the authority concerned.'

Part B – Statement of Special Educational Needs, says:
'Part 3: Special Educational Provision – here specify the special educational provision which the authority consider appropriate to meet the needs specified in Part 2 . . .' (i.e. the special educational needs)

Case 24

2

What the courts have said

In a judgement known as *R vs The Secretary of State for Education and Science, ex parte E [1992] 1 ELR 377*, the Court of Appeal ruled that Part 2 of a statement ('special educational needs') must set out all of a child's special educational needs identified during an assessment; and, that Part 3 of a statement must specify the provision required to meet each of the needs identified in Part 2, whether that provision was to be made by the LEA or by the child's own school. For more information on this judgement, see page 212).

What the Code of Practice says

'Speech and language therapy may be regarded as either educational or non-educational provision, depending upon the health or developmental history of each child.'

(Paragraph 4:34)

'Where the NHS does not provide speech and language therapy for a child whose statement specifies such therapy as educational provision, ultimate responsibility for ensuring that the provision is made rests with the LEA, unless the child's parents have made appropriate alternative arrangements.'

(Paragraph 4:35)

PostScript

It is only if speech therapy is specified as a special educational provision under Part 3 of a statement that your child is guaranteed to receive the provision. This is because LEAs have a strict duty to arrange the provision set out in Part 3. They are entitled to get another body, such as the local health authority, to actually provide or pay for speech therapists. But if, for whatever reason, the health authority won't or can't make the provision, then the LEA *must* do so.

If speech therapy is set out only under Part 6 of a statement, as a non-educational need, however, then no-one – neither the LEA nor the health authority – has a legal duty to make the provision a child needs.

2

Case 24

Whenever you believe that your LEA is not following the law, you should try to get an opinion on the situation from one of the Helpline organisations listed in part 7 of this guide, or from a solicitor familiar with educational law.

Case 25

66 The LEA have sent us a proposed statement on our son, Tony, who has language and communication problems. The speech therapist's advice says his need for speech therapy is educational and that it should be provided for him in an educational setting. However, the draft statement lists 'Speech therapy' under Part 5 as 'Non-educational needs' and under Part 6 as 'Non-educational provision'. We understand that the LEA have a duty to make special educational provision, but not 'non-educational' provision. What can we do to make sure that Tony's needs are written in his statement under the right part and that the LEA accepts responsibility for meeting them? 99

The first step

You should write immediately to the officer, asking for a meeting to discuss the proposed statement. You have to write within 15 days of receiving the proposed statement.

At your meeting, ask the officer:

● What evidence have you got for saying that Tony's need for speech therapy is non-educational rather than educational?
● On what grounds are you ignoring the speech therapist's advice?
● Will you agree to amend the proposed statement in order to list Tony's need for speech therapy under Part 2, as a special educational need, and then specify the provision necessary under Part 3 as a special educational provision?

Write your questions on a sheet of paper which you can leave with the officer at the end of the meeting as a reminder. Ask for the answers to be confirmed in writing as soon as possible in order that you can decide what further action you might want to take.

If that doesn't work

If the LEA refuse to amend the statement, you will probably have to appeal against it to the Special Educational Needs Tribunal. You cannot appeal against the fact that speech therapy is referred to in Parts 5 and 6 of the statement, because there is no appeal against Parts 5 and 6; however, you can appeal on the grounds that Part 2 is incomplete in failing to specify speech therapy as a special educational provision necessary to meet his needs.

See part 3 of this book for advice on appealing to the Tribunal. At this stage it might help to speak to someone from one of the Helpline organisations listed in part 7.

What the law says

Regulation 13 of the Education (Special Educational Needs) Regulations 1994 says:

'A statement of a child's special educational needs made under section 324(1) shall be in a form substantially corresponding to that set out in part B of the schedule, shall contain the information therein specified, and shall be dated and authenticated by the signature of a duly authorised officer of the authority concerned.'

Part B – Statement of Special Educational Needs, says:

'Part 3: Special educational provision – here specify the special educational provision which the authority consider appropriate to meet the needs specified in part 2 . . .' (i.e. the special educational needs)

What the courts have said

The judgement in the case of *R vs Lancashire County Council Ex parte M [1989] 2 ELR 279* included this comment:

Case 2 25

"To teach an adult who has lost his larynx because of cancer might be considered as treatment rather than education. But to teach a child who has never been able to communicate by language, whether because of some chromosomal disorder . . . or because of social cause . . . seems to us just as much educational provision as to teach a child to communicate in writing."

What the Code of Practice says

'Speech and language therapy may be regarded as either educational or non-educational provision, depending upon the health or developmental history of each child.'

(Paragraph 4:34)

'Where the NHS does not provide speech and language therapy for a child whose statement specifies such therapy as educational provision, ultimate responsibility for ensuring that the provision is made rests with the LEA, unless the child's parents have made appropriate alternative arrangements.'

(Paragraph 4:35)

Post Script

There may come a point, when you are arguing over your child's proposed statement with the LEA, when you realise that they are not going to change it. To continue to ask for meetings with professionals after this point will only delay finalising the statement and therefore the point when you can appeal. So, once you sense you are wasting your time, ask the LEA to finalise the statement so that you can appeal to the Tribunal.

If the LEA's own professional advice is on your side, you have a strong case and will not need additional independent professional advice. You are not able to appeal against Parts 5 and 6 of a statement, as these deal with 'non-educational needs and provision'. Your appeal must be based on the fact that speech therapy has not been referred to in Parts 2 and 3 as 'educational needs and provision'.

If in doubt about wording your Notice of Appeal, contact one of the Helpline organisations listed in part 7.

Note that physiotherapy and occupational therapy, like speech therapy, may be educational or medical, depending on the individual child's needs (see *B vs Isle of Wight Council [1997] ELR 279* in part 5: Case Law).

2

Case 25

Case 26

❝ We're at the proposed statement stage and have found a mainstream school we really like for our son, Saul. There's a really good special needs department which works closely with all subject departments so children spend most of their time being supported in the mainstream. At our meeting with the special needs officer to discuss the proposed statement, we expressed a preference for this school, but we were told we'd be wasting our time as it is in a neighbouring LEA's area and that LEA have said that the school is full. **❞**

The first step

Your own LEA are under a legal duty to place Saul in the school of your choice, provided it is a maintained school (i.e. not a private school) and provided that:

- it is suitable to his age, ability or aptitude and his special educational needs;
- his attendance there will not affect the education of other children;
- there is an efficient use of resources.

This is the law, regardless of which LEA are responsible for the school you prefer. It is true that your own LEA must consult the governing body of the school and consult the neighbouring LEA but, after this consultation, the decision has to be made by *your* LEA – not the school itself or the neighbouring LEA.

The first step is to write to your own LEA reminding them that they (and no-one else) have the duty in law to make the decision (see *What the law says* below).

Also, you need to ask your LEA to explain in writing exactly why they are denying you a place for Saul in the school of your preference. Is it because they believe his needs cannot be met in that school, or that other children's education will suffer, or that it would not be an efficient use of resources?

Your letter could go something like this:

> To: The Chief Education Officer,
>
> Dear Sir or Madam,
>
> We are writing to you as the parents of Saul Williams, who has a proposed statement of special educational needs. We wish to express a preference for . . . School, in . . . , and want this school to be named in Saul's statement. We understand that under the 1996 Education Act, your Authority must make the decision about whether to name this school on Saul's statement, even though a different LEA maintain the school.
>
> We also understand that you are under a legal duty to name . . . School on Saul's statement, this being our preference as parents, unless you can show that the school cannot meet his needs, or that other children's education would be prejudiced or that there would be an inefficient use of resources. We do not believe that any of these conditions would arise if Saul were to go to . . . School, and we ask you to set out in writing which conditions you believe would arise and to provide us with your reasons and evidence for believing this . . .

If that doesn't work

If you are unhappy with the reply you receive to this letter, and the LEA go ahead and finalise Saul's statement without naming the school of your preference, you will be able to appeal to the Special Educational Needs Tribunal. It is advisable to consider appealing against Parts 2 and 4 of a statement, as well as Part 4 (which names the school). You should get advice on this straight away (see part 7 of this guide).

What the law says

The 1996 Education Act says:

Case 26

'(1) Every local education authority shall make arrangements for enabling a parent on whom a copy of a proposed statement has been served . . . to express a preference as to the maintained, grant-maintained or grant-maintained special school at which he wishes education to be provided for his child and to give reasons for his preference.

(2) any such preference must be expressed or made within the period of 15 days beginning –

(a) with the date on which the written notice mentioned in paragraph 2(b) above was served on the parent, or
(b) if a meeting has (or meetings have) been arranged under paragraph 4(1)(b) or (2) . . . with the date fixed for that meeting (or the last of those meetings).

(3) Where a local education authority make a statement in a case where the parent of the child concerned has expressed a preference in pursuance of such arrangements as to the school at which he wishes education to be provided for his child, they shall specify the name of that school in the statement unless –

(a) the school is unsuitable to the child's age, ability or aptitude or to his special educational needs, or
(b) the attendance of the child at the school would be incompatible with the provision of efficient education for the children with whom he would be educated or the efficient use of resources.'

(Schedule 27)

'(b) if the name of a maintained, grant-maintained or grant-maintained special school is specified in the statement, the governing body of the school shall admit the child to the school.'

(Section 324(5))

PostScript

There is no definition in law of what it means for a school to be 'full'. Schools have a 'standard, or approved, number' of pupils for the purposes of admissions, but LEAs are able to go over these numbers – and may have no choice when the Special Educational Needs Tribunal orders them to admit a child. In order to convince the Tribunal that the school the parents want simply cannot take another child, the LEA have to show that because of the high numbers of pupils in the school, the child's needs won't be met, or that other children's needs would not be met or that there would be an inefficient use of resources (for example, as a result of them having to appoint another teacher or build another classroom).

2

Case 26

Case 27

66 The statement has been finalised and we disagree with the description of our child's needs in Part 2. All it says is that he 'has moderate learning difficulties and is in need of a curriculum modified to meet his particular needs'. How do we appeal against this? 99

The first step

The arguments you must use to challenge the way your child's special educational needs have been described in the finalised statement are the same as the ones you would use when a statement is first proposed – see case 21. This time, however, instead of putting your case to an LEA officer, you need to put it to the Special Educational Needs Tribunal (see part 3).

It may be that your child's needs are fully described in the professional advice, but that the LEA have ignored the details in the reports. Or it could be that the professional advice is not detailed enough, in which case you should consider whether you need an independent second professional opinion on his needs (see the Helpline numbers in part 7 for advice on this).

You have two months to send in a Notice of Appeal to the Special Educational Needs Tribunal. Your grounds for appeal could be like this:

> *'Part 2 of the statement does not set out Troy's special educational needs in sufficient detail to make it clear what his actual needs are. Our main worry is that he has not made progress with his reading and number work for three years now. We believe there should be specific reference to these needs in Part 2, and an explanation of the cause . . .'*

Along with the form send a copy of the statement and all of

the professional advice attached to it.

You might also want to appeal against the special education provision in Part 3 of the statement, on the grounds that it is not specific enough (see case 30).

It is important that you get advice on appealing to the Tribunal if you are at all unsure of the arguments you should be making. See part 3 of this guide for how to do this.

2

Case

27

What the law says

The 1996 Education Act says:

'(1) The parent of a child for whom a local education authority maintain a statement under section 324 may –

(a) when the statement is first made,
(b) where the description in the statement of the authority's assessment of the child's special educational needs, or the special educational provision specified in the statement, is amended, or
(c) where, after conducting an assessment of the educational needs of the child under section 323, the local education authority determine not to amend the statement,

– appeal to the Tribunal against the description in the statement of the authority's assessment of the child's special educational needs, the special educational provision specified in the statement or, if no school is named in the statement, that fact.'

(Section 326)

'(3) In particular, the statement shall –

(a) give details of the authority's assessment of the child's special educational needs.'

(Section 324)

The Education (Special Educational Needs) Regulations 1994 say:

'A statement of a child's special educational needs made under section 324(1) shall be in a form substantially corresponding to that set out in part B of the Schedule, shall contain the information therein specified, and shall be dated and authenticated by the signature of a duly authorised officer of the authority concerned.'

(Regulation 13)

'Part 2 . . . Here set out the child's special educational needs, in terms of the child's learning difficulties which call for special educational provision, as assessed by the authority.'

(Part B: Statement of special educational needs)

What the courts have said

In a judgement known as *R vs The Secretary of State for Education and Science, ex parte E [1992] 1 ELR 377*, the court ruled that Part 2 of a statement ('special educational needs') must set out all of a child's special educational needs identified during an assessment; and, that Part 3 of a statement must specify the provision required to meet each of the needs identified in Part 2, whether that provision was to be made by the LEA or by the child's own school. A statement which simply says in Part 2, for example, 'Troy has moderate learning difficulties' has not been written in accordance with the judgement in 'Ex parte E'. Similarly, a statement which says 'Troy needs a moderate curriculum' has not been written in accordance with 'Ex parte E'. In both of these cases the statement is open to legal challenge.

What the Code of Practice says

'Part 2 of the statement should describe all the child's learning difficulties identified during the statutory assessment. It should also include a description of the child's functioning – what the child can and cannot do. The description in Part 2 should draw on and may refer to the professional advice attached in the appendices. Where the LEA adopt that advice in their description of the child's learning difficulties, they should say that they have done so but merely stating that they are adopting the advice in the appendices is not sufficient. The appendices may contain conflicting opinion or opinion open to interpretation, which the LEA must resolve, giving reasons for the conclusions they have reached.'

(Paragraph 4:27)

2

Case 27

PostScript

When children are referred to special schools, their statements often do not contain much detail in sections 3 or 6 because it is assumed by everyone that they will receive whatever provision other children at the school get. This can be dangerous if there are changes in the resourcing of the school and it is always in a child's best interests for their statement to be as detailed as possible when it is first issued. This is true whether a child is in a special school or a mainstream school. Even if you know what provision your child will receive and you are happy with this, you should insist on your child's educational needs being accurately and fully described in Part 2 of the statement.

Case 28

66 The statement has been finalised and we disagree with the special education provision set out under Part 3. All it says is that our son should receive 'regular programmes of support, devised and implemented by the school's special needs staff, in consultation with the area support team'. How do we appeal against this, given that we do not know what it means? 99

The first step

The arguments you must use to challenge the way your child's special educational provision has been described in the finalised statement are the same as the ones you would use when a statement is first proposed – see case 22. This time, however, instead of putting your arguments to an LEA officer, you will be putting them to the Special Educational Needs Tribunal.

You should study the professional advice carefully to find how your child's needs have been described, and also look at the particular needs which have been identified in Part 2 of his statement. The law says that professional advice should include information on the provision necessary to meet a child's needs (see case 17).

You have two months to send in a notice of appeal to the Special Educational Needs Tribunal. Your grounds for appeal could read like this:

> *Part 3 of the statement does not specify Michael's special educational provision in sufficient detail to make it clear what help he will get, and therefore ignores the ruling in 'L vs Clarke and Somerset County Council [1998] ELR 129'. Also, we do not accept that the reference to the band and amount of funding fulfils the requirements of the statement to 'specify'*

the special educational provision ('R vs Cumbria CC ex parte P [1995] COD 267'). Our main worry is that he has not made progress with his reading and number work for three years now. We believe that the provision he needs should be specified and quantified, in order to make it clear what kind of support and how much support the statement guarantees him.

2

Case 28

Along with the form send a copy of the statement and all of the professional advice attached to it.

You might also want to appeal against the account of your son's special education needs given in Part 2 of the statement, on the grounds that it is not detailed enough (see case 27) or against the school named on the statement on the grounds that it cannot make the provision you believe your son needs (see cases 29 and 30).

It is important that you get advice on appealing to the Tribunal if you are at all unsure of the arguments you should be making. See part 7 for the numbers of Helpline organisations.

What happens after that?

The Tribunal will send a copy of the notice of appeal to your LEA, and give them 20 working days to:

- say if they want to oppose your appeal, and
- send a written reply to your appeal.

The LEA's reply will be copied to you and you will then have 15 working days to reply to it and send in any further written evidence or reports for the Tribunal to consider.

At this point you should decide whether you want to ask the president of the Tribunal to 'direct':

- that particular witnesses appear;

- that any particular information or documents should be disclosed by the LEA.

2

You will be asked to fill in an attendance form, giving the names of your own witnesses and your representative, if you have one.

Case 28

What the law says

The 1996 Education Act says:

'(1) The parent of a child for whom a local education authority maintain a statement under section 324 may –

(a) when the statement is first made,
(b) where the description in the statement of the authority's assessment of the child's special educational needs, or the special educational provision specified in the statement, is amended, or
(c) where, after conducting an assessment of the educational needs of the child under section 323, the local education authority determine not to amend the statement,

– appeal to the Tribunal against the description in the statement of the authority's assessment of the child's special educational needs, the special educational provision specified in the statement or, if no school is named in the statement, that fact.'

(Section 326)

'(3) In particular, the statement shall –

(b) specify the special educational provision to be made for the purpose of meeting those needs . . .'

(Section 324)

The Schedule to the Education (Special Educational Needs) Regulations 1994 says:

'Part 3 . . . Objectives . . . Here specify the objectives which the special educational provision for the child should aim to meet.

Educational provision to meet needs and objectives . . . Here specify the special educational provision which the authority consider appropriate to meet the needs specified in Part 2 and to meet the objectives specified in this part, and in particular specify –

2

Case 28

(a) any appropriate facilities and equipment, staffing arrangements and curriculum,
(b) any appropriate modifications to the application of the National Curriculum,
(c) any appropriate exclusions from the application of the National Curriculum, in detail, and the provision which it is proposed to substitute for any such exclusions in order to maintain a balanced and broadly based curriculum, and
(d) where residential accommodation is appropriate, that fact.'

(Part B: Statement of special educational needs)

What the courts have said

In a judgement known as *L vs Clarke and Somerset County Council [1998] ELR 129*, the court ruled on the duty of an LEA to be specific when writing Part 3 of a statement of special educational needs:

"A requirement that the help to be given should be specified in the statement in terms of hours per week was not an absolute and universal precondition of the legality of any statement . . . however . . . in very many cases it will not be possible to fulfil the requirement to specify the special educational provision considered appropriate to meet the child's needs, including specification of staffing arrangements and curriculum, unless hours per week are set out."

In a judgement known as *R vs Cumbria County Council ex parte*

2

P [1995] COD 267, the court ruled that although it was not illegal to refer to a funding level (e.g. 'Band C') in Part 3 of a statement, or a specific amount of money, this did not satisfy the legal duty to 'specify' the provision to be arranged for a child.

Case 28

What the Code of Practice says

'The provision set out in this sub-section should normally be specific, detailed and quantified (in terms, for example, of hours of ancillary or specialist teaching support) although there will be cases where some flexibility should be retained in order to meet the changing special educational needs of the child concerned.'

(Paragraph 4:28 (extract))

Post Script

If you believe that there is information missing from the professional advice which, in law, should be there, then you should ask the president of the Tribunal to issue a direction telling the LEA to go back to the professional or professionals concerned and obtain the missing information.

You have to explain why you want the direction. In the case of an incomplete professional report, the reason is obvious: how can you be sure what your child needs if the professional reports do not spell it out for you? How can you argue effectively against the LEA at the Tribunal unless you know exactly what the professionals think is the appropriate provision for your child? For further information on appealing to the Tribunal, see part 3.

Case 29

66 The statement is finalised and the LEA have refused our request for a place in the local mainstream school for our daughter. Instead they want to taxi her on a round trip of 52 miles a day to a special school. We have no intention of sending her to a special school, whatever we are threatened with. How do we appeal against this decision? Will Mandy have a school to go to while we appeal? Can we keep her at home? 99

The first step

You should have already been given notice of the LEA's reasons for refusing your child a place in the school of your choice, before receiving the final form of the statement (Code of Practice, paragraph 4:54).

The LEA's grounds will be one of the following:

- that the school of your preference is not suitable to your daughter's age, ability, aptitude or special educational needs;
- that your daughter's attendance will prejudice the provision of efficient education for other children;
- that your daughter's attendance at the school would not be an efficient use of resources.

Basically, your appeal will be against whichever of these reasons the LEA have put forward for refusing your child a place in the school of your choice. However, as you have expressed a preference for a mainstream school and not a special school, the LEA have a duty to explore the possibility of your daughter being placed in other mainstream schools, i.e. ones you didn't express a preference for (see 'What the Code of Practice says', below). You should make sure they have done this, rather than just name the nearest special school in the statement.

You have two months to send in a Notice of Appeal to the

Special Educational Needs Tribunal. Your grounds for appeal might read like this:

We are appealing against the LEA's decision not to allow our daughter to attend the local community school, which is our preference, on the grounds that:

1. We believe that Mandy would benefit enormously from being integrated with pupils who do not have learning difficulties, so that in this sense her placement is appropriate to her age, ability and aptitude and her special educational needs. The LEA's letter to us of May 7th fails to show that Mandy would not benefit from a place in the school of our preference. We believe the special educational provision set out in Part 3 of the statement could be made in a mainstream school via 10 hours a week non-teaching assistance and 5 hours a week specialist teaching assistance. The LEA have provided no evidence to the contrary.

2. The LEA have produced no evidence that other children's education would be prejudiced by Mandy's presence in the school.

3. The LEA have produced no figures or costings showing that placing Mandy in the school of our preference would represent an inefficient use of resources. We believe that the saving on school transport costs alone will go a long way towards covering the cost of the teaching and non-teaching assistance needed. But, even if the mainstream placement were more expensive, we do not accept that it would represent an inefficient use of resources. This is because of the additional educational benefits there would be for Mandy at a mainstream school.

4. Not only have the LEA turned down our preference, but we also believe that they have failed to explore the possibility of Mandy attending another mainstream school in the area.

Along with the form send a copy of the statement and all of the professional advice attached to it. You might also want to appeal against the way Mandy's needs have been described in Part 2 (see case 21) and the way the provision has been specified in Part 3 (see case 28).

2

Case 29

An additional ground for your appeal could be that the travelling involved would be so stressful that Mandy would be unable to benefit from the educational provision available at the special school (see *What the courts have said* below).

It is important that you get advice on appealing to the Tribunal if you are at all unsure of the arguments you should be making. See part 7 for the numbers of Helpline organisations.

What happens after that?

The Tribunal will send a copy of the notice of appeal to your LEA and give them 20 working days to:

- say if they want to oppose your appeal, and
- send a written reply to your appeal.

The LEA's reply will be copied to you and you will then have 15 working days to reply to it and send in any further written evidence or reports for the Tribunal to consider. At this point you should decide whether you want to ask the president of the Tribunal to 'direct':

- that any particular witnesses should appear;
- that particular information or documents should be disclosed by the LEA.

You will be asked to fill in an attendance form, giving the names of your own witnesses and your representative, if you have one.

For more information on appealing to the Tribunal, see part 3 of this guide.

2

Case 29

Legally, the LEA do not have to offer Mandy a place in a school other than the one named on the finalised statement, although in practice many LEAs allow children to remain at their present school or nursery when parents are appealing against a statement. You should speak to the head of the school or nursery about this and write to the Chief Education Officer making a formal request, if this is what you think would be best for her.

Legally, you are entitled to educate Mandy at home, but the LEA have a duty to check up to ensure that her needs are being properly met. If you are considering this, speak to one of the Helpline organisations first. If the LEA are not satisfied that you are providing for Mandy's needs at home, it is possible that they may serve an Attendance Order on you, which could end up in your being prosecuted in a magistrates court, and fined. If your LEA send you a notice of Attendance Order, you must seek immediate legal advice from a solicitor.

What the law says

The 1996 Education Act says:

'(1) Any person exercising any functions under this part in respect of a child with special educational needs who should be educated in a school shall secure that, if the conditions mentioned in subsection (2) are satisfied, the child is educated in a school which is not a special school unless that is incompatible with the wishes of his parent.

(2) The conditions are that educating the child in a school which is not a special school is compatible with –

(a) his receiving the special educational provision which his learning difficulty calls for,

(b) the provision of efficient education for the children with whom he will be educated, and

(c) the efficient use of resources.'

(Section 316)

'(1) The parent of a child for whom a local education authority maintain a statement under section 324 may –

(a) when the statement is first made,
(b) where the description in the statement of the authority's assessment of the child's special educational needs, or the special educational provision specified in the statement, is amended, or
(c) where, after conducting an assessment of the educational needs of the child under section 323, the local education authority determine not to amend the statement,

– appeal to the Tribunal against the description in the statement of the authority's assessment of the child's special educational needs, the special educational provision specified in the statement or, if no school is named in the statement, that fact.'

(Section 326)

What the courts have said

In the case known as *C vs Lancashire County Council [1997] ELR 377*, the parents appealed to the High Court on a point of law against the decision of the Tribunal to place their child in a special school, rather than in the mainstream school of their choice. One of the reasons put forward by the LEA, and accepted by the Tribunal, was that placing a child in a mainstream school was not an efficient use of resources. On this point, the judge ruled that the decision was not entirely a question of which option was the least expensive for an LEA:

". . . one has to look at the figures, decide whether there is an additional cost, and then do a balancing exercise weighing the additional cost against the parents' preference ... it is partly a factual exercise and partly a balancing exercise."

In the case known as *R vs Hereford and Worcester County Council ex parte P [1992] 2 ELR 732*, the judge ruled as follows:

2

Case 29

"It is implicit in section 55(1) of the Education Act 1944 that the LEA is under a duty to make such arrangements as it considers necessary for a child to reach school without due stress, strain or difficulty such as would prevent him from benefiting from the education the school has to offer ... It follows that where a child with special educational needs requires transport to get him to school, the transport which the LEA proposes to make available must therefore be non-stressful transport ..."

What the Code of Practice says

'Under section 316 of the Act, LEAs have a qualified duty to secure that children with special educational needs, including children with statements, are educated in mainstream schools. If parents express a preference for a mainstream school, the LEA must comply with that preference so long as the three conditions in paragraph 4:41 are met. If those conditions do not apply in the mainstream school preferred by the child's parents but would apply in another, the LEA must name that alternative school, in fulfilment of its duty under section 316. If, however, the conditions would not apply in any mainstream school, the LEA will look to a special school placement or alternative arrangements.'

(Paragraph 4:42)

PostScript

You may be feeling very angry when you go to the Tribunal if you believe that your LEA have ignored their duty to consider seriously the option of integration for Mandy. Although you should certainly draw the Tribunal's attention to this, do not rest the whole of your case on criticising the LEA.

Try to show how, in practice, your child could receive appropriate education in the school of your choice, without other children's education being prejudiced and without resources being used inefficiently. If you believe a second professional opinion will help you show this, speak to one of the Helpline organisations listed in part 7 immediately.

Case 29

Case 30

❝ Our daughter has cerebral palsy and her statement has just been finalised. We have no problem with Part 2, which says clearly that our daughter will benefit from a programme based on conductive education, or with Part 3, which says that she will be taught by a conductor trained in Peto methods. The problem comes with Part 4, where the LEA names one of its own schools for physically handicapped children. We have visited this school and spoken to the head. Four of the teachers were sent on a two-day introductory course on Peto methods last year, and it is on this basis that the LEA now claims that the school offers conductive education for children. The real training consists of a four-year course, and is only offered by the Peto Institute in Hungary. The school we want is staffed by conductors who are Peto trained, but of course it is independent and fee-paying. How do we prepare our appeal? ❞

The first step

The first step is to put on one side the arguments about the training and qualifications of the teachers at the special school. These are important, but not the most important part of the case you have to argue. In order to be successful at appeal, you will have to show that your daughter's special educational needs include the need for the range of activities, tasks and experiences which are embodied within the conductive education programme. Spell these out in detail. Do not just rely on Tribunal members understanding what you mean by the label 'conductive education'.

Having defined your daughter's needs in these terms, describe the provision required to meet them, again in a series of detailed points. Don't rely on phrases like 'needs to be taught by a Peto-trained conductor', because people will not know what that means. For each need in Part 2, try to specify – and quantify – the provision required to meet it in Part 3 (see *What the courts have said* below).

You will also need to present evidence that the LEA special school is not able to make the provision necessary to meet your daughter's needs as you have described them. You may need a second professional opinion on the provision available in the LEA school to prove your point. See the Helpline numbers listed in part 7 of this book.

2

Case 30

You have two months to send in a Notice of Appeal to the Special Educational Needs Tribunal. Your grounds for appeal need to stick close to the points outlined above.

It will not be enough to prove that the school you want is better than the LEA school. You will have to show that their school cannot make the provision necessary to meet your daughter's needs (see *What the courts have said* below).

What happens after that?

The Tribunal will send a copy of the Notice of Appeal to your LEA, and give them 20 working days to:

- say if they want to oppose your appeal;
- send a written reply to your appeal.

The LEA's reply will be copied to you and you will then have 15 working days to reply to it and send in any further written evidence or reports for the Tribunal to consider.

At this point you should decide whether you want to ask the president of the Tribunal to 'direct':

- that any particular witnesses should appear;
- that any particular information or documents should be disclosed by the LEA.

You will be asked to fill in an attendance form, giving the names of your own witnesses and your representative, if you have one.

For more information on how the Tribunal works, see part 3 of this guide.

2

Case 30

What the law says

Section 326 of the 1993 Education Act says:

'(1) The parent of a child for whom a local education authority maintain a statement under section 324 may –

(a) when the statement is first made,
(b) where the description in the statement of the authority's assessment of the child's special educational needs, or the special educational provision specified in the statement, is amended, or
(c) where, after conducting an assessment of the educational needs of the child under section 323, the local education authority determine not to amend the statement,

– appeal to the Tribunal against the description in the statement of the authority's assessment of the child's special educational needs, the special educational provision specified in the statement or, if no school is named in the statement, that fact.'

What the courts have said

According to the judgement in the case known as *R vs Surrey CC Education Committee ex parte H (1983) 83 LGR 219*: "There is no question of Parliament having placed the local education authority under an obligation to provide a child with the best possible education . . . or to educate him or her to his or her maximum potential."

In a judgement known as *R vs The Secretary of State for Education and Science, ex parte E [1992] 1 ELR 377*, the court ruled that Part 2 of a statement ('special educational needs') must set out all of a child's special educational needs identified during an assessment; and, that Part 3 of a statement must specify the provision required to meet each of the needs identified in Part 2, whether that provision was to be made by the LEA or by the child's own school.

In a judgement known as *L vs Clarke and Somerset County Council [1998] ELR 129*, the court ruled on the duty of an LEA to be specific when writing Part 3 of a statement of special educational needs:

2

Case 30

"A requirement that the help to be given should be specified in the statement in terms of hours per week was not an absolute and universal precondition of the legality of any statement . . . however . . . in very many cases it will not be possible to fulfil the requirement to specify the special educational provision considered appropriate to meet the child's needs, including specification of staffing arrangements and curriculum, unless hours per week are set out."

PostScript

When you are preparing your arguments and your evidence for appeal, remember the basic principles underlying the law on special education. These are that individual children's needs are identified, assessed, described in a statement and then provided for. Your starting point, then, should be trying to get as full a description of your child's needs as possible in Part 2 of a statement. Then, in Part 3, specify in as much detail as possible the exact provision or help necessary to meet each one of her needs.

If you can then show that the LEA's choice of school cannot, in practice, make that provision, you have the basis of a good case. On the other hand, if your only arguments are that your daughter needs 'conductive education' and that only a four-year Peto-trained professional can provide this, then you are not likely to be successful at appeal – not because you are wrong, but because the Tribunal members may not understand the terms well enough to appreciate what you are saying. To be sure, spell it all out!

Case 31

❝Our son's speech therapy needs are listed under Part 5 (non-educational needs) and the provision is set out under part 6 (non-educational provision). We have just heard that we have lost our appeal to the Tribunal, where we tried to get the provision moved to Part 3 of the statement. Now we are worried about how specific the wording of Parts 5 and 6 should be. All the statement says under Part 5 is that he 'needs speech therapy;' all it says under Part 6 is 'regular speech therapy.' Will that be good enough? ❞

The first step

You should get immediate advice on the Tribunal's decision. You can ask for a review of the decision within ten days, or appeal on a point of law within 28 days. Contact one of the Helpline organisations listed in Part 7 for advice on approaching a solicitor.

If that doesn't work

If you are not able to challenge the Tribunal's decision on a point of law, you should ask for an urgent meeting with the Special Needs Officer.

At the meeting, ask the officer these questions:

- What arrangements will be made for the provision of speech therapy?
- What are the objectives of the speech therapy provision?
- What are the arrangements for monitoring progress towards meeting those objectives?

Remind the officer that all this information should, by law, be included in Part 6 of the statement of special educational needs. Ask for an assurance that the statement will be amended in order to bring it into line with the requirements of the law.

Also, if you believe that the LEA should arrange the provision specified under Part 6, then ask. The law allows them to, if they choose.

At the end of the meeting, leave the officer with a written copy of your questions, and ask for the answers to be provided in writing as soon as possible.

2

Case 31

If the LEA refuse to bring the wording of the statement in line with the law, contact one of the Helpline organisations. You may be able to challenge the LEA for the way they have worded Parts 5 and 6 of the statement (see part 4 of this guide, which deals with judicial review and legal aid). Again, you will need advice on contacting a solicitor who knows something about special education law.

What the law says

The Education (Special Educational Needs) Regulations 1994 say:

'A statement of a child's special educational needs made under section 324(1) shall be in a form substantially corresponding to that set out in Part B of the Schedule, shall contain the information therein specified, and shall be dated and authenticated by the signature of a duly authorised officer of the authority concerned.'

(Regulation 13)

'Part 6: Non-educational provision
[Here specify any non-educational provision which the authority propose to make available or which they are satisfied will be made available by a district health authority, a social services authority or some other body, *including the arrangements for its provision. Also specify the objectives of the provision, and the arrangements for monitoring progress in meeting those objectives.*]' (our emphasis)

(Part B of the Schedule: Statement
of special educational needs)

What the Code of Practice says

'The designated medical officer for special educational needs should liaise as necessary to ensure that the health service contribution has been confirmed. Part 6 should also state the objectives to be achieved by such non-educational provision and should set out the arrangements which have been agreed by the LEA and the providing body for its delivery.'

(Paragraph 4:32)

'When considering a child's non-educational needs and provision, the LEA should ensure that the needs are clearly and accurately described and that there is full agreement on the nature and quantity of the provision necessary to meet those needs, consulting the relevant responsible professionals as necessary.'

(Paragraph 4:33)

PostScript

You do not need to let the matter rest when you lose an appeal. Even if there are no grounds for taking legal action, you should try to speak to the LEA again about the situation. You could, for example, ask for an early review of the statement (see case 38 for advice on influencing reviews).

If you feel strongly that your child's needs are not being met, talk the situation through with someone from one of the Helpline organisations listed in part 7 of this book.

Case 32

❝ Our son's statement was issued last year and things went fine to begin with. Part 3 of the statement said he should have two hours individual specialist teaching, one to one, every week from a member of the learning support team. This teacher has just unexpectedly resigned, leaving Mark without his teaching. The school say they have no-one who can take the first teacher's place. The LEA says that, because Mark's statement is due for review in six months time, the need for continued support will be looked at afresh then. Is there anything I can do in this situation which will get Mark back his help quickly? I have been told I cannot appeal to the Special Educational Needs Tribunal. ❞

The first step

You can't appeal to the Tribunal in this situation, but luckily the law is very clear. Your local education authority has a binding duty to 'arrange' that the special educational provision set out in Mark's statement (under Part 3) is made. They can ask the school to provide Mark's specialist teaching, or they can ask for another member of the learning support team to take over. But if neither of these is possible the LEA, will have to take action on its own to provide Mark with his special education provision.

The LEA will be fully aware of their duty to 'arrange' Mark's special educational provision. After all, this is the whole point and purpose of statements of special educational needs. You should not delay in pointing their legal duty out to them, by writing a letter to the Chief Education Officer. It could go like this:

Dear Chief Education Officer,

I am writing to inform you that your LEA are in breach of their duty to arrange the special education

2

Case 32

provision for my son, Mark . . . , which is set out under Part 3 of his statement of special educational needs. This is specified as 'two hours per week one-to-one tuition with a member of the learning support service'.

The provision was discontinued with the resignation of the original teacher, and the Special Needs Officer has informed me that the LEA intend to wait until Mark's review (not due for six months) before deciding whether to replace the teacher.

I am sorry to have to inform you that if I do not receive assurance from you within three days of my delivering this letter that the provision specified for Mark will be immediately re-instated, I shall be placing the matter in the hands of a solicitor.

Deliver this letter by hand and get a written receipt from the receptionist at the Education Department when you hand it in. Keep a copy.

If that doesn't work

See a solicitor. If you don't know a solicitor who specialises in education law, ask one of the Helpline organisations listed in part 7 if they can recommend one.

What the law says

Section 324 of the 1996 Education Act says:

'(5) Where a local education authority maintain a statement under this section, then –

(a) unless the child's parent has made suitable arrangements, the authority –

   (i)   shall arrange that the special educational provision

specified in the statement is made for the child, and

(ii) may arrange that any non-educational provision specified in the statement is made for him in such manner as they consider appropriate, and

(b) if the name of a maintained, grant-maintained or grant-maintained special school is specified in the statement, the governing body of the school shall admit the child to the school.'

2

Case 32

PostScript

As with most problems, it is best to discuss them with your child's teacher and headteacher first, to see if a quick and local solution can be found. However, if your child is not receiving the special educational provision specified in his or her statement, you should not delay too long before seeking legal advice.

You can see from this problem how important it is that Part 3 of a statement is worded in specific terms. If it had just said: 'extra provision to be determined and provided by the school's special needs department' then the legal position would have been much less clear – and your chances of putting the matter right much less strong.

LEAs have been known, in the past, to argue that they have no legal duty to 'arrange' the provision under Part 3 of a statement when it relies on professionals employed by the Health Authority. One LEA, the London Borough of Harrow, were taken to court over this issue. They argued that because they had made the request to the Health Authority, their own duty had been fulfilled. The court disagreed and in a judgement known as *R vs London Borough of Harrow ex parte M [1997] ELR 62* the judges ruled:

"In clear terms the obligation upon a LEA under s 168 (5) [1993] (now s 324 (5) EA 1996. ed) is simply expressed and subject to no qualification whether express or implied."

Case 33

❝We've just had a letter from the LEA telling us they propose to amend our son's statement. It says that agreement has been reached with the school for them to provide the first five hours of his 12 hours of welfare support to be paid for from the school's own special needs budget. I've spoken to the head and she says there is no way the school can meet this cost and she has advised me to appeal. Is that right? ❞

The first step

You don't have a right of appeal yet, if all that has happened is that the LEA have proposed the amendment. Their letter should have told you that you have 15 days to 'make representations'. This means writing to them and letting them know what you think. This is what you should do, as well as asking for a meeting with the Special Needs Officer and the head. Take someone with you to the meeting, to support you and take notes on what is said.

At the meeting, ask the officer:

- Did you get any professional advice on the school's ability to fund five hours of Alan's welfare support, before you proposed this amendment?
- If so, could I have copies of those reports, in line with paragraph 6:34 of the Code of Practice?
- Will you confirm that it is still the LEA's view that Alan's needs call for the level of help which is being made for him at present and which is specified in Part 3 of the statement i.e. 12 hours of non-teaching assistance?
- Do you accept that section 324 of the 1996 Education Act places a duty on the LEA to 'arrange' the special education provision set out in Part 3 of Alan's statement?
- If the school informs you that they are not able to fund the first five hours of this provision, will the LEA withdraw the proposed amendment?

Take a written copy of these questions to the meeting. After the meeting, leave a copy with the officer and ask him to write to you to confirm his answers.

Then ask the headteacher these questions:

- Is there money unspent under the school's special educational needs budget?
- If not, where will the school get the money to pay for five hours of welfare support? Will it come from provision being made presently for children with special needs who do not have statements?

After the meeting, write to the head asking her to inform you in writing whether the school intends to agree with the LEA's proposal and accept responsibility for funding five hours of welfare support for Alan.

Case
33

If that doesn't work

If the LEA presses ahead and confirms that the statement has been amended, despite whatever was said at your meeting or in letters afterwards, you will need to appeal to the Special Educational Needs Tribunal, which is your right under special education law (see part 3 of this guide).

It may be possible to get legal aid to pay for the preparation of your appeal. Contact one of the Helpline organisations listed in part 7 for advice on this.

What the law says

Section 324 of the 1996 Education Act says;

'(5) Where a local education authority maintain a statement under this section, then –

(a) unless the child's parent has made suitable arrangements, the authority –

(i) shall arrange that the special educational provision specified in the statement is made for the child, and
(ii) may arrange that any non-educational provision specified in the statement is made for him in such manner as they consider appropriate, and

(b) if the name of a maintained, grant-maintained or grant-maintained special school is specified in the statement the governing body of the school shall admit the child to the school.'

Schedule 27(10)

'(1) Before amending a statement, a local education authority shall serve on the parent of the child concerned a notice informing him –

(a) of their proposal, and
(b) of his right to make representations under sub-paragraph (2) below

(2) A parent on whom a notice has been served under sub-paragraph (1) above may, within the period of fifteen days beginning with the date on which the notice is served, make representations to the local education authority about their proposal.

(3) The local education authority –

(a) shall consider any representations made to them under sub-paragraph (2) above, and
(b) on taking a decision on the proposal to which the representations relate, shall give notice in writing to the parent of their decision.

(4) Where a local education authority make an amendment under this paragraph to the description in a statement of the

authority's assessment of a child's special educational needs or to the special educational provision specified in a statement, they shall give notice in writing to the parent of his right under section 326(1) of the Act to appeal against the description in the statement of the authority's assessment of the child's special educational needs, the special educational provision specified in the statement or, if no school is named in the statement, that fact.

2

Case 33

(5) A local education authority may only amend a statement under this paragraph within the prescribed period beginning with the service of the notice under sub-paragraph (1) above.'

Regulation 14(6) of the Education (Special Education Needs) Regulations 1994 says:

'Where under paragraph 10(1) of Schedule 10 of the Act an authority serve a notice on the child's parent informing him of their proposal to amend a statement, they shall not amend the statement after the expiry of 8 weeks from the date on which the notice was served.'

What the courts have said

In the case of *R vs Oxfordshire County Council ex parte P[1996] ELR 153*, the judge ruled that it was not unlawful for the LEA to obtain agreement from a school, after a statement had been finalised, that part of the cost of the special educational provision set out on the statement should be met from the school's own budget. The judge said:

". . . the (LEA's) decision . . . could, of course, only be put into effect with the concurrence of the school . . . But if . . . the school were suddenly to turn round and say that they were no longer prepared to apply any part of their budget to the cost of the 20 hours extra support, it is undoubted that the (LEA) would immediately have to meet the full cost. The provision would in any event be secure."

2

Case

33

What the Code of Practice says

'Where the LEA propose to amend a statement, whether to change the name of the school in Part 4 or for any other reason, they must write to the child's parents, informing them of that proposal and of their right to make representations within 15 days of the receipt of that proposal. LEAs should always explain the reasons for the proposal and ensure that the parents have copies of any evidence which prompted the proposal . . .'

(Paragraph 6:34)

PostScript

The law does not give parents the right to insist on a meeting with an officer when an amendment to a statement is proposed, unlike the situation when a new statement is issued in proposed form. But there is no reason why you should not ask for a meeting. If your objections to the proposed amendment are well founded, most LEAs would in any case want a meeting with you before going further.

Always make a practice of leaving a written record of the questions you have asked. Also, ask people to confirm in writing what they have said at a meeting as soon as possible afterwards.

Case 34

66 Our 10-year-old son, Gerry, has refused to go to school now for the past month. He's had a statement since he started nursery, but of late he has not been making progress and his behaviour has gone from bad to worse both at school and at home. On Monday last week we wrote to the LEA asking for a fresh assessment of his needs. On Thursday we received a letter from them threatening us with an Attendance Order and court if Gerry didn't return to school. Do they not understand Gerry's problems? Or do they just not care? 99

The first step

This could well be a case of the left hand not knowing what the right hand is doing. The first step, then, is to write and tell the person or department who threatened you with the attendance order that Gerry has special educational needs and that you have asked for a fresh assessment of his needs. Suggest to them that serving an Attendance Order would be premature, given that a fresh assessment may well identify a different school for Gerry.

The second step is to follow up on your request for assessment and find out when the LEA intend to reply to you. You should tell them about the threatened Attendance Order and ask them, in these circumstances, to reach a decision about an assessment as a matter of urgency, rather than waiting the full six weeks allowed in law.

If you want, you could also ask for an emergency placement to be arranged for Gerry for the purposes of a fresh assessment.

Hopefully, once everyone involved realises that Gerry's non-attendance is to do with his special needs rather than with you deliberately keeping him away from school, the decision to reassess will be taken quickly and the threat of issuing an attendance order will be withdrawn.

If that doesn't work

If the LEA continue with the threat of serving an attendance order, or actually do serve it, you will need to speak to a solicitor who is familiar with education law. You should contact the appropriate Helpline number which you will find in part 7 of this book.

If the LEA refuse your request for a fresh assessment, you should get advice on appealing to the Special Educational Needs Tribunal (see part 3).

What the law says

Section 443 of the 1996 Education Act says:

'(1) If a parent on whom a school attendance order is served fails to comply with the requirements of the order, he is guilty of an offence, unless he proves that he is causing the child to receive suitable education otherwise than at school ...

(4) A person guilty of an offence under this section is liable on summary conviction to a fine not exceeding level 3 on the standard scale.'

Regulation 11 of the Education (Special Educational Needs) Regulations 1994 says:

'(3) Where under sections 328(2) or 329(1) a parent asks the authority to arrange for an assessment to be made under section 323, they shall within 6 weeks of the date of receipt of the request give notice to the child's parent –

(a) under section 323(4) of their decision to make an assessment, or
(b) under section 328(3)(a) or 329(2)(a) respectively of their decision not to comply with the request and of the

parent's right to appeal to the Tribunal against the determination.'

PostScript

If you make a positive decision to educate your child at home, and can show that you have made adequate arrangements to do this, then it is unlikely that your LEA would serve an attendance order, or that a court would convict you. However, you should get independent advice on home education before you make a decision – see part 7 for a Helpline number.

Case 34

Case 35

66 Jane is nine. She's just been permanently excluded from her special school. We've been arguing for some time now that this would happen if she didn't get more help, but no one listened. We think this is unfair on her and us, but what can we do about it? 99

The first step

Where you go from here depends on what has gone wrong in the past and what you want for Jane from this point on.

For example, if you want Jane to go back to the school which has excluded her, you should write to the governing body and appeal against the exclusion (see part 7 for a Helpline organisation which can help you with an appeal against exclusion).

If you do not want Jane to go back to that school, but still want to register a complaint because of the unfairness of the exclusion, you should write to the governing body with your complaint. In this case, however, make it clear that you are complaining about the unfairness of the exclusion, but *not* appealing for Jane to be allowed to go back.

Perhaps Jane's statement was not well enough written in the first place, i.e. her needs may not be fully described; or perhaps there is not enough provision specified on the statement. In this case, you may need to think about asking the LEA for another assessment of her special educational needs.

Perhaps the statement is well enough written but Jane has not been getting the provision specified in Part 3. In this case, you may need legal advice to get the LEA to fulfil their duty towards Jane by arranging that she does get the provision specified in the statement.

Perhaps the statement is well enough written and Jane has

been getting the help as specified in Part 3, but you believe there should be a change of school for her. In this case, you could ask the LEA to change the statement to name a different maintained school in Part 4.

Whichever of these applies to you, remember that the LEA continues to have a duty to 'arrange' the special education provision in Part 3 of Jane's statement even though she has been excluded. In practice, what this means is that they should be trying their best to resolve the situation as quickly as they can in order that her special educational provision continues. So, you could, if you wish, contact the LEA straight away and ask what it intends to do to fulfil its duty to 'arrange' Jane's special educational provision.

2

Case 35

If that doesn't work

The main danger in this situation is that things are allowed to drift, with Jane missing more and more school. Unless you are absolutely clear what you want, and how to achieve it, you should ring the appropriate Helpline in part 7 and get advice.

What the law says

Section 324 of the 1996 Education Act says:

'(5) Where a local education authority maintain a statement under this section, then –

(a) unless the child's parent has made suitable arrangements, the authority –

(i) shall arrange that the special educational provision specified in the statement is made for the child . . . '

Post Script

You should get advice from one of the organisations listed in part 7, but this is the kind of situation where it can also help to inform a local councillor of what is going on and, hopefully, get them on your side. If the LEA moves quickly to find another school for Jane which you feel is suitable then you won't need the help of a councillor. However, if weeks turn to months and Jane is still out of school, there is a danger that she will get into the habit of not going to school! You might also find it useful to read cases 29 and 34, which discuss the issue of home education for children who are out of school.

Case 36

66 We moved home about two months ago. Six weeks after we moved we got a letter from the new LEA telling us that they had received a copy of Roger's statement from the old authority and that they would be reviewing it in three months time. The letter also said that the LEA had no plans to re-assess Roger. Before we moved, he was getting four hours of specialist teaching support a week. Since we moved he has been getting nothing, despite the fact that we have spoken to the headteacher about his problems on a number of occasions. Do we have to wait for the review before anything happens? 99

The first step

No. Once the statement has been transferred to your new LEA they have the same duties in law as if it they had issued it themselves. The most important duty is to arrange that Roger gets the four hours special education provision specified in Part 3 of the statement. The fact that the LEA have decided to review the statement in three months time is irrelevant. They should be making the special education provision set out in the statement right now.

You should write immediately to the Chief Education Officer, along these lines:

To: The Chief Education Officer

Dear Sir or Madam,

I am writing to inform you that my son, Roger, has a statement of special educational needs, but that he is not getting the special educational provision specified in Part 3 of that statement, i.e. four hours a week teaching support. I understand that it is your legal duty to arrange that he gets this provision, and I would be grateful if you would reply to this letter immediately, informing me of your proposals for fulfilling your duty towards Roger.

Our family moved into your authority's area last October, and we received a letter on November 25th informing us that Roger's statement has been transferred from the old LEA to your education office. However, he has not received help of any kind with his literacy problems since arriving at his new school.

I have been advised that, failing a satisfactory answer to this letter, I should consult a solicitor. I hope that this will not be necessary, and look forward to your reply.

Yours,

If that doesn't work

You should see a solicitor. One of the Helpline organisations listed in part 7 of this book should be able to recommend one who knows about education law.

What the law says

The Education (Special Education Needs) Regulations 1994 say:

'(1) This regulation applies where a child in respect of whom a statement is maintained moves from the area of the authority which maintains the statement ('the old authority') into that of another ('the new authority').

(2) The old authority shall transfer the statement to the new authority, and from the date of the transfer –

(a) the statement shall be treated for the purposes of the new authority's duties and functions under Part III of the Act and these Regulations as if it had been made by the new authority on the date on which it was made by the old authority, and

(b) where the new authority make an assessment under section 323 and the old authority have supplied the new authority with advice obtained in pursuance of a previous assessment regulations 6(5) shall apply as if the new authority had obtained the advice on the date on which the old authority obtained it.

(3) The new authority shall within 6 weeks of the date of the transfer serve a notice on the child's parent informing him –

(a) that the statement has been transferred

(b) whether they propose to make an assessment under section 323, and

(c) when they propose to review the statement in accordance with paragraph (4).

(4) The new authority shall review the statement under section 328(5) before the expiry of whichever of the following two periods expires later –

(a) the period of twelve months beginning with the making of the statement, or as the case may be, with the previous review, or

(b) the period of three months beginning with the date of the transfer.

(5) Where by virtue of the transfer the new authority come under a duty to arrange the child's attendance at a school specified in the statement but in light of the child's move that attendance is no longer practicable the new authority may arrange for the child's attendance at another school appropriate for the child until such time as it is possible to amend the statement in accordance with paragraph 10 of Schedule 27 to the Act.'

(Regulation 18)

'(5) The authority need not seek the advice referred to in paragraph (1)(b), (c), (d), (e) or (f) if –

(a) the authority have obtained advice under paragraph (1)(b), (c), (d), (e) or (f) respectively within the preceding 12 months, and

(b) the authority, the person from whom the advice was obtained and the child's parent are satisfied that the existing advice is sufficient for the purpose of arriving at a satisfactory assessment.'

(Regulation 6)

PostScript

The new authority must review a statement within 12 months of the date it was issued, or last reviewed, by the old LEA, or within three months of the date of transfer whichever is the later date.

If it is practicable for a child to continue attending the same school, after moving home, then she should do so. If it is not practicable, e.g. because the school is now too far away, the new LEA must arrange for the child to attend another 'appropriate' school.

If your new LEA assess your child, they may use advice collected by the old LEA, provided it is not more than 12 months old, and provided you, as parents, agree.

Case 37

66 This is the start of our daughter's last year in primary school and we are getting worried about her transfer to secondary school. Sarah has moderate learning difficulties and we have been led to believe that she will have to transfer to a special school once she reaches secondary school age – which is next September. We want her to transfer to mainstream secondary school with her friends and be supported there. Also, we are a Catholic family, and we want Sarah to attend a Catholic school – which the mainstream school happens to be. Is there anything we can do to increase the chance of getting what we want for her? 99

The first step

Rather than wait for the LEA to propose the special school, you should ask for the name of the school on the statement to be changed to the name of the secondary school you want, 'as from September . . .' The LEA have a duty to comply with this request unless it believes that the school you have named is not appropriate to Sarah's age, ability, aptitude or special educational needs, or that what you are asking for will prejudice either the education of other children or the efficient use of resources. If the LEA refuse your request you will be able to appeal to the Special Educational Needs Tribunal.

The LEA should take your request for the school on religious grounds seriously, but it does not overrule the conditions which have to be met before they are obliged in law to give you the school of your preference for Sarah (see *What the Code of Practice says* below).

If that doesn't work

If you are not able to ask for the name of the school on the statement to be changed (for example, because you have already made this request within the last 12 months) then you should write to the LEA asking them to amend the statement to name the school you want. If they refuse, ask them to issue an amended statement naming the school they think *is* appropriate as soon as possible.

Case 37

The Code of Practice says that 'arrangements for a child's placement should be finalised by the beginning of the last term before transfer'. As Sarah's transfer is set for September, the placement decision should be made by the first day of the summer term. If it is any later, the Tribunal may not have the time to hear your appeal, and your child could be out of school come the beginning of the new school year.

In order for arrangements to be finalised by the beginning of the term before transfer, discussions about the transfer need to begin *a year* before it is due to happen. So, if nothing is happening by the autumn half term of your child's last year before transfer, you should ring one of the Helpline organisations listed in part 7 to discuss the steps you need to take.

What the law says

Schedule 27 of the 1996 Education Act says:

'(8)(1) Sub-paragraph (2) below applies where –

(a) the parent of a child for whom a statement is maintained which specifies the name of a school or institution asks the local education authority to substitute for that name the name of a maintained, grant-maintained or grant-maintained special school specified by the parent, and

(b) the request is not made less than twelve months after –

(i) a request under this paragraph,

(ii) the service of a copy of the statement under paragraph 6 above,

(iii) if the statement has been amended, the date when

notice of the amendment is given under paragraph 10(3)(b) below, or

(iv) if the parent has appealed to the Tribunal under section 170 of this Act or this paragraph, the date when the appeal is concluded, whichever is the later.

(2) The local education authority shall comply with the request unless –

(a) the school is unsuitable to the child's age, ability or aptitude or to his special educational needs, or
(b) the attendance of the child at the school would be incompatible with the provision of efficient education for the children with whom he would be educated or the efficient use of resources.

(3) Where the local education authority determine not to comply with the request –

(a) they shall give notice of that fact and of the effect of paragraph (b) below to the parent of the child, and
(b) the parent of the child may appeal to the Tribunal against the determination.'

What the Code of Practice says

'All concerned with the child should give careful thought to transfer between phases. Advance planning is essential. The move should be considered at the review meeting during the child's last year in his or her current school. If necessary, that review should be brought forward to allow sufficient time for consideration of the school which will be appropriate for the child in the next phase. *Arrangements for a child's placement should be finalised by the beginning of the child's last term before transfer.* It is important for placements to be finalised as early as possible in order for any advance arrangements relating to that placement to be made and to ensure that parents feel confident and secure about the arrangements in question. Secondary and primary schools in an area should consider

2

Case 37

developing a common system of record-keeping to ease transfer of pupils between schools.'

(Paragraph 6:30)

2

Case 37

'Under paragraph 8 of schedule 27 of the Act, parents have the right to request the LEA to substitute the name of a maintained, grant-maintained or grant-maintained special school for the name of the school in part 4 of the statement. The LEA must comply with the request.'

(Paragraph 6:31)

'If the conditions set out under Schedule 27(8) apply, before naming the school, the LEA must first consult the governing body, and, if the school is maintained by another authority, that LEA. The eight-week time limit allows for this consultation. The LEA may specify in the statement the date on which the child is to start attending the new school. That date might coincide with the start of a new term, or give sufficient time for the school to make necessary preparations for the child's arrival.'

(Paragraph 6:32)

'If the LEA conclude that they cannot name the school proposed by the parents, they must tell the parents, in writing, of their right to appeal to the Tribunal against the decision and should also explain why they have turned down the request. This letter should also be sent to the parents within eight weeks of their initial request (Regulation 14(5)).

If the child is due to transfer between phases, the LEA must name a school which will be appropriate for that child. They should do so in the closest consultation with the child's parents and must follow the procedures for amending statements set out in paragraph 10 of schedule 27 to the Act.'

(Paragraph 6:33)

'The LEA should consider very carefully a preference stated by parents for a denominational mainstream maintained school and representations made by parents for a denominational non-maintained special school or independent school. Denominational considerations cannot override the three criteria which the LEA apply in deciding the school which should be named in the statement – appropriateness to the child's needs, compatibility with the efficient education of other children and compatibility with the efficient use of resources. But denominational considerations may influence the appropriateness of a school for meeting the child's needs and the child's ability to thrive in and benefit from a particular school. The LEA should take such considerations into account when two or more schools, one of which has a denominational affiliation favoured by the parents, could meet the three governing criteria.'

(Paragraph 4:50)

2

Case 37

Post Script

Parents' organisations should be pressing local councillors to get their LEA to adopt, as a policy, a strict timetable for making decisions with regard to the transfer of school for children with statements of special educational needs. The Code of Practice says that the question of transfer should feature on the agenda at the review meeting held in the year before transfer is due, but this is too vague to base a policy on. A better policy would be for all parents of statemented children coming up to transfer to be written to one year before the transfer is due, with clear information on how and when the decision about their child's next school will be made.

Often, parents of children with statements are sent the same information on school transfer as parents whose children do not have statements. This can be very confusing. If this happens to you, ring one of the Helpline organisations listed in part 7 without delay.

When you are seeking a place in a school partly for religious reasons, you should seek to enlist the support of the church

153

concerned. In some cases, diocesan boards have policies on welcoming children with special educational needs in their schools, and you may find that the school you want will, in turn, be particularly positive about accepting your child. If so, this is likely to influence the LEA in your favour.

2

Case 37

Case 38

66 I've heard that the new arrangements for reviewing statements are much more thorough than they used to be, but won't it still be a case of my lone voice as a parent against everyone else? How can we have an influence? 99

The first step

The first step is to find out how the basic review procedure works (there are variations for children who are not at school and children having their first review after reaching the age of 14).

The LEA have a duty to review a statement, and do this in practice by considering a report sent to them by the headteacher of the child's school.

Before writing this report, the headteacher must get written reports on the child from the parents, from anyone the LEA tell him to get advice from and from anyone the head himself or herself considers appropriate.

These reports must refer to:

1. the child's progress;
2. the application of the National Curriculum and substitutions for the National Curriculum;
3. the transition plan, where one exists (i.e. for older students);
4. whether the statement is still appropriate, or needs to be amended or dropped.

The head must invite the following people to a meeting (and send them, beforehand, copies of all reports received):

- a representative of the LEA, if asked to do so by the LEA;
- any teacher who teaches the child or is responsible for the

child's provision, and anyone else in the school the head thinks appropriate;

- anyone else who the LEA or the headteacher thinks is appropriate.

Case 38

The meeting will consider points 1 to 4 above. If there are disagreements, individuals present will be able to report their own views to the LEA. When the headteacher sends the report on the meeting, he or she must indicate any lack of agreement between their report and the views of others at the meeting.

Copies of the headteacher's report to the LEA are sent to everyone who has been involved, including the parents, and the LEA's final recommendations are also copied to everyone as the last stage of the review.

As a parent you can influence your child's reviews in the following ways:

- By making your own report for the review as full and detailed as possible, arguing for what you want for your child and providing as much evidence as possible to back up your view.
- By getting the child to put his/her own views forward for the review, in whatever way is most appropriate. The Code of Practice emphasises the importance of the young person's contributions to statement reviews.
- By asking the headteacher to write for advice to any independent professional who knows your child and shares your views. If the head agrees, then this person should automatically be invited to the review meeting and have the opportunity, later, to write directly to the LEA if they disagree with the report produced by the headteacher after the meeting.
- When you receive copies of the other professionals' reports, study them carefully and try to find out who agrees with you and who disagrees with you. Work out questions for the people who have written the reports you disagree with.
- If you disagree with the head's account of recommendations

made at the meeting, send your own report on the meeting to the LEA. Ask other professionals involved who share your view to do the same.

You might find it useful to discuss how best to present your views at a review of a statement with someone from one of the Helpline organisations listed in part 7 of this guide.

2

Case 38

If that doesn't work

If, following the review, the LEA propose an amendment to the statement which you are not happy with, see case 33 for advice.

If you are disappointed because the LEA refuse to amend the statement in the way you wanted following a review, you might consider asking for a fresh assessment of your child's needs (see case 11 for an example of a letter you could write). Or, if you decide to ask for a change of the school named on the statement, see case 39.

What the law says

Regulation 15 of the Education (Special Educational Needs) Regulations 1994 sets out the procedure for review of a statement for a child under 14 years old who attends a school (See page 281 for the procedures in detail).

Regulation 16 sets out the procedure for review of a statement for a child over 14 who attends a school. (See page 284)

Regulation 17 sets out the procedure for review of a statement for a child who does not attend a school. (See page 286)

What the Code of Practice says

The whole of chapter 6 of the Code of Practice deals with reviews. Contact one of the Helpline organisations (part 7) if you have difficulty getting hold of the Code or if you do not understand any part of it.

PostScript

Case 38

It is always important to get professional support for your views on your child's needs whenever possible. As part of your preparation for a review, try to find out who, amongst the professionals who have worked with your child, agrees with you. Ask the headteacher and the LEA to invite a report from them for the purposes of the review. This will ensure that they are also invited to the review meeting .

Case 39

“We want a different school for our son Michael. He has been in a special school for children with moderate learning difficulties for six years and we feel he deserves a chance in mainstream. We argued this at his last review, but the LEA have just written their recommendations following the review and they say that they believe that his statement, and the special school, are still ‘appropriate’ and they do not intend to amend his statement. What do we do?”

The first step

You cannot appeal to the Tribunal against a decision not to amend a statement, but you can either:

- write to the LEA asking them to change the name of the school on Michael's statement to your local mainstream school (see case 37); or
- write to the LEA asking them to do a fresh assessment of Michael's needs.

If you have support from the professionals for the change of school (for example, if the reports prepared for the most recent review agree with you), then you should consider asking for the name of the school on the statement to be changed. This could be the quickest way to get the change you want.

However, if you do not have any professional support (for example, if all of the reports produced for the most recent review say that Michael is correctly placed in the special school) then the LEA are not likely to agree to your request. Nor are you likely to be successful at appeal. Therefore, it might be better to ask for a reassessment, in the hope that this will produce some new, and different, professional advice – hopefully advice which will support you in arguing for mainstream placement.

Before deciding what to do, speak to someone from one of the Helpline organisations listed in part 7. Whether you ask for a change of school on the existing statement or for a new assessment, it would help to get a second professional opinion from an independent professional as to the support which Michael would need in the mainstream school you want.

Case 39

If that doesn't work

If the LEA refuse to change Michael's school, or refuse to undertake a fresh assessment, you will have the right to appeal to the Tribunal (see part 3).

What the law says

The 1996 Education Act says:

'(1) Sub-paragraph (2) below applies where –

(a) the parent of a child for whom a statement is maintained which specifies the name of a school or institution asks the local education authority to substitute for that name the name of a maintained, grant-maintained or grant-maintained special school specified by the parent, and

(b) the request is not made less than twelve months after –

    (i) a request under this paragraph,

    (ii) the service of a copy of the statement under paragraph 6 above,

    (iii) if the statement has been amended, the date when notice of the amendment is given under paragraph 10(3)(b) below, or

    (iv) if the parent has appealed to the Tribunal under section 326 of this Act or this paragraph, the date when the appeal is concluded, whichever is the later.

(2) The local education authority shall comply with the request unless –

(a)   the school is unsuitable to the child's age, ability or aptitude or to his special educational needs, or

(b)   the attendance of the child at the school would be incompatible with the provision of efficient education for the children with whom he would be educated or the efficient use of resources.

2

Case 39

(3) Where the local education authority determine not to comply with the request –

(a)   they shall give notice of that fact and of the effect of paragraph (b) below to the parent of the child, and

(b)   the parent of the child may appeal to the Tribunal against the determination.'

(Schedule 27(8))

'(2) Where –

(a)   the parent of a child for whom a statement is maintained under section 324 asks the local education authority to arrange for an assessment to be made in respect of the child under section 323,

(b)   no such assessment has been made within the period of six months ending with the date on which the request is made, and

(c)   it is necessary for the authority to make a further assessment under section 323,

– the authority shall comply with the request.'

(Section 328)

PostScript

Remember, you can only ask for a change of school to a maintained (LEA) school or a grant-maintained (opted-out) school.

Although the decision is made by the LEA, not the head or governors of the school you want your child placed in, your chances are greatly increased if you have talked to the head and if she believes her school is an appropriate one for your child. If there is a possibility of your child attending more than one mainstream school, it is worth making visits to them all before actually writing and asking for a change to the statement.

**Case
39**

Case 40

❝ We've just had the annual review of our son's statement. He will be 16 this school year and the officer at the review meeting informed us that he would have to leave school in the summer and that his statement would then cease to exist. We have spent a long time arguing with the LEA to get this statement right for Richard. We do not believe that he will cope in a college and want him to continue his education in a school environment. Is it true that he will just lose his statement and that we will not be able to do anything about it? ❞

The first step

Your first step must be to get some advice immediately from one of the Helpline organisations listed in part 7 of this guide. This is because the law is not clear with regard to special educational provision beyond the age of 16 and judges in two court rulings have disagreed over an LEA's duty with regard to maintaining statements.

In 1994, in a case involving Dorset County Council, the High Court ruled that a statement could not simply cease to exist just because a young person reached the age of 16; an LEA would have to go through the proper process of ceasing to maintain the statement, which now includes giving parents the right to appeal.

However, in 1997, in a case involving Oxfordshire, the Court of Appeal (which is a higher court) ruled that, once a child was beyond the age of 16 and not on the roll of a school, an LEA were not responsible for them, nor for maintaining their statement, and that it was not necessary for an LEA to go through the process of ceasing to maintain a statement (or giving parents the right of appeal).

This apparent contradiction between judgements may only

2

**Case
40**

be cleared up by a further court case or by the Government amending the law to clarify it.

With regard to Richard, if you believe that he should attend a school beyond the age of 16, but your LEA has a policy of all children leaving schools at 16, you will need to get an appeal in to the Tribunal early in Richard's last year at school in the hope of persuading the Tribunal to order a different school to be named in Part 4 of his statement. This may have to be a school in a neighbouring LEA (where children attend beyond 16) or an independent school.

It is vital that you take action as early as possible in the school year. This is because it can take five to six months to get to a Tribunal hearing stage and, once Richard has reached 16 and left school, the Tribunal will have no power to order the LEA to change the statement or continue to maintain it.

You will need advice not only on how to get an appeal to the Tribunal, but also on how to get to a hearing quickly (see part 3).

If that doesn't work

If Richard reaches his 16th birthday and leaves school, he may no longer be the responsibility of the LEA. You will need to consider how his education can best continue at a college. Many colleges make excellent provision for students with special educational needs. If you need advice on Richard's continuing educational career, you should contact SKILL, which supports students with disabilities and their parents (see part 7).

What the courts have said

In the judgement known as *R vs Dorset County Council and Further Education Funding Council Ex parte M [1995] ELR 109,* the judge ruled:

"... a local education authority cannot divest itself of responsibility for a pupil's schooling when he reaches 16 by wrongfully failing to specify it, either by silence or express exclusion, in his statement and by refusing to provide it when he reaches 16 so that he cannot then satisfy the condition of the authority's continuing responsibility under Section 4(2)(a) of the 1981 Education Act, namely by being a registered pupil at a school appropriate to his needs ...

Case 40

Dorset's duty under Section 7(1) and (2) of the Education Act 1981 to maintain the 1992 statement of Mark's special educational needs and to arrange for him the special educational provision specified in it continues until Dorset amends or ceases to maintain the statement in accordance with the procedures set out in paragraphs 6 and 7 of schedule 1 to, and section 8 of, the 1981 Act."

In the judgement known as *R vs Oxfordshire County Council ex parte B [1997] ELR 90* the judge ruled:

"... insofar as Auld J (the judge in the Dorset case, above) was suggesting that there remained a duty upon all LEAs to continue to maintain a statement until it was amended or ceased to be maintained on a proper proposal by the authority, that proposition is expressed in my view far too widely ... In my judgement the responsibility for the registered child ends upon the child ceasing to be registered and the maintenance of the statement ... would cease with the cessation of that responsibility and registration ..."

PostScript

The law on special education changes regularly as a result of rulings in the High Court. A book such as this can therefore be out of date in some respects before it even reaches the bookshop. This is all the more reason for contacting the Helpline organisations listed in part 7 for advice if you are having a problem getting the special educational provision your child needs.

Part 3

Appealing to the Special Educational Needs Tribunal

Appealing to the
Special Educational Needs Tribunal

If your negotiations with the LEA do not achieve what you want for your child, you may need to appeal to the Special Educational Needs Tribunal.

When can I appeal?

The law provides a right of appeal in the following situations:

When your child does not have a statement . . .

When your child does not have a statement, and the LEA refuse to do an assessment under the 1996 Education Act (see cases 2, 9 and 10)

When your child does not have a statement, and the LEA do an assessment under the 1996 Education Act but refuse to issue a statement (see case 16)

When the LEA finalise a first statement . . .

When the LEA first send you a final statement, you can appeal if:

- you disagree with the description of your child's needs in Part 2 of the statement (see case 27);
- you disagree with special educational provision in Part 3 of the statement (see case 28);
- you are unhappy with the school named in Part 4 of the statement (see cases 29 and 30);
- there is no school named in Part 4 and you are unhappy about this.

When your child has a statement . . .

When your child has a statement and the LEA refuse to carry out a further assessment under the 1996 Education Act.

When your child has a statement and the LEA do an assessment under the 1996 Education Act but refuse to amend the existing statement. If this happens, you can appeal if:

- you disagree with the description of your child's needs in Part 2;
- you disagree with special educational provision in Part 3;
- you are unhappy with the school named in Part 4;
- there is no school named in Part 4 and you are unhappy about this.

When your child has a statement, and the LEA do an assessment under the 1996 Education Act and amend the existing statement. If this happens, you can appeal if:

- you disagree with the description of your child's needs in Part 2;
- you disagree with special educational provision in Part 3;
- you are unhappy with the school named in Part 4;
- there is no school named in Part 4 and you are unhappy about this.

Note: You are not limited to appealing against the specific amendment made.

When the LEA amend your child's statement without doing an assessment, you can appeal if:

- you disagree with the description of your child's needs in Part 2;
- you disagree with special educational provision in Part 3;
- you are unhappy with the school named in Part 4;
- there is no school named in Part 4 and you are unhappy about this.

Note: You are not limited to appealing against the specific amendment made (see case 33).

When the LEA cease to maintain your child's statement.

When the LEA refuse to change the name of the school on your child's statement (see case 39).

How do I appeal?

Your LEA should let you know of your right to appeal when they inform you of their decision. You should also receive a booklet called *Special Educational Needs Tribunal – How to appeal.* If you have not been sent this, ask the LEA to send you one or telephone the Tribunal office (0207-925 6925) and you'll be posted a copy free of charge. The booklet is easy to understand and contains much of the information about appeals that you will need. The staff at the Tribunal office are also able to answer queries.

At the back of the booklet you will find a form to fill in and send to the Tribunal. This form is called the *Notice of Appeal,* and you must make sure you provide all the information it asks for. It must arrive at the Tribunal within two months of your LEA telling you of your right to appeal.

You will need to set out your reasons for appeal. You can use a separate sheet for these, but try to keep them brief and to the point. There is no need to set out your full argument; just let the Tribunal know the main issues that you are unhappy with. Concentrate on what are now the main issues of the case and what you are asking for, rather than dwelling on what has gone wrong in the past.

Can I succeed against the LEA?

It is not possible to know for sure if any case will be successful. The Special Educational Needs Tribunal is independent of the LEA, though, and many parents are successful in their appeals. A high proportion of cases do not reach a hearing – usually because the LEA back down or a reasonable solution is found with which all concerned are happy. Many LEAs begin to negotiate once an appeal is started.

Do I need a solicitor?

Legal aid is not available for representation by a solicitor or barrister at the Special Educational Needs Tribunal. If you are receiving income support, job-seekers allowance or have very low income, you will be entitled to free legal advice which could help with preparing your case but will not cover representation at the hearing. Most cases are likely to be decided on the facts rather than on points of law, however, and most parents should be able to represent themselves in the informal setting of the Tribunal. If you do decide to pay for a solicitor, make sure it is one of the few who have experience of special education law.

Where might I go wrong?

It is important to remember that the Tribunal rules have to be strictly followed. For example, the Notice of Appeal must be sent to the Tribunal within two months from the day you received the letter telling you of your right to appeal. This applies even if you are negotiating with the LEA and hope to manage without an appeal.

You need to get your written evidence ready as soon as possible as this must be sent in with your response to the LEA reply within the time limit of 15 working days from receiving the reply.

The case will be decided on the evidence before the tribunal on the day. You are unlikely to succeed without relevant evidence. If the LEA are disputing the nature and extent of your child's learning difficulties, you will need professional evidence from someone suitably qualified who knows or has met your child. This could be a teacher, for example, and may be someone who has already provided advice that the LEA have ignored. The professional evidence should specify and quantify the provision your child needs if this is in dispute. The tribunal will be unwilling to name a school unless they have evidence from someone who knows about what it can offer. If the LEA's case turns on what the school can reasonably provide from within its resources, you will need someone who knows about the school budget to give evidence.

Remember, too, that the tribunal will look at the whole statement, even though you may want only to change part of it. In general, when you are appealing against the school named in Part 4, it is best to appeal against Parts 2 and 3 as well.

What if I don't succeed?

If you do not succeed in your appeal, there is a possibility of a further appeal to the High Court, but only on a point of law. You will need legal advice to decide whether you have an appeal in law, and then, if you do appeal, legal representation in the High Court. Unless you are on a low income which brings you within the legal aid bracket, you are likely to face difficulties in taking an appeal. Legal costs are likely to be large and, even if you can afford to pay your own solicitors, you run the risk of being made to pay the LEA's costs if you are unsuccessful.

The decision of the tribunal can sometimes be reviewed if, for example, there has been a procedural error or fraud discovered after the decision. An application to review the decision must be made in writing not less than ten working days after the decision was sent.

Part 4

Judicial review and legal aid

Judicial review and legal aid

This part of the guide has five sections:

1. What is judicial review?
2. The principles of administrative law
3. What can the court do for your child?
4. Judicial review procedure
5. Costs and legal aid

What is judicial review?

Judicial review is a special type of legal action in which the High Court looks at an action, decision or omission of a public body to see whether it is within the law.

In the field of special educational needs, the public body (the 'respondent' in legal jargon) may be either:

- the local education authority;
- the Secretary of State for Education;
- the president of the Special Educational Needs Tribunal;
- the governing body of a particular school.

However, judicial review is not restricted to the area of education. Most decisions of public bodies such as central and local government which affect the public are subject to the control of the courts in this way. For example, the High Court regularly looks at decisions on subjects such as immigration, homelessness and community care using the judicial review procedure.

In the course of reviewing all these different types of decision, the Court has developed a set of rules which apply generally to the activities of people and institutions carrying out statutory duties. Lawyers call these rules the principles of *administrative law*.

Administrative law has two important features. The first is that

174

its rules apply irrespective of what the public body's decision is about. So, for example, a decision by the High Court on the powers of one local authority to license a cinema may be relevant to the question of whether a different authority can legally adopt a policy of never placing a child with special educational needs in a school outside its area.

The second important feature of administrative law is that its rules are not written down anywhere in a convenient and definitive form. They are not like the rules in the Act or the Regulations (see part 8) which are set out in black and white. Although it is possible to summarise them, they ultimately depend upon *precedent* – that is, what judges have said in previous cases. And, of course, different lawyers will interpret this in different ways.

This aspect of administrative law causes a lot of confusion both for parents and for administrators. It is difficult enough to get to grips with the detailed rules in the Act and the Regulations, and many people are completely unaware that – in addition to those rules – their rights and obligations are affected by general legal principles which are not written down.

This part of the book explains:

- the rules which the High Court applies when it is reviewing decisions about the education of children with special educational needs;
- what happens in an application for judicial review.

We hope this will give parents a better idea of when and how to use judicial review to protect the legal rights of their children.

In the next section we summarise *the principles of administrative law* which everyone making decisions about a child's education must follow. Then, we look at what *the court can do for your child*. Following this, we explain the stages in an application for judicial review. Finally, as expense is a major worry for people who have to retain lawyers, we describe the help which may be available through the legal aid and Legal Advice and Assistance schemes.

The principles of administrative law

To succeed in an application for judicial review about special educational needs, you must show either:

- that the LEA (or other public body) do not have the legal power to make the decision or to take the action which you object to; or
- that the LEA (etc.) are under a legal duty to act or make a decision in a certain way and are refusing or failing to do so.

Lawyers refer to such a decision, action or failure to act as being *ultra vires*. This is a Latin phrase which, in English, literally means 'beyond the powers'.

Ultra vires is a difficult legal concept. The basic idea is that, in the United Kingdom, Parliament is a sovereign body. This means that, in contrast with the governments of countries like the USA, which have written constitutions and built-in protections for minority rights, the UK Parliament can legally do whatever it wishes.

It follows that:

- no other person or public body in the United Kingdom can have sovereign powers;
- every other person or institution which has public powers has them only because Parliament has given those powers to them. They only have the limited powers which Parliament has permitted and no more.

The constitutional basis of judicial review is that the court (acting on behalf of the Crown) is supervising the exercise of the powers delegated by Parliament and ensuring that those powers have not been exceeded.

This is reflected in the names of judicial review cases which always take the form: *The Queen* (usually abbreviated to the letter 'R' which is short for the Latin *Regina*) *vs A County Council ex parte B*. This means that the Crown, on behalf of B, is calling on A County Council to account for the way it has used the powers which have been entrusted to it.

There is no definitive list of the ways in which the people and institutions which govern us can exceed the powers which Parliament has given them. However, the cases in which the courts have decided that public bodies have acted *ultra vires* can be divided into a number of broad categories:

Excess of power: cases where (whether deliberately or because they have misunderstood what their powers are) public bodies have done something which, legally, they simply cannot do.

Error of law: cases where public bodies have made an error of law in reaching their decision.

Improper exercise of discretion: cases involving the improper exercise of discretionary powers by public bodies.

Irrationality: cases in which the decision is completely unreasonable (or *irrational* or *Wednesbury unreasonable* to use the legal jargon).

Procedural errors: cases in which the procedures which public bodies have adopted have not followed the rules laid down by Parliament or have otherwise been unfair.

Excess of power

The first ground upon which a judge can say that an LEA, the Secretary of State or the Tribunal have acted *ultra vires* is that they have done something which they simply have no power to do.

This is comparatively rare, because public bodies normally

have a fairly good idea of what their powers are and take advice from their lawyers if they are not sure. But the point can be illustrated with two made-up examples:

- an LEA name speech therapy in Part 4 of a child's statement and insist that the parents must pay the therapist's fees;
- an LEA insist on parents paying for transport when the school is the nearest one at which the disabled child's needs can be met.

In both of these cases the public body would have no power to act in this way and, on an application for judicial review, the High Court could intervene and nullify the decision.

Examples of this type of *ultra vires* do occur from time to time in real life. For example, it is not unknown for LEAs to fail to arrange for the special educational provision which is required by a statement. For further discussion of this problem see case 32.

Error of law

A public body does not have to be exceeding its powers deliberately in order to be acting *ultra vires*. What it is legally allowed to do can be a difficult question.

For example:

An LEA make a statement which lists 'weekly counselling' under Part 6 as 'non-educational provision'. When the counselling does not materialise, the parents raise the matter with the LEA, who reply: 'because this is listed under Part 6 of the statement as "non-educational provision", the law does not allow us, as an LEA, to make the arrangements for it.'

This is an error in law, in that although the law does not insist on an LEA arranging non-educational provision, it does not actually prohibit it.

Judicial review for error of law is possible because the court assumes that Parliament does not intend the public bodies to which it has delegated powers to apply the wrong law when reaching decisions. The court has therefore decided that no public body has any power to make an error of law upon which the outcome of a decision depends. A decision based on an error of law is therefore *ultra vires.*

'Error of law' can be justified as a ground of judicial review on the basis that if an LEA, etc. misinterpret the law, they cannot be doing what Parliament wanted them to do and must instead be doing something which Parliament has not given them powers to do.

The error must be a legal one. You cannot win an application for judicial review by proving an error of *fact.*

It is often difficult to tell a legal error from a factual one. Perhaps the easiest way for someone who is not a lawyer to understand the distinction is to think of the difference between asking the wrong question and giving the wrong answer.

For example, if an LEA looks at the wrong issues (perhaps its own policy of reducing out-county placements rather than a child's individual needs), it is asking the wrong question ('Can we afford this?' rather than 'What does this child need?') and making a legal error.

However, if two experts disagree on whether your daughter *needs* an out-county placement and the LEA or Tribunal decide that she does not, that is, at most, simply giving the wrong answer to the right question ('What does this child need?'). This, if it is an error at all, is an error of fact and the court cannot interfere with the decision (but see the section on 'Irrationality').

Judicial review is not about whether a decision is *right* but whether it is *legal* in the sense of being within the powers of the person or body which made it.

179

For example:

4

> Following an annual review meeting at a school, the headteacher completes the annual review report and sends it to the LEA. The report strongly recommends an increase in the amount of help the child is receiving under the statement and recommends an amendment to Part 3 so that 'three hours of support per week' is replaced by 'five hours of support per week'. The report refers to the fact that all of the professionals who were present at the review meeting believed this increase to be necessary.
>
> After considering the review report, the LEA decides to make no amendments to the statement and they write informing the parents of this decision.

The LEA have made no legal error in these circumstances. Although they have to await the review report before reviewing the statement, and although they have to make their decision 'in the light of' the report, they are not under a legal duty to follow the recommendations in the report and, therefore, are not making an error in law by choosing not to do so.

Improper exercise of discretion

Parliament often confers powers on public bodies which they do not have to use in every case, but may use when they consider it appropriate.

An example occurs in section 164(1) of the 1993 Education Act which reads:

'A local education authority may make such arrangements as they think fit to enable a child for whom they maintain a statement . . . to attend an institution outside England and Wales which specialises in providing for children with special needs.'

Reading that section, an LEA might think that, as Parliament has said 'may' and not 'shall', they can do whatever they like.

But that would not be correct – discretionary powers must be exercised in accordance with the general principles of administrative law.

Like the other rules of administrative law, the principles which apply to the use of discretionary powers can only be found by reading the reported decisions of the court. The following is a summary, but applying the principles to particular cases can be difficult and (unless there is a right of appeal to the Tribunal against the decision) it may be worth contacting one of the Helpline organisations for advice (see part 7).

The basic principles are that discretionary powers must be exercised by the person or body to whom they were given and not by someone else.

For example:

> Your daughter has Down's Syndrome. You want her to be educated in a mainstream school and the law says that this is what should happen unless:
>
> - the provision she needs cannot be made in that school;
> - the education of other children would be harmed; or
> - there would be an inefficient use of resources.
>
> The LEA's educational psychologist agrees with you that none of these present any problem in your daughter's case, but the headteacher and governing body of the school are unwilling to admit her. When the statement is finalised, it says that your daughter should attend a special school and, when you complain about this, the LEA write back to say that it is not their policy to force schools to admit children with special educational needs against their wishes.
> This is not a proper exercise of the LEA's discretion to decide on your daughter's placement. They must consult the school, but they must make the final decision themselves. In this case, the effect of their policy is that the decision

4

on your daughter's placement has been made by the school, not by the LEA. Although you will have to appeal to the Tribunal, you may also be able to bring a judicial review against the LEA if it has a policy of *never* ordering a school to admit a child with special educational needs.

This example also shows that discretionary powers must be exercised on an individual basis, not on the basis of a policy which is applied inflexibly whatever the personal circumstances of the people affected by the decision. These powers must also be exercised in good faith and to promote the purposes for which the power has been given (in this case to promote the education of children with special needs).

For example:

Your son is now 14 and has been recognised as being autistic since he was five. There has been a long history of trouble between you and the LEA over the special educational provision which he needs.

Three years ago, you successfully appealed to the Special Educational Needs Tribunal to increase the provision in your son's statement. More recently, relations with the education officer in charge of your son's case have deteriorated still further and you complained to the Ombudsman. Last week the Ombudsman reported in your favour, heavily criticising the way in which your son's case had been handled and awarding you £3,000 compensation. Today you received a letter from the education officer proposing an amendment which would halve the help your son is receiving in school. Your son's statement is not due for a review and nothing suggests that his condition has improved recently.

You should see a solicitor about applying for judicial review immediately. There seems to be a strong case for saying that the education officer has made his decision in order to 'punish' you for complaining. That is not allowed. He must exercise the LEA's powers in good faith and not for non-educational purposes.

When discretionary powers are exercised, they must take into account all relevant circumstances and no irrelevant ones.

4

For example:

Your GP recently raised concerns with you about your six-year-old's development and arranged a referral for an examination by an occupational therapist. The therapist's report suggested that your daughter was experiencing problems with fine motor control of a kind which would impact on her classroom work. However, when the school was asked to read the report and to consider whether your daughter should be entered on the special needs register, the answer was 'no', on the grounds that because the referral to the therapist came from your GP, this was a medical not an educational report. The head and the governing body repeated this decision and reasoning.

Although it is true that the governing body ultimately has discretion over which children are placed on the school's special needs register, in this case they are basing their decision on an irrelevant factor. Whether a child has special educational needs or not depends on whether she has a learning difficulty or a disability which calls for additional or different provision to that normally available in schools. The fact that it was a medical professional (a GP), not an educational professional (such as a teacher or an educational psychologist), who first picked up on the child's needs is irrelevant. Also, by failing even to consider the occupational therapist's report, the governors are failing to take account of information which is clearly relevant to their decision.

Taken cumulatively, these principles mean that, far from having a free hand when an Act of Parliament says that they 'may' do something, LEAs and the Secretary of State are in fact operating under heavy restrictions and can only use their discretionary powers in a way and for a purpose which the courts recognise as proper.

Irrationality

Generally, the High Court will not use their powers of judicial review to interfere with a decision just because they disagree with it or because they think that the LEA, etc. got their facts wrong. It is usually necessary to prove that some sort of legal or procedural error has occurred.

But there is a residue of cases where the decision is so bizarre that the High Court has been prepared to say that it was so utterly unreasonable that it could not be allowed to stand. Almost by definition, decisions like this will be very rare: one Law Lord has described the test as being that the decision must be so unreasonable that 'the decision maker must have taken leave of his senses' before the court will strike it down.

Lawyers refer to decisions that are challenged on this ground as *irrational* or *Wednesbury unreasonable*. This is a reference to the decision of the court of appeal in *Associated Provincial Picture Houses Limited vs Wednesbury Corporation*[1] in which it was said that the court could set aside a decision which was 'so absurd that no sensible person could ever dream that it lay within the powers of the authority'.

Nowadays, the courts usually describe an irrational decision as being one 'which no reasonable authority, acting in good faith and properly directing itself as to the applicable law, could have reached'.

For example:

An example of Wednesbury unreasonableness can be found in a recent case[1]:

The applicant was a 16-year-old boy with severe language

---

[1] [1947] 2 ALL ER 680

difficulties. He had previously attended a special school outside the county which was suitable but which did not take pupils over 16. The local authority suggested that he should attend the local College of Further Education even though it had no facilities whatsoever to meet his language needs. The background to the case indicated that the reason for this suggestion was to force the Further Education Funding Council to assume responsibility for, and pay for, his education.

The judge found that the LEA were wrong and that they were still responsible for the applicant's education even though he was over 16. He therefore did not have to decide about the suggestion that the applicant should attend the local college but added that if he had had to make a decision on that point he would have found that it was Wednesbury unreasonable.

Wednesbury cases are a very limited exception to the rule that judicial review is about whether a decision is legal and not about whether the court agrees with it or whether it is factually correct. It is rare for a case which relies solely on this ground to succeed.

Procedural errors

Procedural errors can lead to judicial reviews in two ways. Most obviously, there may be a breach of a written rule in the Regulations about how the assessment or appeal processes must be conducted. But even if there is not, the procedure taken as a whole must not be unfair by being biased against one side or by failing to take account of what both sides have to say.

Although you should always take proper legal advice before starting a judicial review, it is particularly important to do so if you are going to rely on mistakes of procedure. This is because the judge may refuse to make the order you want even if he agrees with you that a procedural mistake has been made. You will probably have to convince him in addition

---

[1] *R vs Dorset CC ex parte Goddard* [1995] ELR 109

that the error is more than trivial and has influenced the eventual decision or prejudiced you in some other way.

You should also remember that, even if you win a judicial review on procedural grounds, the LEA, etc. will then have to go through the process again and may lawfully reach exactly the same decision as long as it complies with the proper procedures.

The Regulations

The Special Educational Needs Regulations contain detailed rules about the steps which an LEA must follow when assessing educational needs as special or reviewing a statement. Similarly, the Tribunal Regulations govern what happens at hearings of the Tribunal and give parents rights to call witnesses and to ask questions of the witnesses who are called by the LEA.

These rules are designed to ensure that parents have a maximum opportunity to consider the views of other people – and to put their own views – at each stage. A failure to follow the procedure set down will be an error of law and may be subject to judicial review.

Normally such a judicial review would be for an order to nullify the resulting decision but, if you are quick enough, it might be possible to get an order to prevent the assessment process from going any further until the error has been corrected.

The duty to act fairly

The duty to act fairly is also sometimes referred to as the rules of 'natural justice' which often leads to misunderstandings.

A decision is not contrary to natural justice just because you think it is unfair.

As explained above, Parliament is a sovereign body and legally can be as unfair as it likes. Provided an unfair law is unambiguous, public bodies such as LEAs must obey it and courts and tribunals must enforce it. It may therefore be that the LEA, the Secretary of State and the Tribunal not only can, but must, make a decision which you think is unfair.

One reason for this is that unfairness is in the eye of the beholder. Parents of children who do not have special educational needs may think it is extremely unfair that the provision for your child is protected because s/he has a statement while the provision for their children can be cut. The point here is not who is right, but that this sort of disagreement about unfairness is economic and political rather than legal. Courts and tribunals simply cannot make that sort of decision: they have to go by the letter of the law.

So, what do lawyers mean when they talk about 'natural justice' or the 'duty to act fairly'? The answer is that those concepts are about *procedural fairness* – that is to say, the way in which decisions are made and not the content of those decisions.

There are two basic rules. The first is that decision-makers should not be biased. The second is that decision-makers should hear what everyone involved has to say in an even-handed way.

The rule against bias
Some parents feel that the whole system of assessing the educational needs of their children – and in particular the fact that the assessment is carried out by the same LEA which will then have to find the resources from a limited budget to make any provision which is assessed as being necessary – is biased against them. But that type of bias is not sufficient for judicial review.

What you need to prove is the sort of bias which occurs when the person making the decision has a direct financial interest in the outcome or is a relative, friend or associate of one of those affected.

Proving that there has been actual bias against you would be very difficult. Fortunately that is not necessary. To succeed, you only have to show that there is a real danger that the decision may have been influenced by bias.

For example:

> Your son attends a school for children with severe learning difficulties which has been selected for closure from the two SLD schools maintained by the LEA. Naturally, all of the parents at your son's school are unhappy. But you are also confused, for the school which is to be retained, and to which your child must transfer, is an older building, in need of extensive repairs, whereas your son's school is modern and was purpose-built only nine years ago. The Secretary of State has yet to give his approval for the closure, although the decision as to which one to recommend has been made by the County Council.

> You discover that the Special Needs Officer wrote the report presented to the councillors by the Chief Education Officer, and that his wife is the headteacher of the school to remain open.

There is a real danger that the report prepared by the Special Educational Needs Officer, and its recommendation, has been influenced by a desire to protect his wife's position. This danger in itself may be sufficient for the court to accept an application for judicial review.

A fair hearing
The requirement of a fair hearing means that there should be an equal opportunity for both sides to put their case. What is necessary in any given case depends upon the nature of the decision which is being made. In the context of special educational needs, the standards which the courts might have insisted upon have largely been pre-empted by the procedures which Parliament and the Secretary of State have laid down in the Act and the Regulations.

However, there may still be occasions where, say, a tribunal falls below the standards which normally apply and fails to give a parent (or possibly an LEA) even-handed treatment, without actually breaking any written rule.

For example:

> Three days before the date of your Special Educational Needs Tribunal hearing, an elderly relative falls gravely ill and you have to go to take care of them. The tribunal refuses an application for an adjournment of the hearing and goes ahead without you being present. Your representative turns up in your place, but it is clear that the members of the tribunal panel are irritated by your absence and you believe that this colours their judgement of the case, which you lose.

> The court may consider that the tribunal has denied you a fair hearing by refusing to fix a new date for the hearing.

Because there are so many possible ways in which public bodies might fall short of fairness, it is hard to be dogmatic about what would or would not be a breach of the duty to act fairly. As a general rule, if you feel you have not been given an opportunity to put your case in your own way, or that the LEA have adopted an unfair procedure or have been given 'an extra crack of the whip' by the Tribunal or the Secretary of State, and if the Act does not allow an appeal against the decision, then you should contact one of the Helpline organisations listed in part 7 of this guide for further advice and, if appropriate, a referral to a solicitor.

What can the court do for your child?

First of all, what do you want the court to do?

Obviously this will depend upon which of the problems

described in part 2 of this book you are encountering. In general terms however there are four types of problems which can arise:

- Something has been done that you disagree with and you want it to be undone – for example, the LEA have changed the person providing support for your child from a teaching assistant to a non-teaching assistant.

- Something has not been done which should have been done and you want to ensure that it is done. For example, having made a statement of your son's special educational needs, the LEA then fail to make the provision which the statement calls for.[1]

- The LEA are threatening to do something which you feel is not in your child's interests and which you think is contrary to the Act, the Regulations or the Code of Practice. For example, your son has been placed in an independent special school. Your LEA is now threatening to stop paying the independent school because they say one of their own special schools can meet his needs just as well. They are basing their argument on the advice of their own special school headteacher, who does not know your child. You suspect that the LEA are simply trying to save money and you want the court to stop them in their tracks.

- The LEA have already fallen short of what is required of them and you think that your child has been harmed as a result. For example, your daughter has been sent to an assessment centre, but after two years no steps have been taken to carry out an assessment. In the meantime, she has been diagnosed as autistic. An educational psychologist tells you that if she had had proper help years ago she would not now be as far behind her age group as she is, and would probably not have developed the behavioural difficulties which she is now displaying. You want compensation for

---

[1] Contrary to the Education Act 1996, section 324(5)(a)

her.

A judge hearing a judicial review application has powers to deal with all of these situations. There are six different orders which he can make if he decides in favour of a child or his or her parents (or the 'applicant', to use the legal jargon). These are:

● Certiorari
● Mandamus
● Prohibition
● Injunction
● Declaration
● Damages

Each of these is dealt with below.

Certiorari

The most important order the court can make is certiorari (pronounced 'sir-sure-air-eye', with the stress on the third syllable). This order deals with the first type of situation described above by depriving the decision which is being challenged of all legal effect. From a legal point of view, the decision does not exist once an order of certiorari has been made. Lawyers call this 'quashing' the decision.

For example:

> The LEA has produced a statement for your son without obtaining up-to-date advice from his school. Instead, they have simply annexed copies of his old school reports to the statement.
> The LEA have acted *ultra vires* . They must take fresh advice from all the relevant professionals listed in the Regulations. The court may grant certiorari to quash the statement.

Mandamus

The second order which the judge can make is called mandamus (pronounced 'man-day-mus', with the stress on the second syllable). It tells the LEA or other public body to perform their legal duties if they are refusing or failing to do so.

For example:

> Your daughter's statement says that she is to receive ten hours of teaching support each week. When it arrives, there is a covering letter from the LEA saying that they do not have enough money in their budget at present to pay for another teacher, but your daughter's name will be placed on a waiting list and she will receive the extra help 'as soon as resources permit, possibly in the next financial year'.

> The LEA cannot do this, and have a legal duty to arrange the educational provision specified in Part 3 of the statement. They must find the necessary resources now and the court may issue an order of mandamus to compel them to do so.

Prohibition

The third order, prohibition, is like certiorari but operates at an earlier stage – i.e. before the decision which is being challenged is actually made. If an LEA or other public body is threatening to make an illegal decision – i.e. one which could be quashed by certiorari, if it had been made – the court may make an order of prohibition to stop it.

For example:

> Case 40 provides an example of a situation in which prohibition might help. In that case, the LEA are threatening to cease to make the provision in your son's statement as soon as he reaches 16 and for no reason other than his age. Following the Goddard case (see above and part 5) it is clear that this would be illegal. Applying for an order of prohibition now may ensure that the position is sorted out before your son's 16th birthday.

The same effect could also be achieved by an interim injunction and, perhaps as a result of this overlap, prohibition is quite a rare order in practice.

Injunctions

An injunction is an order from the Court telling an LEA, the Secretary of State or the Tribunal either to do something or not to do it.

In either case, disobedience or failure to comply is a contempt of court and can be punished by a fine, imprisonment or by sequestration (confiscation of assets) – or in the case of the Secretary of State, by parliamentary censure.

There are two types of injunction – interim (temporary) and final (permanent). Final injunctions are made at the end of a case, after a full hearing, and govern the relationships of the parties for the indefinite future.

For example:

> Your son has cerebral palsy and needs to be taken the six miles to his special school by car. The LEA refuse to arrange and pay for transport on the grounds that you – his father – are registered as unemployed and are therefore available to take and collect your son from school yourself.
>
> However, you are also registered disabled, following an industrial accident, and it is impossible for you to drive. An injunction can compel the LEA to provide transport for your son at their own expense.

Interim injunctions deal with the period between the start of the case and the final hearing and, sometimes, the whole case depends on whether or not you manage to get one.

For historical reasons there is a large overlap between injunctions and the other orders. For example, if you want to compel an LEA to make the provision set out in your child's statement, you could do it either by obtaining an order of mandamus or by getting a mandatory injunction. If you want the LEA not to go ahead with a reassessment of your child's needs you could ask for prohibition or for an injunction ordering them not to do so.

Declarations

As its name suggests, a declaration declares the legal rights and obligations of the parties or the legal status of a decision or act. Unlike an injunction, it does not tell anyone to do or not to do something, nor does it threaten them with punishment if they disobey.

However, there are occasions when parents need an authoritative and binding statement of their or their child's legal rights. It is then that the declaration comes into its own.

For example:

A good example of the use of a declaration can be found in *ex parte M*, the 'Lancashire' case on speech therapy (see part 5). M's parents obtained a declaration from the court that speech therapy could amount to 'educational provision'. It followed from this that Lancashire were correct to have included it in M's Statement and were obliged to arrange and pay for the therapy .

Similarly in the Goddard case (above and part 5), the judge made a declaration that Dorset's duty to maintain the applicant's statement continued after his 16th birthday and that Dorset were in breach of it.

Again, there is considerable overlap with other remedies. For example, if you disagree with a ruling of the Secretary of State, you could either ask the court to quash it by an order of certiorari or to declare that it is legally incorrect.

Damages

If you are in the fourth situation – that is you feel your child has been harmed by something illegal which has been done in the past – you can also use the judicial review procedure to claim damages. However, there are a number of restrictive rules which make this difficult in practice.

First of all, you are only allowed to claim damages in a judicial review application if you could have claimed them in an ordinary court action started at the same time. In other words, your child will not automatically get compensation just because you have won the judicial review. You have to prove what lawyers call a 'tort' as well as at least one of the grounds for judicial review. A tort is a civil wrong in private law such as negligence, breach of statutory duty or misfeasance in a public office.

The need to prove one of these leads to a second difficulty which is specific to the law on education, namely that not all the duties imposed in Acts of Parliament are the same. Some duties certainly give rise to a claim for damages, but others do not.

The House of Lords have decided that an LEA cannot be held liable to pay damages to a child or to parents because of the way it has carried out its legal duties under the rules on special educational needs. This is so, even if the LEA have behaved unreasonably or carelessly. However, the judgement left open the possibility that a child might be able to sue individual members of staff, e.g. if an educational psychologist gives bad advice or if a headteacher behaves carelessly towards a child in relation to her special needs (see page 225). At the time of writing, the House of Lords is set to look at the decision again, following a court of appeal ruling. The position is uncertain, and any parent who believes their child has suffered as a result of educational negligence should get expert legal advice.

Judicial review procedure

Parents who decide to start a judicial review are strongly advised to instruct a solicitor to handle the case. If you do not know of a solicitor with experience of judicial review and the law governing special educational needs, you should contact one of the Helpline organisations listed in part 7, who will be able to refer you to one. Your child will probably be entitled to legal aid to pay the legal costs.

What follows is a brief outline of the various stages in a judicial review and is designed to help parents understand the advice and information which they will receive from their lawyers. It is not a do-it-yourself guide for litigants in person; we strongly advise you not to start a judicial review without legal advice.

It is also important to remember that every case is different and that what follows is only general advice. If your lawyers advise you to do something which goes against what is said in this section or to do something which is not mentioned, it is likely that there are good reasons for this.

There are three stages to an application for judicial review. The first is the application for permission. If permission is granted then there is a second stage (sometimes called the 'interlocutory stage') when the parties exchange their evidence and in which the court may sometimes give directions about the full hearing of the application. Finally there is the hearing.

The application for permission

Unlike other types of legal action, before you can start an application for judicial review, you first have to get permission from the court.

Time limits

The time limit for applying for permission is very short. You must apply promptly and in any event within three months from the date of the decision you are challenging. This means that the application should be made as soon as possible; there have been cases in which parents who have applied within the three months period have not been allowed to go ahead because they were too late.

If you think you may need to apply for judicial review, you

196

should therefore approach a solicitor as soon as possible. He or she will then be able to tell you how quickly an application should be made in practice, given your particular problem.

The court does have the power to extend the time limit if there is a good reason for the delay, but it does not have to do so. One common cause of delay is getting legal aid (particularly if you have to appeal). The court will usually extend the time limit if this has been a problem in your case, but only if you have not contributed to the delay in any way. It is therefore important for your solicitor to keep careful records of all communications with the Legal Aid Board.

The documents
Once legal aid has been granted, your solicitor needs two formal legal documents to make the application for permission. He/she will probably send the papers on the case to a barrister, who will draft these documents.

The first document is called *Form 86A* and is a statement of the decision which you want to challenge, the facts of your case and the reasons why you say the decision is unlawful.

The second document is a witness statement called an *affidavit*. This will confirm the truth of the facts set out in Form 86A and will contain a written statement of your evidence. Copies of all the documents which are relevant to your case (e.g., the statement of special educational needs and the reports of the teachers and educational psychologists, etc.) will be *exhibited* to the witness statement. This means that they will be put into separate marked bundles and referred to in the main text of the witness statement.

Ideally, a witness statement should be signed by someone who has first-hand knowledge of what is stated in it. This means that one of the parents will probably have to sign the witness statement, and it also means that in a complex case there may be two or more such statements.

197

The application for permission is usually made *ex parte*. This means that the judge makes his decision on the basis of what the applicant tells him without hearing the respondents' side of the case. Because of this, you are under a strict obligation to tell the judge everything which is relevant to the case even if it is not in your favour. If you do not do this, the risk is that the judge will throw your case out without considering it once he realises that he has been misled. For this reason, the witness statement which your solicitor asks you to sign may contain things which you would prefer not to tell the court.

It is extremely important that you should read the witness statement before you sign it and that everything you say in it is correct. This is for two reasons:

- if you sign something that you either know is untrue, or you do not believe to be true, you can be prosecuted for perjury and possibly sent to prison;

- although in most judicial reviews all the evidence is given by witness statement so that no-one has to go into the witness box, the court does have the power to order you to attend the hearing and be cross-examined. This would mean that you would have to go into the witness box, where the respondents' barrister would ask you questions about what you have said in the statement. Such orders are very rare in practice, but one of the occasions on which they may be made is when there is a reason for thinking that what is said in the witness statement is not the truth.

So, you should not assume that the witness statement is correct just because your solicitor or barrister has drafted it for you. Check for yourself and ask your solicitor to have it changed if it is wrong.

Because children under 18 cannot usually bring court actions in their own name, one or both of the parents (or some other appropriate adult) has to put their name on the papers as the child's *litigation friend*. Your solicitor will be able to explain the legal implications of this in more detail, but what it means in practice is that you will have to sign a consent form, agreeing to act as litigation friend. Your solicitor will also have to sign a certificate saying that there is no conflict of interest between you and your child.

Making the application for permission
When the documents are ready, your solicitor will file them at the Crown Office in the High Court in London.

Sometimes the judge will simply read the papers and make a decision without a hearing: this is called a *table application*. However, it is possible to ask for a hearing, and this happens quite often in education cases because they are often urgent and you will often be asking the judge to make other orders (e.g. expedition, abridgement of time or an interim injunction – see below) as well as to grant permission. In this case, there will be a short hearing where your barrister will explain the case to the judge and ask him to make the orders you want.

Although the application is usually made without any contribution from the respondents, the court will sometimes ask for them to be served with the papers and attend the hearing. And sometimes your lawyers may decide that it is in your interests to tell the respondents about the hearing voluntarily. This is because a hearing will make your opponents concentrate on your application and possibly try to settle it out of court. If you are asking for an interim injunction as well as for permission, your solicitors will almost always have to tell the other side.

If the judge refuses to give you permission after a table application, you can ask to have it reconsidered at a hearing. This is called *renewing* the application.

If the judge refuses you permission after a hearing (whether or not there has first been a table application), you can make another application to the court of appeal. This has to be done within seven working days of the refusal and you will need to have your legal aid extended before you can do so.

If the court of appeal refuses to give you permission, there is no further appeal and that is the end of the case.

After permission is granted

If you are successful in obtaining permission, your solicitor will serve your opponents with a document called a *claim form* and copies of all the other documents referred to above. He or she will also lodge a copy with the court, together with a witness statement confirming that he or she has served papers on the correspondent.

In the meantime, your opponents will have received the papers on your case and will have to consider what they should do. Very often, they will try to settle the case without the need for another hearing, possibly by agreeing to look again at the decision you object to.

If they decide to fight the case, they will usually want to prepare a witness statement(s) of their own, explaining their side of the case. They have 56 days in which to prepare this evidence, unless the judge has shortened this period at the permission stage.

When you receive the respondents' evidence you will need to consider it carefully with your lawyers. What they have said may be a complete answer to your case from a legal point of view, in which case the Legal Aid Board will insist that you withdraw it.

On the other hand, you may need to put in another witness statement replying to the points they have made, and your lawyers may want to amend Form 86A in the light of any new information which the respondents may have disclosed. Occasionally, your lawyers may decide to ask the court to make orders (called *directions*) about what should happen before or at the hearing. For example, they may ask for an order for *disclosure* (i.e. that the respondents should disclose more documents) or requests for further information (i.e. that they should answer written questions about their evidence on oath) or that those people who have signed witness statements should attend the hearing and be cross-examined about them.

The hearing

The hearing takes place before a High Court judge or, occasionally, before a *divisional court* of two judges. The hearing is in public and the media may be in court, but it is possible to ask the court for an order that your child should not be identified in any publicity about the case.

Unless one of the solicitors involved in the case is one of the very few who have the right to speak in the High Court, both sides will be represented by a barrister (or, occasionally, more than one).

The barristers on each side will have prepared a *skeleton argument*, a written outline of the points which they will be making to the court. The applicant's barrister will begin by explaining the background to the case to the judge and will then make legal submissions. The respondents' barrister then puts his or her case and the applicant's barrister has the right to reply. The hearing will normally take a day or so.

By this time the whole process is in the hands of the lawyers. It is very unusual for parents to have to give oral evidence, and unless they have been ordered to do this there is no need for them even to be in court (although they will usually want to be present).

Although the judge may give his decision at the end of the argument, it is more usual for him to *reserve judgement*. This means that he will take time to think about the case and give a longer, reasoned judgement. If this happens, there will be a further short hearing at the court when the judge reads out his decision and then deals with questions of costs and permission to appeal.

Appeals

Either side can appeal to the court of appeal against the judge's decision, but they first have to get permission to appeal. This can be, and usually is, requested from the judge immediately after he has announced his decision (although it is possible to make the application later).

If permission is refused, you can make another application to the court of appeal. The application will be considered by a single court of appeal judge (known as a Lord Justice of Appeal). If he or she also refuses permission, that is the end of the case.

If permission is granted, there will be a further hearing before the court of appeal, probably about a year later (although sooner in urgent cases). In most cases, the court of appeal's decision will be final. It is possible for there to be a further appeal (again with permission) to the House of Lords but in education cases this is very rare indeed.

The timescale

At the moment, a routine application for judicial review usually takes about 12 months from the application for permission to judgement. This is not necessarily because of delay on the part of the lawyers. The bulk of the time is spent sitting in the queue (or the 'list', as it is called) waiting for an appointment with the judge.

A delay of 12 months is rarely acceptable, but in education cases it can cause particular problems: a year is a long time in the education of any child, and delay can be particularly damaging if the child has special needs. You should therefore discuss with your lawyers what can be done to speed things up.

For example, it may be possible to persuade the judge who grants permission that the case is urgent and should be *expedited*. Expedition is a polite way of describing queue-jumping and, as all the cases in the queue are likely to be important, some judges may be reluctant to agree to this. Other judges, however, may agree that a case about a child's education is particularly urgent, so an application for expedition is always worth considering.

If you are asking for expedition, you should also consider asking for the time limits to be *abridged* (i.e. shortened). For example, the respondents normally have 56 days in which to prepare their evidence. The judge may be prepared to reduce this to 21 days or possibly even less. You will also have to agree to reduction in your own time limits for serving the documents and replying to the respondents' affidavit.

Alternatively, you may be able to protect your child's position by applying for an interim injunction to cover the period between the application for permission and the hearing. These are discussed in more detail earlier in the section on injunctions on page 195.

Costs and legal aid

Costs

Unfortunately, like most legal actions, judicial review is potentially expensive. Although the precise costs will depend upon the circumstances of the particular case, it is safe to say that most ordinary people could not afford to start judicial review proceedings without legal aid.

If you do not qualify for legal aid, it is vital that you obtain a quote before any legal action is taken.
The costs risk is increased by the rule that *costs follow the event*. This means that if you win your judicial review, the LEA etc. will have to pay most, but not all, of your legal costs; but if you lose, you will have to pay most, but not all, of theirs.

Even if you are advised that you have a very strong case (and therefore that your opponent will probably end up paying your costs), there are still a number of problems:

- Lawyers can only predict the result of cases based on what they know about the facts and on their previous experience of similar cases. No lawyer can guarantee the outcome of a case so, however strong your advisers think your case may be, there is always a risk that you will lose and have to pay your own costs and those of your opponents.

- Even if you win, your opponent will only pay your costs at the end of the case, and possibly only after the amount they have to pay has been assessed (or 'taxed', as lawyers call it) by the court. Unless you have particularly understanding lawyers, they will want to be paid more often than this – probably every three months or so. This means that you will have to find the money for your lawyers fees long before you have any chance of getting it back.

- if you win, the other side will probably not have to pay all your legal costs. Even so, you will still be liable to pay all your legal bills in full.

- if the case is settled before conclusion it may be difficult to get costs.

At the moment, it is illegal for lawyers in England and Wales to agree that they will only get paid for a case about special educational needs if they win. This is a pretty depressing picture. Fortunately, it is not as bad as it seems, because of the rule that children under the age of 16 are entitled to legal aid on the basis of their own income and capital.

Legal aid

There are two types of legal aid which may be relevant in cases involving special educational needs – advice and assistance using a Claim 10 form (previously called the Green Form Scheme), and representation under civil legal aid.

The Legal Advice and Assistance Scheme

The Legal Advice and Assistance Scheme allows a solicitor to be paid to do a very limited amount of work advising or helping a client on legal issues. The scheme is often used to do the preliminary work needed for a full application for civil legal aid. It does not allow a solicitor to be paid for representing the client in court.

The Claim 10 form asks for details of the income and savings of the client and his or her family, and the solicitor then carries out a simple means test following the instructions on a 'Claim 10 Key Card' issued by the Legal Aid Board.

If the client qualifies, the solicitor can do approximately two hours of work under the scheme. After that, it is necessary to obtain permission from the local area office of the Legal Aid Board before doing any further work. This will only be given if the board is satisfied that further expenditure of public money would be justified.

In the area of special educational needs, the main problem with the Legal Advice and Assistance Scheme is that, unlike civil legal aid, it is difficult for a child aged less than 16 to apply for assistance in his or her own name. Before a solicitor can accept such an application, he or she must obtain prior authority from the Legal Aid Board, and this will only be given if there is a good reason why one of the child's parents is not applying (e.g. if there is a conflict of interest) and the child is old enough to instruct, and understand the advice given by, the solicitor. If the Legal Aid Board does give permission for Claim 10 advice to be given directly to a child under 16, the solicitor will usually carry out the means test on the basis of the child's resources rather than those of the parents.

For Claim 10 applications made by the parents, the means test is not generous. You and your family must:

- either be on income support, job-seeker's allowance, or have disposable income of less than £83 per week; and
- have less than £1,000 in savings and other capital (more if

you have dependants).

When calculating disposable income, the following are deducted:

- income tax;
- National Insurance contributions;
- £29.25 per week if you are married or cohabiting;
- an amount varying between £20.25 and £30.95 per week for each child, depending on their age;
- some (but not all) social security benefits payable to severely disabled people;
- payments received from the Social Fund.

There are no other deductions.

In very general terms, the effect of these rules is that a parent who is in work will not usually be eligible for help under the Scheme. It is therefore likely that parents will have to pay privately for any preliminary work, even if civil legal aid will eventually be available. You should make sure that you agree a fee with your solicitors for this before they start work.

Although the Scheme will not pay solicitors for representing their clients at hearings of the Special Educational Needs Tribunal, it is possible – provided the parents are financially eligible – for the Legal Aid Board to grant an extension to allow a solicitor to act as a *McKenzie adviser*. This is someone who sits with the parents at a Tribunal hearing, takes notes and advises them about what questions to ask and which points to make. A solicitor acting as a McKenzie adviser under the Claim 10 Scheme is not allowed to speak to the Tribunal on the parents' behalf.

From January 2000, new arrangements will be introduced so that only solicitors who have legal aid contracts will be able to do Claim 10 work.

Civil legal aid is not available for Tribunal hearings and – unless one of the Helpline organisations (see part 7) is able to represent you – a McKenzie adviser is the only type of free legal help available.

Civil legal aid

Civil legal aid is available to pay for legal representation in education cases (including judicial reviews and appeals from the Tribunal) in the High Court, the court of appeal and the House of Lords. It does not cover the cost of legal representation before the Tribunal.

Civil legal aid is administered by local area offices of the Legal Aid Board. To get it, you have to convince the staff of those offices that you have a reasonable chance of winning your case and that it is appropriate for you to receive help from public funds.

Unless the person applying for legal aid is on income support, there may also be a means test.

If you get legal aid, the Legal Aid Board will pay all your legal fees and your lawyers are not allowed to charge you anything extra for work which is covered by the legal aid certificate. The only circumstances in which you may have to pay are if:

- you are assessed as liable to pay a contribution;
- the statutory charge applies at the end of your case.

The means test

As long as the case is being brought to enforce the rights of the child, the civil legal aid means test is based on the child's income and savings, not those of his or her parents. In cases involving special educational needs, this will almost always be the case when judicial review is being sought. When parents are appealing to the High Court against a decision of the Tribunal, however, legal aid is not available in the child's name because it is the parent – and not the child – who has the right of appeal. Such appeals must therefore be made in the names of the parents and the legal aid means test will be carried out on the basis of their financial circumstances.

Children (or, as the case may be, parents) will be financially eligible as long as they have disposable income of less than £7,940 per annum and capital of less than £6,750 in their own name.[1] The rules for calculating disposable income are more generous than for the Claim 10 Scheme.

The question of whether a child (or parent) is financially eligible for legal aid is kept continuously under review throughout the case. Parents must report any change in their (or their children's) finances to the Legal Aid Board. If the change means that the parent or child is better off, the board may either:

- require the payment of a contribution or an increased contribution;
- (if the change means that the child or parent is no longer financially eligible) withdraw legal aid for the future.

The statutory charge
If you are asking the court to give you damages (see page 197) then you may have to pay the Legal Aid Board back out of any damages you receive.

This is known as the *Statutory Charge* or the *Legal Aid Charge.* Your solicitor should give you a leaflet published by the Legal Aid Board explaining this, and you should ensure that he or she advises you in writing about what it means in the particular circumstances of your case.

Normally you should not worry too much about the charge. The worst that can happen is that the legal costs may cancel out any damages you are awarded so there is a risk that you will get nothing. If you do not apply for legal aid and therefore do not take your case to court, you will certainly get nothing (although see part 6 regarding complaints to the Ombudsman).

---

[1] These figures are for the financial years 1999/2000. If a child (or parent) has disposable income of between £2,680 and £7,940 per annum or capital of between £3,000 and £6,750 they will have to pay a contribution. Your solicitor will be able to advise you about what this means in practice.

The charge only applies if you are claiming damages. It does not apply to the other judicial review remedies.

How to apply

The application for legal aid will be made on your behalf by your solicitor, but you will need to complete the forms with his or her help and sign a declaration that the contents are true.

Emergency legal aid

As the time limits for applying for judicial review are so short (see page 198), you will have to make an application for emergency legal aid. This means that you will get legal aid as soon as the area office is persuaded that you have a good case without waiting for the DSS to carry out the means test. In return, you have to agree that if you fail the means test you will pay the legal costs personally. This will not usually be a problem, because you can normally be sure whether or not a child will qualify. If you think there might be a difficulty in your case, you should ask your solicitor for more detailed advice.

Your opponent's legal costs

Legal aid only covers your own legal costs. If you lose the case, you would normally be liable to contribute to the legal costs of your opponents (see page 206). Fortunately, this rule is modified if you are on legal aid. The court is not allowed to make an order for costs against you in respect of a period during which you were on legal aid unless it is reasonable to do so.

What the Court thinks is reasonable in this context differs from case to case and from judge to judge. Quite often, no order for costs at all will be made against you if you are on legal aid. This reflects the reality that a child or parent would not have qualified for legal aid if they had any substantial assets, so it would be very difficult to enforce a costs order even if the court decides to make one.

If you had to pay a contribution towards your legal aid, the court sometimes orders you to pay a similar amount – in addition to your contribution – towards your opponents' legal costs.

The most usual order in these circumstances is probably that you should pay your opponent's costs but that the order should not be enforced against you without leave. This is sometimes called a 'football pools' order (i.e. if you subsequently win the pools, the respondents can come back to the court and ask the judge to make you pay their costs), but the name is misleading as any improvement in your financial circumstances might, in theory, lead to such an application. In practice it is very rare indeed for costs orders to be enforced against people who were on legal aid.

Part 5

Case law

Case law

'Case law' is the law which is developed by the courts as they make their judgements on cases brought to them by parents who believe that either the LEA or the Secretary of State for Education is failing to fulfil their legal duties, or that the Special Educational Needs Tribunal has made an 'error in law' in judging their appeal.

Not all judgements have implications for other children. The ones summarised below do, however, and we have referred to them all in the cases as part of our advice to parents.

R vs The Secretary of State for Education and Science, ex parte E [1992] 1 ELR 377

E was a 13-year-old boy with literacy and numeracy problems. His statement referred to both of these as special educational needs in Part 2, but only specified provision to meet the literacy problems in Part 3. The LEA's explanation was that as the numeracy difficulties were not serious enough for them to have to make any provision (i.e. they could be met from the school's own resources), they did not have to specify this provision in Part 3. The parents disagreed and appealed to the Secretary of State and then applied for judicial review. The court upheld their application.

The Secretary of State appealed to the court of appeal, and lost.

The final judgement included these rulings:

"A child has special educational needs if he has a learning difficulty which requires special educational provision. Of course a child may have more than one learning difficulty. If the special educational provision which the child requires for all his needs can be determined, and provided, by his ordinary school, then no statement is necessary. But once the local education authority have decided that they are required to determine that some special educational

212

5

provision is provided for him, they have to maintain a statement for him under section 7 in respect of that child, not in respect of any particular learning difficulty that he may have. Then the statement must specify in Part 2 the authority's assessment of the special educational needs of the child . . . and in Part 3 the special educational provision to be made for the purpose of meeting those needs . . .

The local education authority is obliged to determine the special educational provision that should be made for the child in respect of each and every educational need identified in the statement . . .

. . . the duty of the authority is then to arrange that the special educational provision specified in the statement is made for the child. It may be that in some cases, or in relation to some particular needs, it will not be possible for the authority to fulfil that duty without themselves providing the requisite special educational provision. But where the authority take the view that the school is able to provide some part of the special educational provision which the child requires, then they will fulfil their duty by arranging that the school do so provide that part of the special educational provision."

The *ex parte E* judgement means that Part 2 of a statement should not be worded vaguely, like this: 'Jenny has a variety of special educational needs, as revealed by her assessment.'

Also, Part 3 of a statement should not be written like this: 'Jenny should receive the help appropriate to her needs.'

If your child's statement does not spell out each of her special educational needs in Part 2, or if it doesn't describe provision to meet each of those needs in Part 3, you should challenge it on the grounds that it is contrary to the judgement in *Ex parte E*.

(See cases 21, 22, 24, 27 and 30)

L vs Clarke and Somerset County Council [1998] ELR 129

The parents of a boy with dyslexia appealed to the Tribunal against Parts 3 and 4 of his statement. Their concern with Part 3 was that it failed to set out the number of hours of help the boy should receive under the statement. The Tribunal refused to order that the statement be made more specific by the help being quantified and the parents appealed to the High Court on this point, which they considered to be an error in law.

The judge ruled:

> "A requirement that the help to be given should be specified in the statement in terms of hours per week was not an absolute and universal precondition of the legality of a statement . . . however . . . in very many cases it will not be possible to fulfil the requirement to specify the special educational provision considered appropriate to meet the child's needs, including specification of staffing arrangements and curriculum, unless hours per week are set out."

(See cases 22, 28 and 30)

R vs Hereford and Worcester County Council, ex parte P [1992] 2 ELR 732

This was a challenge to the arrangements made for transporting a boy with Down's Syndrome to a special school. The parents believed that the journey would take so long that their son would arrive at school in no fit state to learn anything.

The judge ruled as follows:

> "It is implicit in section 55(1) of the Education Act 1944 that the LEA is under a duty to make such arrangements as it considers necessary for a child to reach school without undue stress, strain or difficulty such as would prevent him from benefiting from the education the school has to offer . . . it follows that where a child with special educational needs requires transport to get him to school

the transport which the LEA proposes to make available must therefore be non-stressful transport . . ."

(See case 29)

R vs Surrey County Council Education Committee ex parte H (1985) 83 LGR 219

In this case, the High Court ruled:

"There is no question of Parliament having placed the local education authority under an obligation to provide a child with the best possible education ... or to educate him or her to his or her maximum potential."

This is an important judgement to bear in mind if you are arguing for a place in a specialist independent school for your child. You must not rest your case only on proving how good the school is or how well it will meet your child's needs. Both the LEA and the Tribunal may agree with you that the independent school is the best possible option for your child, but they may still decide that one of the LEA's schools can meet his needs.

So, your task is to present as much evidence as you can which shows that the school the LEA are offering, or any other school they could offer, cannot meet your child's needs as these are described in the statement. It helps if you have a full and detailed Part 2.

(See cases 23 and 30)

R vs Lancashire County Council ex parte M [1989] 2 ELR 279

In this case, known as 'the Lancashire judgement', M had a statement which specified speech therapy provision under Part 3 as 'special educational provision'. When that provision was not made, the LEA claimed that they had made a clerical error when writing the statement and that speech therapy must always be 'non-educational provision' on the grounds that speech therapists are employed by health authorities.

M's parents challenged this interpretation of the law by seeking judicial review and were successful, in that the court ruled that speech therapy could be either a medical provision or an educational provision, depending on the nature of the child's needs for the therapy; and, that the question of who employed the therapists was irrelevant to this decision.

The LEA appealed against this judgement, but it was upheld by the court of appeal.

The judgement included this comment, which is useful as guidance as to whether a child's need for any kind of therapy is 'medical' or 'educational':

> "To teach an adult who has lost his larynx because of cancer might be considered as treatment rather than education. But to teach a child who has never been able to communicate by language, whether because of some chromosomal disorder . . . or because of social cause . . . seems to us just as much educational provision as to teach a child to communicate in writing."

Many LEAs still tell parents that speech therapy always belongs under the heading 'non-educational provision' (i.e. Part 6 of a statement, where no-one has a strict legal duty to provide it). They still tell parents that this is because speech therapists are employed by health authorities. However, the Lancashire judgement specifically rejected this argument. It is the child's need for therapy which is of key importance. The main task for parents is to argue that their child's need for speech therapy is 'educational' rather than 'medical'.

All you have to go on is the judge's example, drawing the distinction between a need for speech therapy following surgery on your larynx (medical) and the need for speech therapy due to chromosomal disorder (educational).

Obviously, under this distinction, the majority of children with special educational needs have speech therapy needs which are 'educational' and which therefore should be set out in

Part 2 of a statement. All Down's Syndrome children, for example, have an 'educational' not 'medical' need for speech therapy, according to the distinction made in the Lancashire judgement.

Many LEAs openly disregard the Lancashire judgement. Why? Because once the need for speech therapy is accepted as 'educational', it must be set out under Part 2 of the statement as one of the child's 'special educational needs.' And, once the need is set out under Part 2, then according to *ex parte E*, the speech therapy provision *must* be specified under Part 3, so that the ultimate responsibility for making the provision then rests with the LEA. They may *ask* the health service to provide the therapists but, if that isn't possible, the LEA themselves must make the arrangements needed and cover the cost.

The message for parents is: 'Get your child's need for speech therapy written into Part 2, as a special educational need, and the rest should follow.'

Although there is no equivalent to the Lancashire judgement covering other therapies (e.g. occupational therapy), the same argument has been used successfully by parents wanting to make their child's occupational therapy secure. That is, by arguing that the need for occupational therapy is educational rather than medical, getting the need written into Part 2 of the statement. The provision to meet that need must then be specified under Part 3, which guarantees the help, as the LEA is ultimately responsible for making the 'special educational provision'.

(See case 25)

B vs Isle of Wight Council [1997] ELR 279

This is probably the only case to reach the High Court on the issue of whether physiotherapy and occupational therapy can be special educational provisions, as opposed to medical provisions. In giving his decision, the judge made the following comment:

> "No doubt the council were right to accept that some occupational therapy and some physiotherapy might be educational in some cases, but I cannot think this would be other than exceptional."

This is an unfortunate comment and reveals a certain lack of experience on the judge's part, given that for a great many children with special educational needs (for example, those with cerebral palsy), therapies are central to the special educational provision. Not surprisingly, this is the part of the judgement most often quoted by LEA officers.

Parents and their advisers, however, should be aware of a further comment made by the judge, which can be quoted in support of the view that these decisions can only be made on an individual basis:

> "All that anyone can do when judging whether a 'provision' is educational or 'non-educational' is to recognise that there is an obvious spectrum from the clearly educational (in the ordinary sense of that word) at one end to the clearly medical at the other, take all the relevant facts into account, apply common sense and do one's best."

By putting it this way, the judge was establishing criteria for making a decision on occupational therapy and physiotherapy very similar to the criteria set out in the Lancashire judgement on speech therapy (see above) – that is, it all depends on the nature of the needs of the individual child.

(See case 25)

R vs London Borough of Harrow ex parte M [1997] ELR 62

M was a six-year-old girl with cerebral palsy who had a statement of special educational needs. Part 3 of the statement specified occupational therapy, physiotherapy and speech therapy, but these provisions had only ever been partially arranged, and for a period M had had no therapies at all. The LEA argued that, because they had made a formal request of the Health Authority to provide these therapies, they were themselves relieved of any further duty to 'arrange' these provisions. The court disagreed and ruled:

> "In clear terms the obligation upon a LEA under s 168 (5) 1993 (now s 324 (5) EA 1996. ed) is simply expressed and subject to no qualification whether express or implied. The construction of the section for which the respondents contended would have involved writing words into the statute which not only are not there, but, more importantly, would manifestly fail to serve the child for whose benefit this part of the 1993 (now 1996) Act exists."

(See case 32)

C vs Lancashire County Council [1997] ELR 377

The parents in this case appealed to the High Court when they lost a Tribunal appeal to have their child placed in a mainstream school. The judge dismissed the appeal but, in a comment on the issue of efficient use of resources, set out how LEAs and Tribunals must address this issue in future.

In summary, the judge ruled that a two-stage process was required in reaching a decision. First, an LEA or Tribunal must establish whether one alternative was in fact more expensive than another. Then, if so, they must make the decision as to whether the additional expenditure involved in meeting the parent's preference was justified:

> ". . . one has to look at the figures, decide whether there is an additional cost, and then do a balancing exercise weighing the additional cost against the parents' preference . . . it is partly a factual exercise and partly a balancing exercise."

(See case 29)

R vs Oxfordshire County Council ex parte
P [1996] ELR 153

Sam Pittick attended his local mainstream school, with a statement which provided him with 20 hours of learning support. His parents were happy with the level of support and with his placement, believing that Sam, like other children with Down's Syndrome, could have his needs best met in a mainstream school.

Then his parents heard from other parents that the LEA, Oxfordshire, were informing schools that they would, in future, have to meet the cost of the first five hours of a child's statemented provision. It seemed to Sam's parents that this would jeopardise his chances of being accepted by a mainstream secondary school come the time for transfer as, in doing so, the school would be also accepting responsibility for meeting the cost of five hours of his learning support. Also, Sam's parents were unhappy at his present school having suddenly to find extra money for Sam from their special needs budget, and particularly concerned that this should not result in provision being reduced for other pupils at the school who also had special educational needs but who did not have the protection of statements.

Sam's mother, Ann Pittick, advised and supported by IPSEA, approached a solicitor in order to apply for judicial review of the LEA's actions. It took over a year for the case to be heard.

The judge ruled that it was not unlawful for the LEA to obtain agreement from a school, after a statement had been finalised, that part of the cost of the special educational provision set out on the statement should be met from the school's own budget. The judge said:

> "So far as can be gleaned from the papers, it was in about mid-1992 that the (LEA) began to explore the possibility that the school might pay out of its own budget for five hours of the ancillary support; and this was in the context

of a wider initiative by which the cost of special provision being made for children with statements who were being educated in mainstream schools might, in part, be funded by the school, rather than in its entirety by the authority out of its central budget . . .

The (LEA's) decision . . . could, of course, only be put into effect with the concurrence of the school . . .

In the ordinary course of things, before the advent of the Education Reform Act 1988, it was no doubt factually inherent in the day-to-day administration of section 7(2) of the 1981 Education Act (which places on LEAs the duty to arrange the special educational provision set out in a statement) that the local authority would be bound to pay for the provision. Under the system of delegated budgets provided for by the Act of 1988, local authority schools . . . have the power, within the limits of their budget, to decide how the money allocated to them shall be spent . . . if in a particular case the school agrees to deploy some of its budget resources towards the cost of special educational provision for one of its children, there is no conceivable breach of section 7(2) . . .

But if ... the school were suddenly to turn round and say that they were no longer prepared to apply any part of their budget to the cost of the 20 hours extra support, it is undoubted that the (LEA) would immediately have to meet the full cost. The provision would in any event be secure."

(See Case 33)

R vs Cumbria County Council ex parte P [1995] COD 267

P's statement referred to speech therapy under Part 3 but in such vague terms that his father did not have a clear idea of how much help to expect for his son. The speech therapist's advice recommended three hours a week. P received one hour per week.

The statement did seem to be specific, however, about the

money that would be spent on P's provision: 'P's needs entitle him to extra funding at Band Level 3. This is now £6,000 a year'.

P's father obtained professional advice that three hours of speech therapy a week could not be obtained for the annual sum of £6,000. He therefore concluded that the reason why his son could not have the therapy he needed was that the figure of £6,000 acted as a ceiling on the spending that could be made on his son's special educational provision. He therefore sought judicial review in order to challenge the legality of the LEA's banding policy, in that it seemed to place a fetter on the LEA's ability to give P the provision which his needs called for.

The application failed, but the judge's comments on the situation provide useful guidance to other parents facing a similar problem. This is an extract from the judgement:

> "... the County has a policy of allocating pupils with special educational needs into various bands or categories. All but one of these of these have a cash figure against them. Pupils are categorised according to the degree of impairment as assessed by the authority into 12 categories set out in a document entitled the Cumbria Scheme for Local Management of Schools ...
>
> I am not persuaded that it is illegal. The scheme does not indicate any unwillingness by the authority to have regard to the need for securing that special education provision is made for pupils who have special educational needs ... Nor does the scheme as such fetter the authority's discretion as to what is contained in the statements of any of its statemented pupils ...
>
> I am not persuaded that the authority regarded itself in any way as being fettered by the figure of £6,000 ... There is, in my judgement, no need to specify such a figure in the statement. I am told, and can well believe, that many

parents are pleased to know the amount of extra money which their offspring received compared with the generality of pupils. If in the present case nothing other than a sentence on the lines of '£6,000 is allocated to pay for all P's needs' has appeared in Part 3 of the statement I would have regarded this as not complying with the requirements of specificity contained in the statute and regulations. The reason for that is that the appeal process becomes impossible to operate if the parent, and indeed the Secretary of State, does not know what the nature of the provision is which the authority intends to make. However, that is not this case . . .

Failure to have appropriate material in the statement and appendices: I have already touched on part of this and found room for criticism. There are other matters in respect of which there seems further such room . . . I understand and sympathise with the uncertainty in which the parents found themselves following the way in which their son's statement has been dealt with . . .

The statement is unsatisfactory in several respects and the authority ought to produce a new statement as soon as is compatible with their duties of consultation and consideration and the authority ought to produce it in such a form as makes it clear to P's parents what the authority consider their son ought to receive by way of special educational provision and non-educational provision for his profound communication difficulties. Then the parents will be in a position to appeal if they wish to."

(See case 28)

R vs Dorset County Council and Further Education Funding Council ex parte M [1995] ELR 109

This was a challenge to an LEA's attempt to argue that it had no responsibility for a pupil with a statement once he had reached the age of 16. This is what the judge decided:

". . . a local education authority cannot divest itself of

responsibility for a pupil's schooling when he reaches 16 by wrongfully failing to specify it, either by silence or express exclusion, in his statement and by refusing to provide it when he reaches 16 so that he cannot then satisfy the condition of the authority's continuing responsibility under Section 4(2)(a) of the 1981 Education Act, namely by being a registered pupil at a school appropriate to his needs . . .

Dorset's duty under Section 7(1) and (2) of the Education Act 1981 to maintain the 1992 statement of Mark's special educational needs and to arrange for him the special educational provision specified in it continues until Dorset amends or ceases to maintain the statement in accordance with the procedures set out in paragraphs 6 and 7 of schedule 1 to, and section 8 of, the 1981 Act."

(See case 40)

R vs Oxfordshire County Council ex parte B, Court Of Appeal [1997] ELR 90

B was a boy with autism and severe learning difficulties. His LEA operated a policy of all children leaving school at the age of 16 and continuing their education at local colleges. B's mother was not sure that the college could meet B's needs and, when the LEA ceased to maintain his statement, she challenged the LEA via judicial review on the grounds that they should have followed the appropriate procedure for ceasing to maintain a statement.

The judge made reference to the earlier Dorset judgement, made by Auld J (see above) but distinguished his opinion from it by ruling:

". . . insofar as Auld J (the judge in the Dorset case, above) was suggesting that there remained a duty upon all LEAs to continue to maintain a statement until it was amended or ceased to be maintained on a proper proposal by the authority, that proposition is expressed in my view far too widely . . . In my judgement the responsibility for the registered child ends upon the child ceasing to be registered and the maintenance of the statement . . . would cease with the cessation of that responsibility and registration . . ."

(See case 40)

P vs Hillingdon London Borough Council [1998] ELR 38

Ms Phelps, as an adult, sued her LEA for failing to diagnose her dyslexia. The judge ruled that an educational psychologist had been negligent in failing to detect dyslexia and awarded damages.

P vs London Borough of Hillingdon, [1998] ELR 587 CA

Hillingdon appealed against the judgement above and the court overturned the original ruling, on the grounds that failing to ameliorate the effects of dyslexia is not 'an injury' and that the educational psychologist did not owe a duty of care directly to the child.

The outcome of an appeal to the House of Lords for a final ruling on the question of 'educational negligence' is expected at the time of writing. The judgement is not expected to emerge for a further year. For up-to-date information on the progress of this case, contact one of the Helplines listed in part 7 of this guide.

Part 6

Complaining

6

If you are unhappy about the way your LEA is acting, you could consider making a complaint, either to the Secretary of State for Education or to the Local Government Ombudsman. This part of the guide will help you decide who to complain to, and how to do it. However, before you write your complaint, it is a good idea to discuss the options with one of the Helpline organisations listed in part 7.

Complaining to the Secretary of State

There are two situations in which you can make a formal complaint to the Secretary of State against your LEA or the governors of your child's school: when they are failing to fulfil a legal duty and when they are acting unreasonably.

Failing to fulfil a legal duty

When you write a letter complaining that your LEA or your child's school are failing to fulfil a legal duty, you must:

- say that you are making the complaint under *Section 497 of the 1996 Education Act*;

- quote the specific legal duty which your LEA or school have failed to fulfil;

- give the evidence, including copies of any letters which you have received which show what has happened.

Case 11, where an LEA is not fulfilling its legal duty to keep to the time limits set out in the Regulations, is an example of a situation in which a parent would be able to make a complaint under section 497 of the 1996 Education Act. The letter of complaint might look something like this:

6

Secretary of State for Education
Department for Education
Sanctuary Buildings
Great Smith Street
London
SW1P 3BT

Dear Secretary of State,

I am writing to make a formal complaint under Section 497 of the 1996 Education Act against . . . local education authority on the grounds that they have failed to fulfil their legal duty to complete my child's assessment of special educational needs in the period set out in the 1994 Regulations.

I received a letter on October 7th telling me that the assessment was due to begin. It is now May, and I have heard nothing further from the LEA, despite having written six times to ask what was happening. So far as I know, the LEA has no reasonable excuse not to have kept to the time limits and completed the statement within ten weeks, which is what the Regulations require.

I enclose copies of all correspondence relating to this complaint . . .

Case 5 describes a situation in which you might want to complain that the governors of your child's school are failing to fulfil their legal duty. Your letter of complaint could start like this:

Secretary of State for Education
Department for Education
Sanctuary Buildings
Great Smith Street
London
SW1P 3BT

Dear Secretary of State,

I am writing to make a formal complaint under Section 497 of the 1996 Education Act against the governors of . . . school on the grounds that they have failed to fulfil their legal duty under Section 317 of the 1996 Education Act to 'use their best endeavours' to ensure that my daughter's special educational needs are provided for.

For the past eight weeks, Shirley has not been getting the support which she is supposed to receive under her individual education plan. I have raised this matter with the headteacher and the chair of the governing body, but without any satisfaction and I enclose copies of correspondence between myself and the school on this issue . . .

If you believe that you have grounds for a complaint under Section 497 of the 1996 Education Act, you should get advice on wording your complaint from one of the Helpline organisations listed in part 7.

Acting 'unreasonably'

Complaints against an LEA or a school acting unreasonably are less easy to make than complaints on the grounds that they have failed to fulfil a legal duty. That is because there is not a clear definition in law of what 'unreasonable' means.

As a general rule, if you can make a complaint under Section 497 of the 1996 Act ('failure to fulfil a legal duty') then do that rather than complaining of unreasonableness. However, in some cases, the complaint of unreasonableness is the only option. For example, in **case 7**, the LEA is acting legally in proposing to assess Lloyd. There is no appeal to the Tribunal either, in this situation. The only option Lloyd's parents have is to try making a complaint of unreasonableness against the LEA to the Secretary of State. The letter could start off like this:

Secretary of State for Education
Department for Education
Sanctuary Buildings
Great Smith Street
London
SW1P 3BT

Dear Secretary of State,

I am writing to make a formal complaint under Section 496 of the 1996 Education Act against . . . local education authority on the grounds that they are acting unreasonably by proposing to assess my son under Section 323 of the 1996 Education Act when there is no evidence that he has special educational needs, nor have any professionals who know Lloyd said that he has special needs, apart from the headteacher of his school. And, when I asked the headteacher to provide evidence for his opinion, he was unable to do so.

I have complained both to Lloyd's school about them

referring Lloyd for assessment and to the Chief Education Officer. Copies of the correspondence are enclosed for your information . . .

Time

It is difficult to judge how long it will take the Department for Education to investigate a formal complaint. It may be months; it may be a year or more. However, swift action at a local level can follow a formal complaint, and it is always worthwhile copying your complaint to your local councillor and asking him/her to take the matter up directly with the Chief Education Officer.

For further advice and information on making a complaint to the Secretary of State for Education, contact one of the Helpline organisations listed in part 7.

Complaining to the Ombudsman

The official name for the Ombudsman is the Local Commissioner for Administration. You can make a complaint about your local authority to the Ombudsman if you believe that they have caused you (or your child) injustice because of maladministration.

What is maladministration?

Basically, maladministration is the term used when a council either does something wrong, or fails to do something which it should have done. Here are some examples:

- delay, with no good cause;
- failure to follow the council's agreed policies;
- acting with bias or malice;
- failure to take account of matters which they should have considered;
- failure to tell people of their rights.

The most common complaint which parents of children with special educational needs make to the Ombudsman is over their LEA's delay in making the proper provision to meet their child's needs.

What is injustice?

The Ombudsman cannot investigate a complaint of maladministration unless you can also show that it has caused injustice. You can't complain just because the council has done something wrong. You must also explain the bad effect that this has had on you and your family. Some examples of injustice are:

- that your child has missed out on his/her education (e.g. by not being allowed to attend school, or by not receiving the special help needed);
- that you have suffered financial loss;
- that you and your family have suffered stress.

The three months rule

Normally the Ombudsman will not investigate a complaint about maladministration unless it has happened within the preceding three months.

If you think that you might have grounds for complaint to the Ombudsman, you should discuss the situation with one of the Helpline organisations (part 7) before putting your complaint in writing. Or, you can ring the Ombudsman's office direct and they will send you a free booklet explaining how to complain, plus a form. The booklet is also available from libraries.

If you live in England, send your complaint to:

The Commission for Local Administration in England
21 Queen Anne's Gate
London
SW1H 9BU.
Tel: 0207-915 3210
If you live in Wales, send your complaint to:

6

The Commission for Local Administration in Wales
Derwen House
Court Road
Bridgend
CF31 1BN
Tel: 01656-661 325

You do not need the Ombudsman's form to make a complaint. Instead, you can write a letter along these lines:

Dear Sir or Madam,

I am writing to make a complaint of maladministration leading to injustice against ... local education authority.

The maladministration

The maladministration was the failure of the LEA to respond to repeated requests from my daughter's school and from me that she be examined by an educational psychologist. I have a number of letters showing how often the requests were made and copies of LEA acknowledgements and 'promises'. However, despite the fact that both the school and I believed that the advice of a psychologist was needed, no response was made for 18 months, and I believe that this delay was maladministration on the part of the LEA.

The history of my problems with the LEA, and of their maladministration, is set out below.

October 12th 1998: I wrote to the LEA asking to be sent information on special education provision in the county for children under 5 years old.

November 22nd 1998: I telephoned to find out why

my letter in October had not been replied to. I spoke to Mr Simmons, the officer with responsibility for special needs, and was told to ring back and ask for a Miss Jenkins, as she was responsible for all under-5s provision.

November 22nd to December 24th: I made ten phone calls to the Education Department, leaving a message each time asking Miss Jenkins to return my call. She was always 'out of the office' and never did ring me back.

. . . etc.

The injustice

As a result of the maladministration, I was unaware of the existence in the area of two special needs 'opportunity playgroups'. I placed my daughter in the nearest private nursery, and at my own expense paid an occupational therapist and a speech therapist to visit for weekly sessions with her. Although I was happy with the efforts made by the nursery, the staff did not have the training nor the experience of the staff at the LEA's own opportunity playgroups. Therefore:

1. My daughter was deprived of specialist provision which was available to her.

2. The LEA failed to inform me of my rights as a parent of a child with special needs.

3. I was put to unnecessary expense paying for the therapies when I believe now that an assessment would have shown them to be necessary provision for my daughter.

4. For 18 months, my whole family suffered from the

stress involved in trying (in vain) to get the LEA to fulfil their proper duties towards my daughter.

. . . etc.

Time

A complaint to the Ombudsman can take up to a year to be investigated. However, swift action at a local level can follow a formal complaint, and it is always worthwhile copying your complaint to your local councillor and asking her or him to take the matter up directly with the Chief Education Officer.

The Ombudsman publicises his findings and can recommend that LEAs pay parents compensation. These sums are never huge, but LEAs generally award the amount recommended by the Ombudsman.

For further advice and information on making a complaint to the Ombudsman, contact one of the Helpline organisations listed in part 7 or ring the Ombudsman direct (see above for the numbers).

Complaining to the Local Authority Monitoring Officer

Under the Local Government and Housing Act 1989, every local authority must appoint a Monitoring Officer with responsibility for reporting on any act taken or decision made by the Authority which either breaches the law, or may breach the law.

In most local authorities, the role of Monitoring Officer is given to the Chief Executive, or the head of the Legal Department. You could write to the Monitoring Officer if you thought that your LEA were acting in breach of the law with regard to meeting your child's needs, or if the LEA were proposing to bring in a policy which would, when enacted, mean they were breaching the law with regard to meeting all children's special educational needs in your area.

You could start your letter like this:

> *The Monitoring Officer*
> *Town Hall*
> *Etc . . .*
>
> *Dear Sir or Madam,*
>
> *I am writing to request that you use your powers under s5 of the Local Government and Housing Act 1989 to investigate and report on the policy which is being proposed with regard to provision in schools for children with statements of special educational needs. I have attached a letter which all parents of children at . . . received from the Headteacher last week. It informed us that the authority was proposing to reduce LEA support for children with statements, and to require schools to increase their contribution to meeting the costs of statemented provision. Our Headteacher says this is not possible, so after half term non-teaching assistant hours are being cut for all pupils with statements.*
>
> *As a parent, I believe that the LEA will be acting illegally if it creates a situation in which it is failing to provide the special educational provision specified on my child's statement. This is because the LEA will be in breach of s324 of the Education Act 1994. I ask you to investigate and report on this policy as a matter of urgency . . .*

If the Monitoring Officer accepts your argument that there is a breach of law, or a likely breach of law, he or she will investigate the situation and produce a report which must be circulated to all the elected members of the Authority (the councillors).

If the Monitoring Officer refuses to investigate your complaint, or reports that there is no breach of law likely, you should contact one of the Helplines (see part 7) for the name of a solicitor who will give advice on whether there are further steps you can take.

Part 7

Helpline organisations and further reading

Helpline organisations and further reading

Helpline organisations

If you work for an organisation which advises parents of children with special educational needs, but which is not listed here, please let IPSEA know.

Organisations which will advise parents of children with special educational needs, regardless of the specific nature of the child's disability:

Advisory Centre for Education (ACE)
Telephone helpline: 0207 354 8321
Weekdays 2.00pm to 5.00pm

Children's Legal Centre
Telephone helpline: 01206 872 466
Weedays 9.00am to 5.00pm

Contact a Family
Telephone helpline: 0207 383 3555
Weekdays 9.00am to 5.00pm

Education Otherwise (home education)
Telephone helpline: 0870 730 0074

Independent Panel For Special Education Advice (IPSEA)
Telephone helpline: 0800 018 4016
Tribunal support service: 01394-384 711

National Association for Special Educational Needs
Telephone helpline: 01827 311500
Weekdays 9.00am to 5.00pm

Network 81
Telephone helpline: 01279 647 415
Weekdays 10.00am to 2.00pm

Norfolk Network 81
Telephone helpline: 01603 614 647
Weekdays 9.00am to 7.00pm

Parents for Inclusion
Telephone helpline: 0207 582 5008
Tuesday and Thursday 10.00am to 2.00pm

The Rathbone Society
Telephone helpline: 0800 917 6790
Weekdays 1.30pm to 4.30pm

SKILL: National Bureau for Students with Disabilities
Telephone helpline: 0207 274 0565
Weekdays 2.00pm to 5.00pm

Organisations which advise parents of children with specific disabilities:

Association for All Speech Impaired Children (AFASIC)
Telephone helpline 08453 555577
Monday to Wednesday 10.00am to 4.00pm
Thursday 11.00am to 2.00pm

Association for Spina Bifida and Hydrocephalus (ASBAH)
Telephone helpline: 01733 555 988
Weekdays 9.00am to 5.00pm

British Dyslexia Association
Telephone helpline: 0118 966 8271
Weekdays 10.00am to 12.45pm; 2.00pm to 4.45pm

British Epilepsy Association
Telephone helpline: 0808 800 5050
Monday to Thursday 9.00am to 4.30pm (Friday 4.00pm)

Child Growth Foundation
Telephone helpline: 0208 995 0275 or 020 8994 7625
Weekdays 9.00am to 3.30pm

Cystic Fibrosis Trust
Telephone helpline: 0208 464 7211
Weekdays 9.00am to 5.00pm

Down's Syndrome Association
Telephone helpline: 0181 682 4001
Weekdays 9.00am to 5.00pm

Hyperactive Children's Support Group
Telephone helpline: 01903 725 182
Weekdays 10.00am to 1.00pm

The Multiple Sclerosis Society
Telephone helpline: 0808 800 8000
Weekdays 9.00am to 9.00pm

National Autistic Society
Telephone helpline: 0870-600 8585
Weekdays 10.00am to 4.00pm

Royal National Institute for the Blind
Telephone helpline: 0345 669999
Weekdays 9.00am to 5.00pm

SCOPE – for people with cerebral palsy
Telephone helpline: 0207 619 7100
Weekdays 8.30am to 5.30pm

Tuberous Sclerosis Association
Telephone helpline 0199 3881238
Weekdays

Other publications you should have

7

- *Special Educational Needs – a Parents' Guide: Parents' Charter* (Copies are available in Bengali, Chinese, Greek, Gujarati, Hindi, Punjabi, Turkish, Urdu, Vietnamese and Welsh)

- *The Code of Practice (on the identification and assessment of special educational needs)*

- *Special Educational Needs Tribunal – How to Appeal*

All of the above are free publications on special educational needs which are available from the Department for Education and Employment, telephone 0845 602 2260.

- *Sent Ahead* by Sally Capper. IPSEA's guide for parents appealing to the Special Educational Needs Tribunal. £7.50 from: IPSEA, 4 Ancient Horse Mews, Woodbridge IP12 1DH

- *ACE's Special Education Handbook.* This is not free, but it is probably the most popular guide to the law on special education written from the parents' perspective. Available from: ACE, 18 Aberdeen Studios, 22 Highbury Grove, London N5 2EA.

- *Children with Special Needs. Assessment, Law and Practice - Caught in the Acts* by John Friel (Jessica Kingsley Publishers, 1995). This is not so easy to digest as the ACE book, but it is an important source book, particularly for information on important case law judgements.

- *Education, Law and Practice* by David Ruebain, John Ford and Mary Hughes (Legal Action Group 1999).

Part 8

The law

Education Act 1996

(Sections 312 to 336, Schedule 26 and Schedule 27)

Introductory

Section 312

Meaning of "special educational needs" and "special educational provision" etc.

(1) A child has "special educational needs" for the purposes of this Act if he has a learning difficulty which calls for special educational provision to be made for him.

(2) Subject to subsection (3) (and except for the purposes of section 15(5)) a child has a "learning difficulty" for the purposes of this Act if –

   (a) he has a significantly greater difficulty in learning than the majority of children of his age,

   (b) he has a disability which either prevents or hinders him from making use of educational facilities of a kind generally provided for children of his age in schools within the area of the local education authority, or

   (c) he is under the age of five and is, or would be, if special educational provision were not made for him, likely to fall within paragraph (a) or (b) when of or over that age.

(3) A child is not to be taken as having a learning difficulty solely because the language (or form of the language) in which he is, or will be, taught is different from a language (or form of a language) which has at any time been spoken in his home.

(4) In this Act "special educational provision" means –

   (a) in relation to a child who has attained the age of two, educational provision which is additional to, or otherwise different from, the educational provision made generally for children of his age in schools maintained by the local education authority (other than special schools) or grant-maintained schools in their area, and

   (b) in relation to a child under that age, educational provision of any kind.

(5) In this Part –

"child" includes any person who has not attained the age of 19 and is a registered pupil at a school;
"maintained school" means any county or voluntary school or any maintained special school not established in a hospital.

Code of Practice

Section 313

(1) The Secretary of State shall issue, and may from time to time revise, a code of practice giving practical guidance in respect of the discharge by local education authorities and the governing bodies of maintained or grant-maintained schools, or grant-maintained special schools, of their functions under this Part.

Code of
Practice

(2) It shall be the duty of –

    (a) local education authorities, and such governing bodies, exercising functions under this Part, and

    (b) any other person exercising any function for the purpose of the discharge by local education authorities, and such governing bodies, of functions under this Part

– to have regard to the provisions of the code.

(3) On any appeal under this Part to the Tribunal, the Tribunal shall have regard to any provision of the code which appears to the Tribunal to be relevant to any question arising on the appeal.

(4) The Secretary of State shall publish the code as for the time being in force.

(5) In this Part "the Tribunal" means the Special Educational Needs Tribunal.

Section 314

(1) Where the Secretary of State proposes to issue or revise a code of practice, he shall prepare a draft of the code (or revised code).

Making and
approval of
code

(2) The Secretary of State shall consult such persons about the draft as he thinks fit and shall consider any representations made by them.

(3) If he determines to proceed with the draft (either in its original form or with such modifications as he thinks fit) he shall lay it before both Houses of Parliament.

(4) If the draft is approved by resolution of each House, the Secretary of State shall issue the code in the form of the draft, and the code shall come into effect on such day as the Secretary of State may by order appoint.

Special educational provision: general

8

Review of arrangements

Section 315

(1) A local education authority shall keep under review the arrangements made by them for special educational provision.

(2) In doing so the authority shall, to the extent that it appears necessary or desirable for the purpose of co-ordinating provision for children with special educational needs, consult the funding authority and the governing bodies of county, voluntary, maintained special and grant-maintained schools in their area.

Children with special educational needs normally to be educated in mainstream schools

Section 316

(1) Any person exercising any functions under this Part in respect of a child with special educational needs who should be educated in a school shall secure that, if the conditions mentioned in subsection (2) are satisfied, the child is educated in a school which is not a special school unless that is incompatible with the wishes of his parent.

(2) The conditions are that educating the child in a school which is not a special school is compatible with –

(a) his receiving the special educational provision which his learning difficulty calls for,

(b) the provision of efficient education for the children with whom he will be educated, and

(c) the efficient use of resources.

Duties of governing body or LEA in relation to pupils with special educational needs

Section 317

(1) The governing body, in the case of a county, voluntary or grant-maintained school, and the local education authority, in the case of a maintained nursery school, shall –

(a) use their best endeavours, in exercising their functions in relation to the school, to secure that, if any registered pupil has special educational needs, the special educational provision which his learning difficulty calls for is made,

(b) secure that, where the responsible person has been informed by the local education authority that a registered pupil has special educational needs, those needs are made known to all who are likely to teach him, and

(c) secure that the teachers in the school are aware of the importance of identifying, and providing for, those registered pupils who have special educational needs.

(2) In subsection (1)(b) "the responsible person" means –

(a) in the case of a county, voluntary or grant-maintained school, the head teacher or the appropriate governor (that is, the chairman of the governing body or, where the governing body have designated another governor for the purposes of this paragraph, that other governor), and

(b) in the case of a nursery school, the head teacher.

(3) To the extent that it appears necessary or desirable for the purpose of co-ordinating provision for children with special educational needs –

(a) the governing bodies of county, voluntary and grant-maintained schools shall, in exercising functions relating to the provision for such children, consult the local education authority, the funding authority and the governing bodies of other such schools, and

(b) in relation to maintained nursery schools, the local education authority shall, in exercising those functions, consult the funding authority and the governing bodies of county, voluntary and grant-maintained schools.

(4) Where a child who has special educational needs is being educated in a county, voluntary or grant-maintained school or a maintained nursery school, those concerned with making special educational provision for the child shall secure, so far as is reasonably practicable and is compatible with –

(a) the child receiving the special educational provision which his learning difficulty calls for,

(b) the provision of efficient education for the children with whom he will be educated, and

(c) the efficient use of resources,

that the child engages in the activities of the school together with children who do not have special educational needs.

(5) The annual report for each county, voluntary, maintained special or grant-maintained school shall include a report containing such information as may be prescribed about the implementation of the governing body's policy for pupils with special educational needs.

(6) The annual report for each county, voluntary or grant-maintained school shall also include a report containing information as to –

(a) the arrangements for the admission of disabled pupils;

(b) the steps taken to prevent disabled pupils from being treated less favourably than other pupils; and

(c) the facilities provided to assist access to the school by disabled pupils;

– and for this purpose "disabled pupils" means pupils who are disabled persons for the purposes of the Disability Discrimination Act 1995.

1995 c. 50

(7) In this section "annual report" means the report prepared under the

articles of government for the school in accordance with section 161 or, as the case may be, paragraph 7 of Schedule 23.

Section 318

(1) A local education authority may, for the purpose only of assisting –

    (a) the governing bodies of county, voluntary or grant-maintained schools (in their or any other area) in the performance of the governing bodies' duties under section 317(1)(a), or

    (b) the governing bodies of maintained or grant-maintained special schools (in their or any other area) in the performance of the governing bodies' duties,

– supply goods or services to those bodies.

(2) The terms on which goods or services are supplied by local education authorities under this section –

    (a) to the governing bodies of grant-maintained schools or grant-maintained special schools, or

    (b) to the governing bodies of county, voluntary or maintained special schools,

– in any other area may, in such circumstances as may be prescribed, include such terms as to payment as may be prescribed.

(3) A local education authority may supply goods or services to any authority or other person (other than a governing body within subsection (1)) for the purpose only of assisting them in making for any child in respect of whose education grants are (or are to be) made under arrangements under section 1 of the Nursery Education and Grant-Maintained Schools Act 1996 any special educational provision which any learning difficulty of the child calls for.

1996 c. 50.

(4) This section is without prejudice to the generality of any other power of local education authorities to supply goods or services.

Section 319

(1) Where a local education authority are satisfied that it would be inappropriate for –

    (a) the special educational provision which a learning difficulty of a child in their area calls for, or

    (b) any part of any such provision, to be made in a school,

– they may arrange for the provision (or, as the case may be, for that part of it) to be made otherwise than in a school.

(2) Before making an arrangement under this section, a local education

authority shall consult the child's parent.

Section 320

(1) A local education authority may make such arrangements as they think fit to enable a child for whom they maintain a statement under section 324 to attend an institution outside England and Wales which specialises in providing for children with special needs.

(2) In subsection (1) "children with special needs" means children who have particular needs which would be special educational needs if those children were in England and Wales.

(3) Where a local education authority make arrangements under this section in respect of a child, those arrangements may in particular include contributing to or paying –

(a) fees charged by the institution,
(b) expenses reasonably incurred in maintaining him while he is at the institution or travelling to or from it,
(c) his travelling expenses, and
(d) expenses reasonably incurred by any person accompanying him while he is travelling or staying at the institution.

(4) This section is without prejudice to any other powers of a local education authority.

Identification and assessment of children with special educational needs

Section 321

(1) A local education authority shall exercise their powers with a view to securing that, of the children for whom they are responsible, they identify those to whom subsection (2) below applies.

(2) This subsection applies to a child if –

(a) he has special educational needs, and
(b) it is necessary for the authority to determine the special educational provision which any learning difficulty he may have calls for.

(3) For the purposes of this Part a local education authority are responsible for a child if he is in their area and –

(a) he is a registered pupil at a maintained, grant-maintained or grant-maintained special school,
(b) education is provided for him at a school which is not a maintained, grant-maintained or grant-maintained special school but is so provided at the expense of the authority or the funding authority,
(c) he does not come within paragraph (a) or (b) above but is a

8

Provision outside England and Wales for certain children

General duty of local education authority towards children for whom they are responsible

251

registered pupil at a school and has been brought to the authority's attention as having (or probably having) special educational needs, or

(d) he is not a registered pupil at a school but is not under the age of two or over compulsory school age and has been brought to their attention as having (or probably having) special educational needs.

Section 322

Duty of Health Authority or local authority to help local education authority

(1) Where it appears to a local education authority that any Health Authority or local authority could, by taking any specified action, help in the exercise of any of their functions under this Part, they may request the help of the authority, specifying the action in question.

(2) An authority whose help is so requested shall comply with the request unless –

(a) they consider that the help requested is not necessary for the purpose of the exercise by the local education authority of those functions, or

(b) subsection (3) applies.

(3) This subsection applies –

(a) in the case of a Health Authority, if that authority consider that, having regard to the resources available to them for the purpose of the exercise of their functions under the National Health Service Act 1977, it is not reasonable for them to comply with the request, or

1977 c. 49.

(b) in the case of a local authority, if that authority consider that the request is not compatible with their own statutory or other duties and obligations or unduly prejudices the discharge of any of their functions.

(4) Regulations may provide that, where an authority are under a duty by virtue of subsection (2) to comply with a request to help a local education authority in the making of an assessment under section 323 or a statement under section 324 of this Act, they must, subject to prescribed exceptions, comply with the request within the prescribed period.

(5) In this section "local authority" means a county council, a county borough council, a district council (other than one for an area for which there is a county council), a London borough council or the Common Council of the City of London.

Assessment of educational needs

Section 323

(1) Where a local education authority are of the opinion that a child for whom they are responsible falls, or probably falls, within subsection (2), they shall serve a notice on the child's parent informing him –

252

(a) that they propose to make an assessment of the child's educational needs,

(b) of the procedure to be followed in making the assessment,

(c) of the name of the officer of the authority from whom further information may be obtained, and

(d) of the parent's right to make representations, and submit written evidence, to the authority within such period (which must not be less than 29 days beginning with the date on which the notice is served) as may be specified in the notice.

(2) A child falls within this subsection if –

(a) he has special educational needs, and

(b) it is necessary for the authority to determine the special educational provision which any learning difficulty he may have calls for.

(3) Where –

(a) a local education authority have served a notice under subsection (1) and the period specified in the notice in accordance with subsection (1)(d) has expired, and

(b) the authority remain of the opinion, after taking into account any representations made and any evidence submitted to them in response to the notice, that the child falls, or probably falls, within subsection (2),

– they shall make an assessment of his educational needs.

(4) Where a local education authority decide to make an assessment under this section, they shall give notice in writing to the child's parent of that decision and of their reasons for making it.

(5) Schedule 26 has effect in relation to the making of assessments under this section.

(6) Where, at any time after serving a notice under subsection (1), a local education authority decide not to assess the educational needs of the child concerned they shall give notice in writing to the child's parent of their decision.

Section 324

(1) If, in the light of an assessment under section 323 of any child's educational needs and of any representations made by the child's parent in pursuance of Schedule 27, it is necessary for the local education authority to determine the special educational provision which any learning difficulty he may have calls for, the authority shall make and maintain a statement of his special educational needs.

Statement of special educational needs

(2) The statement shall be in such form and contain such information as may be prescribed.

(3) In particular, the statement shall –

(a) give details of the authority's assessment of the child's special educational needs, and

(b) specify the special educational provision to be made for the purpose of meeting those needs, including the particulars required by subsection (4).

(4) The statement shall –

(a) specify the type of school or other institution which the local education authority consider would be appropriate for the child,

(b) if they are not required under Schedule 27 to specify the name of any school in the statement, specify the name of any school or institution (whether in the United Kingdom or elsewhere) which they consider would be appropriate for the child and should be specified in the statement, and

(c) specify any provision for the child for which they make arrangements under section 319 and which they consider should be specified in the statement.

(5) Where a local education authority maintain a statement under this section, then –

(a) unless the child's parent has made suitable arrangements, the authority –

(i) shall arrange that the special educational provision specified in the statement is made for the child, and

(ii) may arrange that any non-educational provision specified in the statement is made for him in such manner as they consider appropriate, and

(b) if the name of a maintained, grant-maintained or grant-maintained special school is specified in the statement, the governing body of the school shall admit the child to the school.

(6) Subsection (5)(b) does not affect any power to exclude from a school a pupil who is already a registered pupil there.

(7) Schedule 27 has effect in relation to the making and maintenance of statements under this section.

Section 325

Appeal against decision not to make statement

(1) If, after making an assessment under section 323 of the educational needs of any child for whom no statement is maintained under section 324, the local education authority do not propose to make such a statement, they shall give notice in writing of their decision, and of the effect of subsection (2) below, to the child's parent.

(2) In such a case, the child's parent may appeal to the Tribunal against the decision.

(3) On an appeal under this section, the Tribunal may –

(a) dismiss the appeal,
(b) order the local education authority to make and maintain such a statement, or
(c) remit the case to the authority for them to reconsider whether, having regard to any observations made by the Tribunal, it is necessary for the authority to determine the special educational provision which any learning difficulty the child may have calls for.

Section 326

(1) The parent of a child for whom a local education authority maintain a statement under section 324 may –

Appeal against contents of statement

(a) when the statement is first made,
(b) where the description in the statement of the authority's assessment of the child's special educational needs, or the special educational provision specified in the statement, is amended, or
(c) where, after conducting an assessment of the educational needs of the child under section 323, the local education authority determine not to amend the statement,

– appeal to the Tribunal against the description in the statement of the authority's assessment of the child's special educational needs, the special educational provision specified in the statement or, if no school is named in the statement, that fact.

(2) Subsection (1)(b) does not apply where the amendment is made in pursuance of –

(a) paragraph 8 (change of named school) or 11(3)(b) (amendment ordered by Tribunal) of Schedule 27, or
(b) directions under section 442 (revocation of school attendance order);

– and subsection (1)(c) does not apply to a determination made following the service of notice under paragraph 10 (amendment by LEA) of Schedule 27 of a proposal to amend the statement.

(3) On an appeal under this section, the Tribunal may –

(a) dismiss the appeal,
(b) order the authority to amend the statement, so far as it describes the authority's assessment of the child's special educational needs or specifies the special educational provision, and make such other consequential amendments to the statement as the Tribunal think

fit, or

(c) order the authority to cease to maintain the statement.

(4) On an appeal under this section the Tribunal shall not order the local education authority to specify the name of any school in the statement (either in substitution for an existing name or in a case where no school is named) unless –

    (a) the parent has expressed a preference for the school in pursuance of arrangements under paragraph 3 (choice of school) of Schedule 27, or

    (b) in the proceedings the parent, the local education authority, or both have proposed the school.

(5) Before determining any appeal under this section the Tribunal may, with the agreement of the parties, correct any deficiency in the statement.

Section 327

Access for local education authority to certain schools

(1) This section applies where –

    (a) a local education authority maintain a statement for a child under section 324, and

    (b) in pursuance of the statement education is provided for the child at –

        (i) a school maintained by another local education authority,

        (ii) a grant-maintained school, or

        (iii) a grant-maintained special school.

(2) Any person authorised by the local education authority shall be entitled to have access at any reasonable time to the premises of any such school for the purpose of monitoring the special educational provision made in pursuance of the statement for the child at the school.

Section 328

Reviews of educational needs

(1) Regulations may prescribe the frequency with which assessments under section 323 are to be repeated in respect of children for whom statements are maintained under section 324.

(2) Where –

    (a) the parent of a child for whom a statement is maintained under section 324 asks the local education authority to arrange for an assessment to be made in respect of the child under section 323,

    (b) no such assessment has been made within the period of six months ending with the date on which the request is made, and

    (c) it is necessary for the authority to make a further assessment under section 323,

– the authority shall comply with the request.

(3) If in any case where subsection (2)(a) and (b) applies the authority determine not to comply with the request –

8

(a) they shall give notice of that fact and of the effect of paragraph (b) below to the child's parent, and
(b) the parent may appeal to the Tribunal against the determination.

(4) On an appeal under subsection (3) the Tribunal may –

(a) dismiss the appeal, or
(b) order the authority to arrange for an assessment to be made in respect of the child under section 323.

(5) A statement under section 324 shall be reviewed by the local education authority –

(a) on the making of an assessment in respect of the child concerned under section 323, and
(b) in any event, within the period of 12 months beginning with the making of the statement or, as the case may be, with the previous review.

(6) Regulations may make provision –

(a) as to the manner in which reviews of such statements are to be conducted,
(b) as to the participation in such reviews of such persons as may be prescribed, and
(c) in connection with such other matters relating to such reviews as the Secretary of State considers appropriate.

Section 329

(1) Where –

Assessment of educational needs at request of child's parent

(a) the parent of a child for whom a local education authority are responsible but for whom no statement is maintained under section 324 asks the authority to arrange for an assessment to be made in respect of the child under section 323,
(b) no such assessment has been made within the period of six months ending with the date on which the request is made, and
(c) it is necessary for the authority to make an assessment under that section,

– the authority shall comply with the request.

(2) If in any case where subsection (1)(a) and (b) applies the authority determine not to comply with the request –

(a) they shall give notice of that fact and of the effect of paragraph (b) below to the child's parent, and

(b) the parent may appeal to the Tribunal against the determination.

(3) On an appeal under subsection (2) the Tribunal may –

(a) dismiss the appeal, or

(b) order the authority to arrange for an assessment to be made in respect of the child under section 323.

Section 330

Assessment of educational needs at request of governing body of grant-maintained school

(1) Where in the case of a child for whom a local education authority are responsible but for whom no statement is maintained under section 324 –

(a) a grant-maintained school is specified in a direction in respect of the child under section 431 (direction to admit child to specified school),

(b) the governing body of the school ask the authority to arrange for an assessment to be made in respect of the child under section 323, and

(c) no such assessment has been made within the period of six months ending with the date on which the request is made,

– the local education authority shall serve a notice under subsection (2) on the child's parent.

(2) The notice shall inform the child's parent –

(a) that the local education authority propose to make an assessment of the child's educational needs,

(b) of the procedure to be followed in making the assessment,

(c) of the name of the officer of the authority from whom further information may be obtained, and

(d) of the parent's right to make representations, and submit written evidence, to the authority within such period (which must not be less than 29 days beginning with the date on which the notice is served) as may be specified in the notice.

(3) Where –

(a) a local education authority have served a notice under subsection (2) and the period specified in the notice in accordance with subsection (2)(d) has expired, and

(b) the authority are of the opinion, after taking into account any representations made and any evidence submitted to them in response to the notice, that the child falls, or probably falls, within subsection (4),

– they shall make an assessment of his educational needs under section 323.

(4) A child falls within this subsection if –

   (a) he has special educational needs, and

   (b) it is necessary to determine the special educational provision which any learning difficulty he may have calls for.

(5) Where a local education authority decide in pursuance of this section to make an assessment under section 323, they shall give notice in writing to the child's parent, and to the governing body of the grant-maintained school, of that decision and of their reasons for making it.

(6) Where, at any time after serving a notice under subsection (2), a local education authority decide not to assess the educational needs of the child concerned, they shall give notice in writing to the child's parent and to the governing body of the grant-maintained school of their decision.

Section 331

(1) Where a local education authority are of the opinion that a child in their area who is under the age of two falls, or probably falls, within subsection (2) –

Assessment of educational needs of children under two

   (a) they may, with the consent of his parent, make an assessment of the child's educational needs, and

   (b) they shall make such an assessment if requested to do so by his parent.

(2) A child falls within this subsection if –

   (a) he has special educational needs, and

   (b) it is necessary for the authority to determine the special educational provision which any learning difficulty he may have calls for.

(3) An assessment under this section shall be made in such manner as the authority consider appropriate.

(4) After making an assessment under this section, the authority –

   (a) may make a statement of the child's special educational needs, and

   (b) may maintain that statement, in such manner as they consider appropriate.

Section 332

(1) This section applies where a Health Authority or a National Health Service trust, in the course of exercising any of their functions in relation to a child who is under the age of five, form the opinion that he has (or probably has) special educational needs.

Duty of Health Authority or National Health Service trust to notify parent etc.

(2) The Authority or trust –

259

(a) shall inform the child's parent of their opinion and of their duty under paragraph (b), and
(b) after giving the parent an opportunity to discuss that opinion with an officer of the Authority or trust, shall bring it to the attention of the appropriate local education authority.

(3) If the Authority or trust are of the opinion that a particular voluntary organisation is likely to be able to give the parent advice or assistance in connection with any special educational needs that the child may have, they shall inform the parent accordingly.

Special Educational Needs Tribunal

Section 333

Constitution of Tribunal

(1) There shall continue to be a tribunal known as the Special Educational Needs Tribunal which shall exercise the jurisdiction conferred on it by this Part.

(2) There shall be appointed –

(a) a President of the Tribunal (referred to in this Part as "the President"),
(b) a panel of persons (referred to in this Part as "the chairmen's panel") who may serve as chairman of the Tribunal, and
(c) a panel of persons (referred to in this Part as "the lay panel") who may serve as the other two members of the Tribunal apart from the chairman.

(3) The President and the members of the chairmen's panel shall each be appointed by the Lord Chancellor.

(4) The members of the lay panel shall each be appointed by the Secretary of State.

(5) Regulations may –

(a) provide for the jurisdiction of the Tribunal to be exercised by such number of tribunals as may be determined from time to time by the President, and
(b) make such other provision in connection with the establishment and continuation of the Tribunal as the Secretary of State considers necessary or desirable.

(6) The Secretary of State may, with the consent of the Treasury, provide such staff and accommodation as the Tribunal may require.

Section 334

1990 c. 41.

(1) No person may be appointed President or member of the chairmen's panel unless he has a seven year general qualification (within the meaning

260

of section 71 of the Courts and Legal Services Act 1990).

(2) No person may be appointed member of the lay panel unless he satisfies such requirements as may be prescribed.

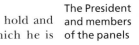

(3) If, in the opinion of the Lord Chancellor, the President is unfit to continue in office or is incapable of performing his duties, the Lord Chancellor may revoke his appointment.

(4) Each member of the chairmen's panel or lay panel shall hold and vacate office under the terms of the instrument under which he is appointed.

The President and members of the panels

(5) The President or a member of the chairmen's panel or lay panel –

(a) may resign office by notice in writing to the Lord Chancellor or (as the case may be) the Secretary of State, and
(b) is eligible for re-appointment if he ceases to hold office.

Section 335

(1) The Secretary of State may pay to the President, and to any other person in respect of his service as a member of the Tribunal, such remuneration and allowances as the Secretary of State may, with the consent of the Treasury, determine.

Remuneration and expenses

(2) The Secretary of State may defray the expenses of the Tribunal to such amount as he may, with the consent of the Treasury, determine.

Section 336

(1) Regulations may make provision about the proceedings of the Tribunal on an appeal under this Part and the initiation of such an appeal.

Tribunal procedure

(2) The regulations may, in particular, include provision –

(a) as to the period within which, and the manner in which, appeals are to be instituted,
(b) where the jurisdiction of the Tribunal is being exercised by more than one tribunal –

(i) for determining by which tribunal any appeal is to be heard, and
(ii) for the transfer of proceedings from one tribunal to another,

(c) for enabling any functions which relate to matters preliminary or incidental to an appeal to be performed by the President, or by the chairman,
(d) for the holding of hearings in private in prescribed circumstances,
(e) for hearings to be conducted in the absence of any member other than the chairman,
(f) as to the persons who may appear on behalf of the parties,

(g) for granting any person such discovery or inspection of documents or right to further particulars as might be granted by a county court,

(h) requiring persons to attend to give evidence and produce documents,

(i) for authorising the administration of oaths to witnesses,

(j) for the determination of appeals without a hearing in prescribed circumstances,

(k) as to the withdrawal of appeals,

(l) for the award of costs or expenses,

(m) for taxing or otherwise settling any such costs or expenses (and, in particular, for enabling such costs to be taxed in the county court),

(n) for the registration and proof of decisions and orders, and

(o) for enabling the Tribunal to review its decisions, or revoke or vary its orders, in such circumstances as may be determined in accordance with the regulations.

(3) The Secretary of State may pay such allowances for the purpose of or in connection with the attendance of persons at the Tribunal as he may, with the consent of the Treasury, determine.

(4) Part I of the Arbitration Act 1996 shall not apply to any proceedings before the Tribunal but regulations may make provision corresponding to any provision of that Act.

(5) Any person who without reasonable excuse fails to comply with –

(a) any requirement in respect of the discovery or inspection of documents imposed by the regulations by virtue of subsection (2)(g), or

(b) any requirement imposed by the regulations by virtue of subsection (2)(h),

– is guilty of an offence.

(6) A person guilty of an offence under subsection (5) is liable on summary conviction to a fine not exceeding level 3 on the standard scale.

Schedule 26

Making of Assessments under Section 323

8

Introductory

1

In this Schedule "assessment" means an assessment of a child's educational needs under section 323.

Medical and other advice

2

(1) Regulations shall make provision as to the advice which a local education authority are to seek in making assessments.

(2) Without prejudice to the generality of sub-paragraph (1), the regulations shall require the authority, except in such circumstances as may be prescribed, to seek medical, psychological and educational advice and such other advice as may be prescribed.

Manner, and timing, of assessments, etc.

3

(1) Regulations may make provision –

    (a) as to the manner in which assessments are to be conducted,

    (b) requiring the local education authority, where, after conducting an assessment under section 323 of the educational needs of a child for whom a statement is maintained under section 324, they determine not to amend the statement, to serve on the parent of the child a notice giving the prescribed information, and

    (c) in connection with such other matters relating to the making of assessments as the Secretary of State considers appropriate.

(2) Sub-paragraph (1)(b) does not apply to a determination made following the service of notice under paragraph 10 of Schedule 27 (amendment of statement by LEA) of a proposal to amend the statement.

(3) Regulations may provide that, where a local education authority are under a duty to make an assessment, the duty must, subject to prescribed exceptions, be performed within the prescribed period.

(4) Such provision shall not relieve the authority of the duty to make an assessment which has not been performed within that period.

Attendance at examinations

4

(1) Where a local education authority propose to make an assessment, they may serve a notice on the parent of the child concerned requiring the child's attendance for examination in accordance with the provisions of the notice.

(2) The parent of a child examined under this paragraph may be present at the examination if he so desires.

(3) A notice under this paragraph shall –

- (a) state the purpose of the examination,
- (b) state the time and place at which the examination will be held,
- (c) name an officer of the authority from whom further information may be obtained,
- (d) inform the parent that he may submit such information to the authority as he may wish, and
- (e) inform the parent of his right to be present at the examination.

Offence

5

(1) Any parent who fails without reasonable excuse to comply with any requirements of a notice served on him under paragraph 4 commits an offence if the notice relates to a child who is not over compulsory school age at the time stated in it as the time for holding the examination.

(2) A person guilty of an offence under this paragraph is liable on summary conviction to a fine not exceeding level 2 on the standard scale.

Schedule 27

Making and Maintenance of Statements under Section 324

Introductory

1

In this Schedule "statement" means a statement of a child's special educational needs under section 324.

Copy of proposed statement

2

Before making a statement, a local education authority shall serve on the parent of the child concerned –

(a) a copy of the proposed statement, and

(b) a written notice explaining the arrangements under paragraph 3, the effect of paragraph 4 and the right to appeal under section 326 and containing such other information as may be prescribed,

– but the copy of the proposed statement shall not specify any matter in pursuance of section 324(4) or any prescribed matter.

Choice of school

3

(1) Every local education authority shall make arrangements for enabling a parent on whom a copy of a proposed statement has been served under paragraph 2 to express a preference as to the maintained, grant-maintained or grant-maintained special school at which he wishes education to be provided for his child and to give reasons for his preference.

(2) Any such preference must be expressed or made within the period of 15 days beginning –

    (a) with the date on which the written notice mentioned in paragraph 2(b) was served on the parent, or

    (b) if a meeting has (or meetings have) been arranged under paragraph 4(1)(b) or (2), with the date fixed for that meeting (or the last of those meetings).

(3) Where a local education authority make a statement in a case where the parent of the child concerned has expressed a preference in pursuance of such arrangements as to the school at which he wishes education to be provided for his child, they shall specify the name of that school in the statement unless –

    (a) the school is unsuitable to the child's age, ability or aptitude or to his special educational needs, or

    (b) the attendance of the child at the school would be incompatible with the provision of efficient education for the children with whom he would be educated or the efficient use of resources.

(4) A local education authority shall, before specifying the name of any maintained, grant-maintained or grant-maintained special school in a statement, consult the governing body of the school and, if the school is maintained by another local education authority, that authority.

Representations

4

(1) A parent on whom a copy of a proposed statement has been served under paragraph 2 may –

    (a) make representations (or further representations) to the local education authority about the content of the statement, and

    (b) require the authority to arrange a meeting between him and an officer of the authority at which the statement can be discussed.

(2) Where a parent, having attended a meeting arranged by a local education authority under sub-paragraph (1)(b), disagrees with any part of the assessment in question, he may require the authority to arrange such meeting or meetings as they consider will enable him to discuss the relevant advice with the appropriate person or persons.

(3) In this paragraph –

- "relevant advice" means such of the advice given to the authority in connection with the assessment as they consider to be relevant to that part of the assessment with which the parent disagrees, and
- "appropriate person" means the person who gave the relevant advice or any other person who, in the opinion of the authority, is the appropriate person to discuss it with the parent.

(4) Any representations under sub-paragraph (1)(a) must be made within the period of 15 days beginning –

    (a) with the date on which the written notice mentioned in paragraph 2(b) was served on the parent, or

    (b) if a meeting has (or meetings have) been arranged under sub-paragraph (1)(b) or (2), with the date fixed for that meeting (or the last of those meetings).

(5) A requirement under sub-paragraph (1)(b) must be made within the period of 15 days beginning with the date on which the written notice mentioned in paragraph 2(b) was served on the parent.

(6) A requirement under sub-paragraph (2) must be made within the period of 15 days beginning with the date fixed for the meeting arranged under sub-paragraph (1)(b).

Making the statement

5

(1) Where representations are made to a local education authority under paragraph 4(1)(a), the authority shall not make the statement until they have considered the representations and the period or the last of the periods allowed by paragraph 4 for making requirements or further representations has expired.

(2) The statement may be in the form originally proposed (except as to the matters required to be excluded from the copy of the proposed statement) or in a form modified in the light of the representations.

(3) Regulations may provide that, where a local education authority are under a duty (subject to compliance with the preceding requirements of this Schedule) to make a statement, the duty, or any step required to be taken for performance of the duty, must, subject to prescribed exceptions,

be performed within the prescribed period.

(4) Such provision shall not relieve the authority of the duty to make a statement, or take any step, which has not been performed or taken within that period.

Service of statement

6
Where a local education authority make a statement they shall serve a copy of the statement on the parent of the child concerned and shall give notice in writing to him –

(a) of his right under section 326(1) to appeal against –

(i) the description in the statement of the authority's assessment of the child's special educational needs,
(ii) the special educational provision specified in the statement, or
(iii) if no school is named in the statement, that fact, and

(b) of the name of the person to whom he may apply for information and advice about the child's special educational needs.

Keeping, disclosure and transfer of statements

7
(1) Regulations may make provision as to the keeping and disclosure of statements.

(2) Regulations may make provision, where a local education authority become responsible for a child for whom a statement is maintained by another authority, for the transfer of the statement to them and for Part IV to have effect as if the duty to maintain the transferred statement were their duty.

Change of named school

8
(1) Sub-paragraph (2) applies where –

(a) the parent of a child for whom a statement is maintained which specifies the name of a school or institution asks the local education authority to substitute for that name the name of a maintained, grant-maintained or grant-maintained special school specified by the parent, and
(b) the request is not made less than 12 months after –

(i) an earlier request under this paragraph,
(ii) the service of a copy of the statement under paragraph 6,
(iii) if the statement has been amended, the date when notice of the amendment is given under paragraph 10(3)(b), or

(iv) if the parent has appealed to the Tribunal under section 326 or this paragraph, the date when the appeal is concluded, whichever is the later.

(2) The local education authority shall comply with the request unless –

(a) the school is unsuitable to the child's age, ability or aptitude or to his special educational needs, or
(b) the attendance of the child at the school would be incompatible with the provision of efficient education for the children with whom he would be educated or the efficient use of resources.

(3) Where the local education authority determine not to comply with the request-

(a) they shall give notice of that fact and of the effect of paragraph (b) below to the parent of the child, and
(b) the parent of the child may appeal to the Tribunal against the determination.

(4) On the appeal the Tribunal may –

(a) dismiss the appeal, or
(b) order the local education authority to substitute for the name of the school or other institution specified in the statement the name of the school specified by the parent.

(5) Regulations may provide that, where a local education authority are under a duty to comply with a request under this paragraph, the duty must, subject to prescribed exceptions, be performed within the prescribed period.

(6) Such provision shall not relieve the authority of the duty to comply with such a request which has not been complied with within that period.

Procedure for amending or ceasing to maintain a statement

9

(1) A local education authority may not amend, or cease to maintain, a statement except in accordance with paragraph 10 or 11.

(2) Sub-paragraph (1) does not apply where the local education authority –

(a) cease to maintain a statement for a child who has ceased to be a child for whom they are responsible,
(b) amend a statement in pursuance of paragraph 8,
(c) are ordered to cease to maintain a statement under section 326(3)(c), or

(d) amend a statement in pursuance of directions under section 442 (revocation of school attendance order).

10

(1) Before amending a statement, a local education authority shall serve on the parent of the child concerned a notice informing him –

(a) of their proposal, and
(b) of his right to make representations under sub-paragraph (2).

(2) A parent on whom a notice has been served under sub-paragraph (1) may, within the period of 15 days beginning with the date on which the notice is served, make representations to the local education authority about their proposal.

(3) The local education authority –

(a) shall consider any representations made to them under sub-paragraph (2), and
(b) on taking a decision on the proposal to which the representations relate, shall give notice in writing to the parent of their decision.

(4) Where a local education authority make an amendment under this paragraph to the description in a statement of the authority's assessment of a child's special educational needs or to the special educational provision specified in a statement, they shall give notice in writing to the parent of his right under section 326(1) to appeal against –

(a) the description in the statement of the authority's assessment of the child's special educational needs,
(b) the special educational provision specified in the statement, or
(c) if no school is named in the statement, that fact.

(5) A local education authority may only amend a statement under this paragraph within the prescribed period beginning with the service of the notice under sub-paragraph (1).

11

(1) A local education authority may cease to maintain a statement only if it is no longer necessary to maintain it.

(2) Where the local education authority determine to cease to maintain a statement –

(a) they shall give notice of that fact and of the effect of paragraph (b) below to the parent of the child, and
(b) the parent of the child may appeal to the Tribunal against the determination.

(3) On an appeal under this paragraph the Tribunal may –

    (a) dismiss the appeal, or

    (b) order the local education authority to continue to maintain the statement in its existing form or with such amendments of –

    (i) the description in the statement of the authority's assessment of the child's special educational needs, or

    (ii) the special educational provision specified in the statement,

    and such other consequential amendments, as the Tribunal may determine.

(4) Except where the parent of the child appeals to the Tribunal under this paragraph, a local education authority may only cease to maintain a statement under this paragraph within the prescribed period beginning with the service of the notice under sub-paragraph (2).

The Education (Special Educational Needs) Regulations 1994*

(S.I. 1994 No. 1047)

ARRANGEMENT OF REGULATIONS

*References to sections of the law are to sections in the Education Act 1996

PART I
General

PART II
Assessments

PART III
Statements

PART IV
Revocation and Transitional Provisions
(Not included)

SCHEDULE

PART I

GENERAL

Title and commencement

1. These Regulations may be cited as the Education (Special Educational Needs) Regulations 1994 and shall come into force on 1st September 1994.

Interpretation

2. (1) In these Regulations –

'the Act' means the Education Act 1996;

'authority' means a local education authority;

'district health authority' has the same meaning as in the National Health Service Act 1977(c);

'head teacher' includes any person to whom the duties or functions of a head teacher under these Regulations have been delegated by the head teacher in accordance with regulation 3.

'social services authority' means a local authority for the purposes of the Local Authority Social Services Act 1970(d) acting in the discharge of such functions as are referred to in section 2(1) of that Act;

'target' means the knowledge, skills and understanding which a child is expected to have by the end of a particular period;

'transition plan' means a document prepared pursuant to regulation 16(9) or 17(9) which sets out the arrangements which an authority consider appropriate for a young person during the period when he is aged 14 to 19 years, including arrangements for special educational provision and for any other necessary provision, for suitable employment and accommodation and for leisure activities and which will facilitate a satisfactory transition from childhood to adulthood;

'working day' means a day other than a Saturday, Sunday, Christmas Day, Good Friday or Bank Holiday within the meaning of the Banking and Financial Dealings Act 1971(e);

'the 1996 Act' means the Education Act 1996;

'the 1994 Regulations' means the Education (Special Educational Needs) Regulations 1994.

(2) In these Regulations any reference to the district health authority or the social services authority is, in relation to a particular child, a reference

to the district health authority or social services authority in whose area that child lives.

(3) Where a thing is required to be done under these Regulations –

    (a) within a period after an action is taken, the day on which that action was taken shall not be counted in the calculation of that period; and

    (b) within a period and the last day of that period is not a working day, the period shall be extended to include the following working day.

(4) References in these Regulations to a section are references to a section of the Act.

(5) References in these Regulations to a regulation are references to a regulation in these Regulations and references to a Schedule are references to the Schedule to these Regulations.

Delegation of functions

3. Where a head teacher has any functions or duties under these Regulations he may delegate those functions or duties –

    (a) generally to a member of the staff of the school who is a qualified teacher, or

    (b) in a particular case to a member of the staff of the school who teaches the child in question.

Service of documents

4. (1) Where provision in Part III of the Act or in these Regulations authorises or requires any document to be served on or sent to a person or any written notice to be given to a person the document may be served or sent or the notice may be given by properly addressing, pre-paying and posting a letter containing the document or notice.

(2) For the purposes of this regulation, the proper address of a person is –

    (a) in the case of the child's parent, his last known address;

    (b) in the case of a head teacher or other member of the staff of a school, the school's address;

    (c) in the case of any other person, the last known address of the place where he carries on his business, profession or other employment.

(3) Where first class post is used, the document or notice shall be treated as served, sent or given on the second working day after the date of posting, unless the contrary is shown.

(4) Where second class post is used, the document or notice shall be treated as served, sent or given on the fourth working day after the date of posting, unless the contrary is shown.

(5) The date of posting shall be presumed, unless the contrary is shown, to be the date shown in the post-mark on the envelope in which the document is contained.

PART II

ASSESSMENTS

Notices relating to assessment

5. (1) Where under section 323(1) or 330(2) an authority give notice to a child's parent that they propose to make an assessment, or under section 323(4) give notice to a child's parent of their decision to make an assessment, they shall send copies of the relevant notice to –

    (a) the social services authority,
    (b) the district health authority, and
    (c) if the child is registered at a school, the head teacher of that school.

(2) Where a copy of a notice is sent under paragraph (1) an endorsement on the copy or a notice accompanying that copy shall inform the recipient what help the authority are likely to request.

(3) Where under section 328(2) or 329(1) a child's parent asks the authority to arrange for an assessment to be made the authority shall give notice in writing to the persons referred to in paragraph (1)(a) to (c) of the fact that the request has been made and inform them what help they are likely to request.

Advice to be sought

6. (1) For the purpose of making an assessment under section 323 an authority shall seek -

    (a) advice from the child's parent;
    (b) educational advice as provided for in regulation 7;
    (c) medical advice from the district health authority as provided for in regulation 8;
    (d) psychological advice as provided for in regulation 9;
    (e) advice from the social services authority; and
    (f) any other advice which the authority consider appropriate for the purpose of arriving at a satisfactory assessment.

(2) The advice referred to in paragraph (1) shall be written advice relating to –

    (a) the educational, medical, psychological or other features of the case (according to the nature of the advice sought) which appear to be relevant to the child's educational needs (including his likely future needs),

(b) how those features could affect the child's educational needs, and

(c) the provision which is appropriate for the child in light of those features of the child's case, whether by way of special educational provision or non-educational provision, but not relating to any matter which is required to be specified in a statement by virtue of section 324(4)(b).

(3) A person from whom the advice referred to in paragraph (1) is sought may in connection therewith consult such persons as it appears to him expedient to consult; and he shall consult such persons, if any, as are specified in the particular case by the authority as persons who have relevant knowledge of, or information relating to, the child.

(4) When seeking the advice referred to in paragraph (1)(b) to (f) an authority shall provide the person from whom it is sought with copies of –

(a) any representations made by the parent, and

(b) any evidence submitted by, or at the request of, the parent under section 323(1)(d).

(5) The authority need not seek the advice referred to in paragraph (1)(b), (c), (d), (e) or (f) if –

(a) the authority have obtained advice under paragraph (1)(b), (c), (d), (e) or (f) respectively within the preceding 12 months, and

(b) the authority, the person from whom the advice was obtained and the child's parent are satisfied that the existing advice is sufficient for the purpose of arriving at a satisfactory assessment.

Educational advice

7. (1) The educational advice referred to in regulation 6(1)(b) shall, subject to paragraphs (2) to (5), be sought –

(a) from the head teacher of each school which the child is currently attending or which he has attended at any time within the preceding 18 months;

(b) if advice cannot be obtained from a head teacher of a school which the child is currently attending (because the child is not attending a school or otherwise) from a person who the authority are satisfied has experience of teaching children with special educational needs or knowledge of the differing provision which may be called for in different cases to meet those needs;

(c) if the child is not currently attending a school and if advice obtained under sub-paragraph (b) is not advice from such a person, from a person responsible for educational provision for him; and

(d) if any of the child's parents is a serving member of Her Majesty's armed forces, from the Service Children's Education Authority.

(2) The advice sought as provided in paragraph (1) shall not be sought

from any person who is not a qualified teacher within the meaning of section 218 of the Educational Reform Act 1988(h).

(3) The advice sought from a head teacher as provided in paragraph (1)(a) shall, if the head teacher has not himself taught the child within the preceding 18 months, be advice given after consultation with a teacher who has so taught the child.

(4) The advice sought from a head teacher as provided in paragraph (1)(a) shall include advice relating to the steps which have been taken by the school to identify and assess the special educational needs of the child and to make provision for the purpose of meeting those needs.

(5) Where it appears to the authority, in consequence of medical advice or otherwise, that the child in question is –

(a) hearing impaired, or
(b) visually impaired, or
(c) both hearing impaired and visually impaired, and any person from whom advice is sought as provided in paragraph (1) is not qualified to teach pupils who are so impaired then the advice sought shall be advice given after consultation with a person who is so qualified.

(6) For the purposes of paragraph (5) a person shall be considered to be qualified to teach pupils who are hearing impaired or visually impaired or who are both hearing impaired and visually impaired if he is qualified to be employed at a school as a teacher of a class for pupils who are so impaired otherwise than to give instruction in a craft, trade, or domestic subject.

(7) Paragraphs (3) and (5) are without prejudice to regulation 6(3).

Medical advice

8. The advice referred to in paragraph 6(1)(c) shall be sought from the district health authority, who shall obtain the advice from a fully registered medical practitioner.

Psychological advice

9. (1) The psychological advice referred to in regulation 6(1)(d) shall be sought from a person –

(a) regularly employed by the authority as an educational psychologist, or
(b) engaged by the authority as an educational psychologist in the case in question.

(2) The advice sought from a person as provided in paragraph (1) shall, if that person has reason to believe that another psychologist has relevant knowledge of, or information relating to, the child, be advice given after

consultation with that other psychologist.

(3) Paragraph (2) is without prejudice to regulation 6(3).

Matters to be taken into account in making an assessment

10. When making an assessment an authority shall take into consideration –

(a) any representations made by the child's parent under section 323(1)(d);
(b) any evidence submitted by, or at the request of, the child's parent under section 323(1)(d); and
(c) the advice obtained under regulation 6.

Time limits

11. (1) Where under section 323(1) the authority serve a notice on the child's parent informing him that they propose to make an assessment of the child's educational needs under section 323 they shall within 6 weeks of the date of service of the notice give notice to the child's parent –

(a) under section 323(4) of their decision to make an assessment, and of their reasons for making that decision, or
(b) under section 323(6) of their decision not to assess the educational needs of the child.

(2) Where under section 330(2) the authority serve a notice on the child's parent informing him that they propose to make an assessment of the child's educational needs under section 323 they shall within 6 weeks of the date of service of the notice give notice to the child's parent and to the governing body of the grant-maintained school which asked the authority to make an assessment –

(a) under section 330(5) of their decision to make an assessment and their reasons for making that decision, or
(b) under section 330(6) of their decision not to assess the educational needs of the child.

(3) Where under sections 328(2) or 329(1) a parent asks the authority to arrange for an assessment to be made under section 323 they shall within 6 weeks of the date of receipt of the request give notice to the child's parent –

(a) under section 323(4) of their decision to make an assessment, or
(b) under section 328(3)(a) or 329(2)(a) respectively of their decision not to comply with the request and of the parent's right to appeal to the Tribunal against the determination.

(4) An authority need not comply with the time limits referred to in

paragraphs (1) to (3) if it is impractical to do so because –

(a) the authority have requested advice from the head teacher of a school during a period beginning one week before any date on which that school was closed for a continuous period of not less than 4 weeks from that date and ending one week before the date on which it reopens;

(b) exceptional personal circumstances affect the child or his parent during the 6 week period referred to in paragraphs (1) to (3); or

(c) the child or his parent are absent from the area of the authority for a continuous period of not less than 4 weeks during the 6 week period referred to in paragraphs (1) to (3).

(5) Subject to paragraph (6), where under section 323(4) an authority have given notice to the child's parent of their decision to make an assessment they shall complete that assessment within 10 weeks of the date on which such notice was given.

(6) An authority need not comply with the time limit referred to in paragraph (5) if it is impractical to do so because –

(a) in exceptional cases after receiving advice sought under regulation 6 it is necessary for the authority to seek further advice;

(b) the child's parent has indicated to the authority that he wishes to provide advice to the authority after the expiry of 6 weeks from the date on which a request for such advice under regulation 6(a) was received, and the authority have agreed to consider such advice before completing the assessment;

(c) The authority have requested advice from the head teacher of a school under regulation 6(1)(b) during a period beginning one week before any date on which that school was closed for a continuous period of not less that 4 weeks from that date and ending one week before the date on which it re-opens;

(d) the authority have requested advice from a district health authority or a social services authority under regulation 6(1)(c) or (e) respectively and the district health authority or the social services authority have not complied with that request within 6 weeks from the date on which it was made;

(e) exceptional personal circumstances affect the child or his parent during the 10 week period referred to in paragraph (5);

(f) the child or his parent are absent from the area of the authority for a continuous period of not less than 4 weeks during the 10 week period referred to in paragraph (5); or

(g) the child fails to keep an appointment for an examination or a test during the 10 week period referred to in paragraph (5).

(7) Subject to paragraph (8), where an authority have requested advice from a district health authority or a social services authority under regulation 6(1)(c) or (e) respectively they shall comply with that request

within 6 weeks of the date on which they receive it.

(8) A district health authority or a social services authority need not comply with the time limit referred to in paragraph (7) if it is impractical to do so because –

(a) exceptional personal circumstances affect the child or his parent during the 6 week period referred to in paragraph (7);

(b) the child or his parent are absent from the area of the authority for a continuous period of not less than 4 weeks during the 6 week period referred to in paragraph (7);

(c) the child fails to keep an appointment for an examination or a test made by the district health authority or the social services authority respectively during the 6 week period referred to in paragraph (7); or

(d) they have not before the date on which a copy of a notice had been served on them in accordance with regulation 5(1) or a notice has been served on them in accordance with regulation 5(3) produced or maintained any information or records relevant to the assessment of the child under section 323.

PART III

STATEMENTS

Notice accompanying a proposed statement

12. The notice which shall accompany a copy of a proposed statement served on the parent pursuant to paragraph 2 of Schedule 27 of the Act shall be in a form substantially corresponding to that set out in Part A of the Schedule and shall contain the information therein specified.

Statement of special educational needs

13. A statement of a child's special educational needs made under section 324(1) shall be in a form substantially corresponding to that set out in Part B of the Schedule, shall contain the information therein specified, and shall be dated and authenticated by the signature of a duly authorised officer of the authority concerned.

Time limits

14. (1) Where under section 323 an authority have made an assessment of the educational needs of a child for whom no statement is maintained they shall within two weeks of the date on which the assessment was completed either –

(a) serve a copy of a proposed statement and a written notice on the child's parent under paragraph 2 of Schedule 27 to the Act, or

(b) give notice in writing to the child's parent under section 169(1) that they have decided not to make a statement and that he may appeal against that decision to the Tribunal.

(2) Where under section 323 an authority have made an assessment of the educational needs of a child for whom a statement is maintained they shall within two weeks of the date on which the assessment was completed –

   (a) under paragraph 10(1) of Schedule 27 to the Act serve on the child's parent a notice that they propose to amend the statement and of his right to make representations; or

   (b) under paragraph 11(2) of Schedule 27 to the Act give notice to the child's parent that they have determined to cease to maintain the statement and of his right of appeal to the Tribunal; or

   (c) serve on the child's parent a notice which informs him that they have determined not to amend the statement and their reasons for that determination, which is accompanied by copies of the professional advice obtained during the assessment, and which informs the child's parent that under section 326(1)(c) he may appeal to the Tribunal against the description in the statement of the authority's assessment of the child's special educational needs, the special educational provision specified in the statement or, if no school is named in the statement, that fact.

(3) Subject to paragraph (4), where an authority have served a copy of a proposed statement on the child's parent under paragraph 2 of Schedule 27 to the Act they shall within 8 weeks of the date on which the proposed statement was served serve a copy of the completed statement and a written notice on the child's parent under paragraph 6 of that Schedule, or give notice to the child's parent that they have decided not to make a statement.

(4) The authority need not comply with the time limit referred to in paragraph (3) if it is impractical to do so because –

   (a) exceptional personal circumstances affect the child or his parent during the 8 week period referred to in paragraph (3);

   (b) the child or his parent are absent from the area of the authority for a continuous period of not less than 4 weeks during the 8 week period referred to in paragraph (3);

   (c) the child's parent indicates that he wishes to make representations to the authority about the content of the statement under paragraph 4(1)(a) of Schedule 27 to the Act after the expiry of the 15 day period for making such representations provided for in paragraph 4(4) of that Schedule;

   (d) a meeting between the child's parent and an officer of the authority has been held pursuant to paragraph 4(1)(b) of Schedule 27 to the Act and the child's parent has required that another such meeting be arranged or under paragraph 4(2) of that Schedule has required a meeting with the appropriate person under to be arranged; or

(e) the authority have sent a written request to the Secretary of State seeking his consent under section 347(5)(b) to the child being educated at an independent school which is not approved by him and such consent has not been received by the authority within two weeks of the date on which the request was sent.

(5) Where under paragraph 8(1) of Schedule 27 to the Act the child's parent asks the authority to substitute for the name of a school or institution specified in a statement the name of another school specified by him and where the condition referred to in paragraph 8(1)(b) of that Schedule has been satisfied the authority shall within 8 weeks of the date on which the request was received either –

(a) comply with the request; or
(b) give notice to the child's parent under paragraph 8(3) of that Schedule that they have determined not to comply with the request and that he may appeal against that determination to the Tribunal.

(6) Where under paragraph 10(1) of Schedule 27 to the Act an authority serve a notice on the child's parent informing him of their proposal to amend a statement they shall not amend the statement after the expiry of 8 weeks from the date on which the notice was served.

(7) Where under paragraph 11(2) of Schedule 27 to the Act an authority give notice to the child's parent that they have determined to cease to maintain a statement they shall not cease to maintain the statement –

(a) before the expiry of the prescribed period during which the parent may appeal to the Tribunal against the determination, or
(b) after the expiry of 4 weeks from the end of that period.

Review of statement where child not aged 14 attends school

15. (1) This regulation applies where –

(a) an authority review a statement under section 328(5) other than on the making of an assessment,
(b) the child concerned attends a school, and
(c) regulation 16 does not apply.

(2) The authority shall by notice in writing require the head teacher of the child's school to submit a report to them under this regulation by a specified date not less than two months from the date the notice is given and shall send a copy of the notice to the child's parent.

(3) The head teacher shall for the purpose of preparing the report referred to in paragraph (2) seek advice as to the matters referred to in paragraph (4) from –

(a) the child's parent;

(b) any person whose advice the authority consider appropriate for the purpose of arriving at a satisfactory report and whom they specify in the notice referred to in paragraph (2), and

(c) any person whose advice the head teacher considers appropriate for the purpose of arriving at a satisfactory report.

(4) The advice referred to in paragraph (3) shall be written advice as to –

(a) the child's progress towards meeting the objectives specified in the statement;

(b) the child's progress towards attaining any targets established in furtherance of the objectives specified in the statement;

(c) where the school is not established in a hospital and is a maintained, grant-maintained or grant-maintained special school, the application of the provisions of the National Curriculum to the child;

(d) where the school is not established in a hospital and is a maintained, grant-maintained or grant-maintained special school, the application of any provisions substituted for the provisions of the National Curriculum in order to maintain a balanced and broadly based curriculum;

(e) where appropriate, and in any case where a transition plan exists, any matters which are the appropriate subject of such a plan;

(f) whether the statement continues to be appropriate;

(g) any amendments to the statement which would be appropriate; and

(h) whether the authority should cease to maintain the statement.

(5) The notice referred to in paragraph (2) shall require the head teacher to invite the following persons to attend a meeting to be held on a date before the report referred to in that paragraph is submitted –

(a) the representative of the authority specified in the notice,

(b) the child's parent,

(c) a member or members of the staff of the school who teach the child or who are otherwise responsible for the provision of education for the child whose attendance the head teacher considers appropriate,

(d) any other person whose attendance the head teacher considers appropriate, and

(e) any person whose attendance the authority consider appropriate and who is specified in the notice.

(6) The head teacher shall not later than two weeks before the date on which a meeting referred to in paragraph (5) is to be held send to all the persons invited to that meeting copies of the advice he has received pursuant to his request under paragraph (3) and by written notice accompanying the copies shall request the recipients to submit to him

before or at the meeting written comments on that advice and any other advice which they think appropriate.

(7) The meeting referred to in paragraph (5) shall consider –

    (a) the matters referred to in paragraph (4); and

    (b) any significant changes in the child's circumstances since the date on which the statement was made or last reviewed.

(8) The meeting shall recommend –

    (a) any steps which it concludes ought to be taken, including whether the authority should amend or cease to maintain the statement,

    (b) any targets to be established in furtherance of the objectives specified in the statement which it concludes the child ought to meet during the period until the next review, and

    (c) where a transition plan exists, the matters which it concludes ought to be included in that plan.

(9) If the meeting cannot agree the recommendations to be made under paragraph (8) the persons who attended the meeting shall make differing recommendations as appears necessary to each of them.

(10) The report to be submitted under paragraph (2) shall be completed after the meeting is held and shall include the head teacher's assessment of the matters referred to in paragraph (7) and his recommendations as to the matters referred to in paragraph (8), and shall refer to any difference between his assessment and recommendations and those of the meeting.

(11) When the head teacher submits his report to the authority under paragraph (2) he shall at the same time send copies to –

    (a) the child's parent,

    (b) the persons from whom the head teacher sought advice under paragraph (3),

    (c) the persons who were invited to attend the meeting in accordance with paragraph (5),

    (d) any other person to whom the authority consider it appropriate that a copy be sent and to whom they direct him to send a copy, and

    (e) any other person to whom the head teacher considers it appropriate that a copy be sent.

(12) The authority shall review the statement under section 328(5) in light of the report and any other information or advice which they consider relevant, shall make written recommendations as to the matters referred to in paragraph (8)(a) and (b) and, where a transition plan exists, shall amend the plan as they consider appropriate.

(13) The authority shall within one week of completing the review under section 328(5) send copies of the recommendations and any transition plan referred to in paragraph (12) to –

(a) the child's parent;
(b) the head teacher;
(c) the persons from whom the head teacher sought advice under paragraph (3);
(d) the persons who were invited to attend the meeting in accordance with paragraph (5); and
(e) any other person to whom the authority consider it appropriate that a copy be sent.

Review of statement where child aged 14 attends school

16. (1) This regulation applies where –

(a) an authority review a statement under section 328(5) other than on the making of an assessment,
(b) the child concerned attends a school, and
(c) the review is the first review commenced after the child has attained the age of 14 years.

(2) The authority shall for the purpose of preparing a report under this regulation by notice in writing require the head teacher of the child's school to seek the advice referred to in regulation 15(4), including in all cases advice as to the matters referred to in regulation 15(4)(e), from –

(a) the child's parent,
(b) any person whose advice the authority consider appropriate for the purpose of arriving at a satisfactory report and whom they specify in the notice referred to above, and
(c) any person whose advice the head teacher considers appropriate for the purpose of arriving at a satisfactory report.

(3) The authority shall invite the following persons to attend a meeting to be held on a date before the review referred to in paragraph (1) is required to be completed –

(a) the child's parent;
(b) a member or members of the staff of the school who teach the child or who are otherwise responsible for the provision of education for the child whose attendance the head teacher considers appropriate and whom he has asked the authority to invite;
(c) a representative of the social services authority;
(d) a person providing careers services under sections 8 to 10 of the Employment and Training Act 1973(i);
(e) any person whose attendance the head teacher considers

appropriate and whom he has asked the authority to invite; and

(f) any person whose attendance the authority consider appropriate.

(4) The head teacher shall not later than two weeks before the date on which the meeting referred to in paragraph (3) is to be held serve on all the persons invited to attend that meeting copies of the advice he has received pursuant to his request under paragraph (2) and shall by written notice request the recipients to submit to him before or at the meeting written comments on that advice and any other advice which they think appropriate.

(5) A representative of the authority shall attend the meeting.

(6) The meeting shall consider the matters referred to in regulation 15(7), in all cases including the matters referred to in regulation 15(4)(e), and shall make recommendations in accordance with regulation 15(8) and (9), in all cases including recommendations as to the matters referred to in regulation 15(8)(c).

(7) The report to be prepared by the authority under paragraph (2) shall be completed after the meeting, shall contain the authority's assessment of the matters required to be considered by the meeting and their recommendations as to the matters required to be recommended by it and shall refer to any difference between their assessment and recommendations and those of the meeting.

(8) The authority shall within one week of the date on which the meeting was held send copies of the report completed under paragraph (7) to –

(a) the child's parent;
(b) the head teacher;
(c) the persons from whom the head teacher sought advice under paragraph (2);
(d) the persons who were invited to attend the meeting under paragraph (3); and
(e) any person to whom they consider it appropriate to send a copy.

(9) The authority shall review the statement under section 328(5) in light of the report and any other information or advice which it considers relevant, shall make written recommendations as to the matters referred to in regulation 15(8)(a) and (b), and shall prepare a transition plan.

(10) The authority shall within one week of completing the review under section 328(5) send copies of the recommendations and the transition plan referred to in paragraph (9) to the persons referred to in paragraph (8).

Review of statement where child does not attend school

17. (1) This regulation applies where an authority review a statement under section 328(5) other than on the making of an assessment and the child concerned does not attend a school.

(2) The authority shall prepare a report addressing the matters referred to in regulation 15(4), including the matters referred to in regulation 15(4)(e) in any case where the review referred to in paragraph (1) is commenced after the child has attained the age of 14 years or older, and for that purpose shall seek advice on these matters from the child's parent and any other person whose advice they consider appropriate in the case in question for the purpose of arriving at a satisfactory report.

(3) The authority shall invite the following persons to attend a meeting to be held on a date before the review referred to in paragraph (1) is required to be completed –

    (a) the child's parent;

    (b) where the review referred to in paragraph (1) is the first review commenced after the child has attained the age of 14 years, a representative of the social services authority;

    (c) where subparagraph (b) applies, a person providing careers services under sections 8 to 10 of the Employment and Training Act 1973; and

    (d) any person or persons whose attendance the authority consider appropriate.

(4) The authority shall not later than two weeks before the date on which the meeting referred to in paragraph (3) is to be held send to all the persons invited to that meeting a copy of the report which they propose to make under paragraph (2) and by written notice accompanying the copies shall request the recipients to submit to the authority written comments on the report and any other advice which they think appropriate.

(5) A representative of the authority shall attend the meeting.

(6) The meeting shall consider the matters referred to in regulation 15(7), including in any case where the review is commenced after the child has attained the age of 14 years the matters referred to in regulation 15(4)(e), and shall make recommendations in accordance with regulation 15(8) and (9), including in any case where the child has attained the age of 14 years or older as aforesaid recommendations as to the matters referred to in regulation 15(8)(c).

(7) The report prepared by the authority under paragraph (2) shall be completed after the meeting referred to in paragraph (3) is held, shall contain the authority's assessment of the matters required to be considered

by the meeting and their recommendations as to the matters required to be recommended by it, and shall refer to any difference between their assessment and recommendations and those of the meeting.

(8) The authority shall within one week of the date on which the meeting referred to in paragraph (3) was held send copies of the report completed under paragraph (7) to –

(a) the child's parent;
(b) the persons from whom they sought advice under paragraph (2);
(c) the persons who were invited to attend the meeting under paragraph (3); and
(d) any person to whom they consider it appropriate to send a copy.

(9) The authority shall review the statement under section 328(5) in light of the report and any other information or advice which it considers relevant, shall make written recommendations as to the matters referred to in regulation 15(8)(a) and (b), in any case where the review is the first review commenced after the child has attained the age of 14 years prepare a transition plan, and in any case where a transition plan exists amend the plan as they consider appropriate.

(10) The authority shall within one week of completing the review under section 328(5) send copies of the recommendations and any transition plan referred to in paragraph (9) to the persons referred to in paragraph (8).

Transfer of statements

18. (1) This regulation applies where a child in respect of whom a statement is maintained moves from the area of the authority which maintains the statement ('the old authority') into that of another ('the new authority').

(2) The old authority shall transfer the statement to the new authority, and from the date of the transfer –

(a) the statement shall be treated for the purposes of the new authority's duties and functions under Part III of the Act and these Regulations as if it had been made by the new authority on the date on which it was made by the old authority, and
(b) where the new authority make an assessment under section 323 and the old authority have supplied the new authority with advice obtained in pursuance of a previous assessment regulation 6(5) shall apply as if the new authority had obtained the advice on the date on which the old authority obtained it.

(3) The new authority shall within 6 weeks of the date of the transfer serve a notice on the child's parent informing him –

(a) that the statement has been transferred,

(b) whether they propose to make an assessment under section 323, and

(c) when they propose to review the statement in accordance with paragraph (4).

(4) The new authority shall review the statement under section 328(5) before the expiry of whichever of the following two periods expires later –

(a) the period of twelve months beginning with the making of the statement, or as the case may be, with the previous review, or

(b) the period of three months beginning with the date of the transfer.

(5) Where by virtue of the transfer the new authority come under a duty to arrange the child's attendance at a school specified in the statement but in light of the child's move that attendance is no longer practicable the new authority may arrange for the child's attendance at another school appropriate for the child until such time as it is possible to amend the statement in accordance with paragraph 10 of Schedule 27 to the Act.

Restriction on disclosure of statements

19. (1) Subject to the provisions of the Act and of these Regulations, a statement in respect of a child shall not be disclosed without the parent's consent except –

(a) to persons to whom, in the opinion of the authority concerned, the statement should be disclosed in the interests of the child;

(b) for the purposes of any appeal under the Act;

(c) for the purposes of educational research which, in the opinion of the authority, may advance the education of children with special educational needs, if, but only if, the person engaged in that research undertakes not to publish anything contained in, or derived from, a statement otherwise than in a form which does not identify any individual concerned including, in particular, the child concerned and his parent;

(d) on the order of any court or for the purposes of any criminal proceedings;

(e) for the purposes of any investigation under Part III of the Local Government Act 1974 (investigation of maladministration) (j);

(f) to the Secretary of State when he requests such disclosure for the purposes of deciding whether to give directions or make an order under section 68 or 99 of the Education Act 1944(k);

(g) for the purposes of an assessment of the needs of the child with respect to the provision of any statutory services for him being carried out by officers of a social services authority by virtue of arrangements made under section 5(5) of the Disabled Persons (Services, Consultation and Representation) Act 1986(1);

(h) for the purposes of a local authority in the performance of their duties under sections 22(3)(a), 85(4)(a), 86(3)(a) and 87(3) of the Children Act 1989(m): or

(i) to one of Her Majesty's Inspectors of Schools, or to a registered inspector or a member of an inspection team, who requests the right to inspect or take copies of a statement in accordance with section 3(3) of or paragraph 7 of Schedule 2 to the Education (Schools) Act 1992(n) respectively.

(2) The arrangements for keeping such statements shall be such as to ensure, so far as is reasonably practicable, that unauthorised persons do not have access to them.

(3) In this regulation any reference to a statement includes a reference to any representations, evidence, advice or information which is set out in the appendices to a statement.

SCHEDULE
Regulations 12 and 13
PART A

NOTICE TO PARENT

To: [*name and address of parent*]

1. Accompanying this notice is a copy of a statement of special educational needs of [*name of child*] which [*name of authority*] ('the authority') propose to make under the Education Act 1996.

2. You may express a preference for the maintained, grant-maintained or grant-maintained special school you wish your child to attend and may give reasons for your preference.

3. If you wish to express such a preference you must do so not later than 15 days from the date on which you receive this notice and the copy of the statement or 15 days from the date on which you last attend a meeting in accordance with paragraph 10 or 11 below, whichever is later. If the 15th day falls on a weekend or a bank holiday you must do so not later than the following working day.

4. If you express a preference in accordance with paragraphs 2 and 3 above the authority are required to specify the name of the school you prefer in the statement, and accordingly to arrange special educational provision at that school, unless –

    (a) the school is unsuitable to your child's age, ability or aptitude or to his/her special educational needs, or

    (b) the attendance of your child at the school would be incompatible with the provision of efficient education for the children with whom he/she would be educated or the efficient use of resources.

5. The authority will normally arrange special educational provision in a maintained, grant-maintained or grant-maintained special school. However, if you believe that the authority should arrange special educational provision for your child at a non-maintained special school or an independent school you may make representations to that effect.

6. The following maintained, grant-maintained and grant-maintained special schools provide [*primary/secondary*] education in the area of the authority:

[*Here list all maintained, grant-maintained, and grant-maintained special schools in the authority's area which provide primary education, or list all such schools which provide secondary education, depending on whether the child requires primary or secondary education. Alternatively, list the required information in a list attached to this notice.*]

7. A list of the non-maintained special schools which make special educational provision for pupils with special educational needs in England and Wales and are approved by the Secretary of State for Education or the Secretary of State for Wales is attached to this notice.

8. A list of the independent schools in England and Wales which are approved by the Secretary of State for Education or the Secretary of State for Wales as suitable for the admission of children for whom statements of special educational needs are maintained is attached to this notice.

9. You are entitled to make representations to the authority about the content of the statement. If you wish to make such representations you must do so not later than 15 days from the date on which you receive this notice, or 15 days from the date on which you last attended a meeting in accordance with the next paragraph, whichever is the later date.

10. You are entitled, not later than 15 days from the date on which you receive this notice, to require the authority to arrange a meeting between you and an officer of the authority at which any part of the statement, or all of it, may be discussed. In particular, any advice on which the statement is based may be discussed.

11. If having attended a meeting in accordance with paragraph 10 above you still disagree with any part of the assessment in question, you may within 15 days of the date of the meeting require the authority to arrange a meeting or meetings to discuss the advice which they consider relevant to the part of the assessment you disagree with. They will arrange for the person who gave the advice, or some other person whom they think appropriate, to attend the meeting.

12. If at the conclusion of the procedure referred to above the authority

serve on you a statement with which you disagree you may appeal to the Special Educational Needs Tribunal against the description of your child's special educational needs, against the special educational provision specified including the school named, or, if no school is named, against that fact.

13. All correspondence with the authority should be addressed to the officer responsible for this case:

[*Here set out name, address and telephone number of case officer, and any reference number which should be quoted.*]

_____   _____
[Date]   [Signature of officer responsible]

PART B: STATEMENT OF SPECIAL EDUCATIONAL NEEDS

Part 1: Introduction

1. In accordance with section 324 of the Education Act 1996 ('the Act') and the Education (Special Educational Needs) Regulations 1994 ('the Regulations'), the following statement is made by [*here set out name of authority*] ('the authority') in respect of the child whose name and other particulars are mentioned below.

Child

Surname   Other names
Home address

                                                    Sex
                                                    Religion
Date of Birth   Home language

Child's parent or person responsible

Surname   Other names
Home address

                                                    Relation to child

Telephone No

2. When assessing the child's special educational needs the authority took

into consideration, in accordance with regulation 10 of the Regulations, the representations, evidence and advice set out in the Appendices to this statement.

PART 2: SPECIAL EDUCATIONAL NEEDS

[Here set out the child's special educational needs, in terms of the child's learning difficulties which call for special educational provision, as assessed by the authority.]

PART 3: SPECIAL EDUCATIONAL PROVISION

Objectives

[Here specify the objectives which the special educational provision for the child should aim to meet.]

Educational provision to meet needs and objectives

[Here specify the special educational provision which the authority consider appropriate to meet the needs specified in Part 2 and to meet the objectives specified in this Part, and in particular specify –

(a) any appropriate facilities and equipment, staffing arrangements and curriculum,

(b) any appropriate modifications to the application of the National Curriculum,

(c) any appropriate exclusions from the application of the National Curriculum, in detail, and the provision which it is proposed to substitute for any such exclusions in order to maintain a balanced and broadly based curriculum; and

(d) where residential accommodation is appropriate, that fact.]

Monitoring

[Here specify the arrangements to be made for –

(a) regularly monitoring progress in meeting the objectives specified in this Part,

(b) establishing targets in furtherance of those objectives,

(c) regularly monitoring the targets referred to in (b),

(d) regularly monitoring the appropriateness of any modifications to the application of the National Curriculum, and

(e) regularly monitoring the appropriateness of any provision substituted for exclusions from the application of the National Curriculum. Here also specify any special arrangements for reviewing this statement.]

PART 4: PLACEMENT

[*Here specify –*

(a) *the type of school which the authority consider appropriate for the child and the name of the school for which the parent has expressed a preference or, where the authority are required to specify the name of a school, the name of the school which they consider would be appropriate for the child and should be specified, or*

(b) *the provision for his education otherwise than at a school which the authority consider appropriate.*]

PART 5: NON-EDUCATIONAL NEEDS

[*Here specify the non-educational needs of the child for which the authority consider provision is appropriate if the child is to properly benefit from the special educational provision specified in Part 3.*]

PART 6: NON-EDUCATIONAL PROVISION

[*Here specify any non-educational provision which the authority propose to make available or which they are satisfied will be made available by a district health authority, a social services authority or some other body, including the arrangements for its provision. Also specify the objectives of the provision, and the arrangements for monitoring progress in meeting those objectives.*]

_____   _____

[Date]   [A duly authorised officer of the authority]

Appendix A: Parental Representations

[*Here set out any written representations made by the parent of the child under section 323(1)(d) of or paragraph 4(1) of Schedule 27 to the Act and a summary which the parent has accepted as accurate of any oral representations so made or record that no such representations were made.*]

Appendix B: Parental Evidence

[*Here set out any written evidence either submitted by the parent of the child under section 323(1)(d) of the Act or record that no such evidence was submitted.*]

Appendix C: Advice from the Child's Parent

[*Here set out the advice obtained under regulation 6(1)(a).*]

Appendix D: Educational Advice

[Here set out the advice obtained under regulation 6(1)(b).]

Appendix E: Medical Advice

[Here set out the advice obtained under regulation 6(1)(c).]

Appendix F: Psychological Advice

[Here set out the advice obtained under regulation 6(1)(d).]

Appendix G: Advice from the Social Services Authority

[Here set out the advice obtained under regulation 6(1)(e).]

Appendix H: Other Advice Obtained by the Authority

[Here set out the advice obtained under regulation 6(1)(f).]

The Special Educational Needs Tribunal Regulations 1995

(S.I. 1995 No. 3133)

8

ARRANGEMENT OF REGULATIONS

PART 4

The determination of appeals

25. Power to determine an appeal without a hearing
26. Hearings to be in private: exceptions
27. Failure of parties to attend hearing
28. Procedure at hearing
29. Evidence at hearing
30. Decision of the tribunal
31. Review of the tribunal's decision
32. Review of President's decision
33. Orders for costs and expenses

PART 5

Additional powers of and provisions relating to the tribunal

34. Transfer of proceedings
35. Miscellaneous powers of the tribunal
36. Power to strike out
37. Power to exercise powers of the President and Chairman
38. The Secretary of the Tribunal
39. Irregularities
40. Method of sending, delivering or serving notices and documents
41. Extension of time
42. Parent's representative
43. Revocation and transitional provisions

The Secretary of State for Education and Employment, in respect of England, and the Secretary of State for Wales, in respect of Wales, in exercise of the powers conferred by sections 333(5), 334(2), 336(1) and (2), 301(6) and 305(1)**(a)** of the Education Act 1996**(b)**, and after consultation with the Council on Tribunals in accordance with section 8 of the Tribunals and Inquiries Act 1992**(c)**, hereby make the following Regulations:

(a) *See* the definitions of "prescribed" and "regulations"
(b) 1993 c.35.
(c) 1992 c.53; Part I of Schedule 1 was amended by section 181(1) of the Education Act 1993.

PART 1

GENERAL

Citation and commencement

1. These Regulations may be cited as the Special Educational Needs Tribunal Regulations 1995 and shall come into force on 1st January 1996.

Interpretation

2. In these Regulations, unless the context otherwise requires –

"the 1996 Act" means the Education Act 1996;

"authority" means the local education authority which made the disputed decision;

"child" means the child in respect of whom the appeal is brought;

"disputed decision" means the decision or determination in respect of which the appeal is brought;

"the clerk to the tribunal" means the person appointed by the Secretary of the Tribunal to act in that capacity at one or more hearings;

"hearing" means a sitting of the tribunal duly constituted for the purpose of receiving evidence, hearing addresses and witnesses or doing anything lawfully requisite to enable the tribunal to reach a decision on any question;

"parent" means a parent who has made an appeal to the Special Educational Needs Tribunal under the 1996 Act;

"records" means the records of the Special Educational Needs Tribunal;

"the Secretary of the Tribunal" means the person for the time being acting as the Secretary of the office of the Special Educational Needs Tribunal;

"the tribunal" means the Special Educational Needs Tribunal but where the President has determined pursuant to regulation 4(1) that the jurisdiction of the Special Educational Needs Tribunal is to be exercised by more than one tribunal, it means, in relation to any proceedings, the tribunal to which the proceedings have been referred by the President;

"working day" , except in Regulation 24, means any day other than –

   (a) a Saturday, a Sunday, Christmas Day, Good Friday or a day which is a bank holiday within the meaning of the Banking and Financial Dealings Act 1971(**a**); or

(a) 1971 c.80.

297

(b) a day in August.

Members of lay panel

3. No person may be appointed as a member of the lay panel unless the Secretary of State is satisfied that he has knowledge and experience in respect of –

(a) children with special educational needs; or
(b) local government.

Establishment of tribunals

4. (1) Such number of tribunals shall be established to exercise the jurisdiction of the Special Educational Needs Tribunal as the President may from time to time determine.

(2) The tribunals shall sit at such times and in such places as may from time to time be determined by the President.

Membership of tribunal

5. (1) Subject to the provisions of regulation 28(5), the tribunal shall consist of a chairman and two other members.

(2) For each hearing –

(a) the chairman shall be the President or a person selected from the chairman's panel by the President; and
(b) the two other members of the tribunal other than the chairman shall be selected from the lay panel by the President.

Proof of documents and certification of decisions

6. (1) A document purporting to be a document issued by the Secretary of the Tribunal on behalf of the Special Educational Needs Tribunal shall, unless the contrary is proved, be deemed to be a document so issued.

(2) A document purporting to be certified by the Secretary of the Tribunal to be a true copy of a document containing a decision of the tribunal shall, unless the contrary is proved, be sufficient evidence of matters contained therein.

PART 2

MAKING AN APPEAL TO THE TRIBUNAL AND REPLY BY THE AUTHORITY

(A) THE PARENT

Notice of appeal

7. (1) An appeal to the Special Educational Needs Tribunal shall be made by notice which –

(a) shall state –

(i) the name and address of the parent making the appeal and, if more than one address is given, the address to which the tribunal should send replies or notices concerning the appeal;

(ii) the name of the child;

(iii) that the notice is a notice of appeal;

(iv) the name of the authority which made the disputed decision and the date on which the parent was notified of it;

(v) the grounds of the appeal;

(vi) if the parent seeks an order that a school (other than one already named in the statement of special educational needs relating to the child) be named in the child's statement, the name and address of that school;

(b) shall be accompanied by –

(i) a copy of the notice of the disputed decision;

(ii) where the appeal is made under section 326 of, or paragraph S of Schedule 27 to, the 1996 Act, a copy of the statement of special educational needs relating to the child; and

(c) may state the name, address and profession of any representative of the parent to whom the tribunal should (subject to any notice under regulation 42(2)(a)) send replies or notices concerning the appeal instead of the parent.

(2) The parent shall sign the notice of appeal.

(3) The parent must deliver the notice of appeal to the Secretary of the Tribunal so that it is received no later than the first working day after the expiry of 2 months from the date on which the authority gave him notice, under Part III of the 1996 Act, that he had a right of appeal.

Response, and supplementary provisions

8. (1) If the authority delivers a reply under regulation 12 the parent may deliver a written response to it.

(2) A response under paragraph (1) above must be delivered to the Secretary of the Tribunal not later than 15 working days from the date on which the parent receives a copy of the authority's written reply from the Secretary of the Tribunal.

(3) Subject to paragraph (5) below a response under paragraph (1) shall include all written evidence which the parent wishes to submit to the tribunal (unless such evidence was delivered with the notice of appeal);

(4) The parent may in exceptional cases (in addition to delivering a response under paragraph (1) above) –

> (a) with the permission of the President, at any time before the hearing; or
> (b) with the permission of the tribunal at the hearing itself

– amend the notice of appeal or any response, deliver a supplementary statement of grounds of appeal or amend a supplementary statement of grounds of appeal.

(5) The parent may in exceptional cases –

> (a) with the permission of the President at any time within 15 working days from the date on which a response under paragraph (2) above could have been delivered, or
> (b) with the permission of the tribunal at the hearing itself

– deliver written evidence (if he has not previously done so) or further written evidence.

(6) The parent shall deliver a copy of every amendment and supplementary statement made under paragraph (4)(a) above and any written evidence delivered under paragraph (5)(a) above to the Secretary of the Tribunal.

Withdrawal of appeal

9. The parent may –

> (a) at any time before the hearing of the appeal withdraw his appeal by sending to the Secretary of the Tribunal a notice signed by him stating that he withdraws his appeal;
> (b) at the hearing of the appeal, withdraw his appeal.

Further action by parent

10. (1) The parent shall supply the Secretary of the Tribunal with the

information requested in the enquiry made under regulation 17.

(2) If the parent does not intend to attend or be represented at the hearing, he may, not less that 5 working days before the hearing, send to the Secretary of the Tribunal additional written representation in support of his appeal.

Representatives of the parent: further provisions

11. (1) Where a parent has not stated the name of a representative in the notice of appeal pursuant to regulation 7(1)(c) he may at any time before the hearing notify the Secretary of the Tribunal in writing of the name, address and profession of a representative to whom the tribunal should (subject to any notice under regulation 42(2)(a)) send any subsequent documents or notices concerning the appeal instead of to the parent;

(2) Where a parent has stated the name of a representative, whether in the notice of appeal pursuant to regulation 7(1)(c) or pursuant to paragraph (1) above, he may at any time notify the Secretary of the Tribunal in writing –

(a) of the name, address and profession of a new representative of the parent to whom the tribunal should send documents or notices concerning the appeal instead of to the representative previously notified; or

(b) that no person is acting as a representative of the parent and accordingly any subsequent documents or notices concerning the appeal should be sent to the parent himself.

(3) If the person named by the parent as a representative under regulation 7(I)(c) or paragraphs (1) or (2)(a) above notifies the Secretary of the Tribunal in writing that he is not prepared, or is no longer prepared, to act in that capacity –

(a) the Secretary of the Tribunal shall notify the parent, and

(b) any subsequent documents or notices concerning the appeal shall be sent to the parent himself.

(4) At a hearing, the parent may conduct his case himself (with assistance from one person if he wishes) or may appear and be represented by one person whether or not legally qualified:

Provided that, if the President gives permission before the hearing or the tribunal gives permission at the hearing, the parent may obtain assistance or be represented by more than one person.

(B) THE REPLY BY THE AUTHORITY

Action by the authority on receipt of a notice of appeal

12. (1) An authority which receives a copy of a notice of appeal shall deliver to the Secretary of the Tribunal a written reply acknowledging service upon it of the notice of appeal and stating –

    (a) whether or not the authority intends to oppose the appeal and, if it does intend to oppose the appeal, the grounds on which it relies; and

    (b) the name and profession of the representative of the authority and the address for service of the authority for the purposes of the appeal.

(2) The authority's reply shall include –

    (a) a statement summarising the facts relating to the disputed decision;

    (b) if they are not part of the decision, the reasons for the disputed decision; and

    (c) subject to regulation 13(3) all written evidence which the authority wishes to submit to the tribunal.

(3) Every such reply shall be signed by an officer of the authority who is authorised to sign such documents and shall be delivered to the Secretary of the Tribunal not later than 20 working days after the date on which the copy of the notice of appeal was received by the authority from the Secretary of the Tribunal.

Amendment of reply by the authority

13. (1) The authority, if it has delivered a reply pursuant to regulation 12, may, in exceptional cases –

    (a) with the permission of the President at any time before the hearing; or

    (b) with the permission of the tribunal at the hearing itself amend its reply,

– deliver a supplementary reply or amend a supplementary reply.

(2) The President or, as the case may be, the tribunal may give permission under paragraph (1) above on such terms as he or it thinks fit including the payment of costs or expenses.

(3) The authority may, in exceptional cases–

    (a) with the permission of the President at any time within 15 working days from the date on which the parent could have delivered a response under regulation 8(1); or

(b) with the permission of the tribunal at the hearing itself

– deliver written evidence (if it has not previously done so) or further written evidence.

(4) The authority shall send a copy of every amendment and supplementary statement made before the hearing to the Secretary of the Tribunal.

Failure to reply and absence of opposition

14. If no reply is received by the Secretary of the Tribunal within the time appointed by regulation 12(3) or if the authority states in writing that it does not resist the appeal, or withdraws its opposition to the appeal, the tribunal shall –

(a) determine the appeal on the basis of the notice of appeal without a hearing; or
(b) without notifying the authority hold a hearing at which the authority is not represented.

Representation at hearing and further action by the authority

15. (1) At a hearing or part of a hearing the authority maybe represented by one person whether or not legally qualified:

Provided that if the President gives permission before the hearing or the tribunal gives permission at the hearing the authority may be represented by more than one person.

(2) The authority shall supply the Secretary of the Tribunal with the information requested in the enquiry made under Regulation 17.

(3) If the authority does not intend to attend or be represented at the hearing it may, not less than 5 working days before the hearing, send to the Secretary of the Tribunal additional written representations in support of its reply.

PART 3

PREPARATION FOR A HEARING

Acknowledgement of appeal and service of documents by the Secretary of the Tribunal

16. (1) Upon receiving a notice of appeal the Secretary of the Tribunal shall –

    (a) enter particulars of it in the records;

    (b) send to the parent –

    (i) an acknowledgement of its receipt and a note of the case number entered in the records;

    (ii) a note of the address to which notices and communications to the Special Educational Needs Tribunal or to the Secretary of the Tribunal should be sent; and

    (iii) notification that advice about the appeal procedure may be obtained from the office of the Special Educational Needs Tribunal;

    (c) subject to paragraph (6) below, send to the authority –

    (i) a copy of the notice of appeal and any accompanying papers;

    (ii) a note of the address to which notices and communications to the Special Educational Needs Tribunal or to the Secretary of the Tribunal should be sent, and

    (iii) a notice stating the time for replying and the consequences of failure to do so.

(2) Where the Secretary of the Tribunal is of the opinion that, on the basis of the notice of appeal, the parent is asking the Special Educational Needs Tribunal to do something which it cannot, he may give notice to that effect to the parent stating the reasons for his opinion and informing him that the notice of appeal will not be entered in the records unless the parent notifies the Secretary of the Tribunal that he wishes to proceed with it.

(3) Where the Secretary of the Tribunal is of the opinion that there is an obvious error in the notice of appeal –

    (a) he may correct that error and if he does so shall notify the parent accordingly and such notification shall state the effect of sub-paragraph (b) below; and

    (b) unless within 5 working days the parent notifies the Secretary of the Tribunal that he objects to the correction, the notice of appeal as so corrected shall be treated as the notice of appeal for the purposes of these Regulations.

(4) An appeal, as respects which a notice has been given under paragraph (2) above, shall only be treated as having been received for the purposes of paragraph (1) when the parent notifies the Secretary of the Tribunal that he wishes to proceed with it.

(5) Subject to paragraph (6) below, the Secretary of the Tribunal shall forthwith send a copy of a reply by the authority under regulation 12 and of a response under regulation 8 together with any amendments or supplementary statements, written representations, written evidence or other documents received from a party, to the other party to the proceedings.

(6) If a notice of appeal, reply by the authority under regulation 12 or response by the parent under regulation 8 is delivered to the Secretary of the Tribunal after the time prescribed by these Regulations, the Secretary of the Tribunal shall defer the sending of the copies referred to in paragraph (1)(c) or (5) above pending a decision by the President as to an extension of the time limit pursuant to regulation 41.

Enquiries by the Secretary of the Tribunal

17. The Secretary of the Tribunal shall, at any time after he has received the notice of appeal –

  (a) enquire of each party –

  (i)   whether or not the party intends to attend the hearing;
  (ii) whether the party wishes to be represented at the hearing in accordance with regulation 11(4) or 15(1) and if so the name of the representative;
  (iii) whether the party wishes the hearing to be in public;
  (iv) whether the party intends to call witnesses and if so the names of the proposed witnesses; and
  (v)   whether the party or a witness will require the assistance of an interpreter; and

  (b) enquire of the parent whether he wishes any persons (other than a person who will represent him or any witness which he proposes to call) to attend the hearing if the hearing is to be in private and if so the names of such persons.

Directions in preparation for a hearing

18. (1) The President may at any time before the hearing give such directions (including the issue of a witness summons) as are provided in this Part of these Regulations to enable the parties to prepare for the hearing or to assist the tribunal to determine the issues.

(2) Directions given pursuant to regulations 20 and 21 may be given on the application of a party or of the President's own motion.

(3) A witness summons issued pursuant to regulation 22 may only be issued on the application of a party.

(4) An application by a party for directions shall be made in writing to the Secretary of the Tribunal and, unless it is accompanied by the written consent of the other party, shall be served by the Secretary of the Tribunal on that other party. If the other party objects to the directions sought, the President shall consider the objection and, if he considers it necessary for the determination of the application, shall give the parties an opportunity of appearing before him.

(5) Directions containing a requirement under this Part of these Regulations shall, as appropriate –

(a) include a statement of the possible consequences for the appeal, as provided by regulation 23, of a party's failure to comply with the requirement within the time allowed by the President; and

(b) contain a reference to the fact that, under section 180(5) of the 1996 Act, any person who without reasonable excuse fails to comply with requirements regarding discovery or inspection of documents, or regarding attendance to give evidence and produce documents, shall be liable on summary conviction to a fine not exceeding level 3 on the standard scale and shall, unless the person to whom the direction is addressed had an opportunity of objecting to the direction, contain a statement to the effect that that person may apply to the President under regulation 19 to vary or set aside the direction.

Varying or setting aside of directions

19. Where a person to whom a direction (including any summons) given under this Part of these Regulations is addressed had no opportunity to object to the giving of such direction, he may apply to the President, by notice to the Secretary of the Tribunal, to vary it or set it aside, but the President shall not so do without first notifying the person who applied for the direction and considering any representations made by him.

Particulars and supplementary statements

20. The President may give directions requiring any party to provide such particulars or supplementary statements as may be reasonably required for the determination of the appeal.

Disclosure of documents and other material

21. (1) The President may give directions requiring a party to deliver to the tribunal any document or other material which the tribunal may require and which it is in the power of that party to deliver. The President shall make such provision as he thinks necessary to supply copies of any document obtained under this paragraph to the other party to the

proceedings, and it shall be a condition of such supply that that party shall use such a document only for the purposes of the appeal.

(2) The President may grant to a party such discovery or inspection of documents (including the taking of copies) as might be granted by a county court.

Summoning of witnesses

22. The President may by summons require any person in England and Wales to attend as a witness at a hearing of an appeal at such time and place as may be specified in the summons and at the hearing to answer any questions or produce any documents or other material in his custody or under his control which relate to any matter in question in the appeal:

Provided that –

    (a) No person shall be compelled to give any evidence or produce any document or other material that he could not be compelled to give or produce at a trial of an action in a court of law;

    (b) In exercising the powers conferred by this regulation, the president shall take into account the need to protect any matter that relates to intimate personal or financial circumstances or consists of information communicated or obtained in confidence;

    (c) no person shall be required to attend in obedience to such a summons unless he has been given at least 5 working days' notice of the hearing or, if less than 5 working days, he has informed the President that he accepts such notice as he has been given; and

    (d) no person shall be required in obedience to such a summons to attend and give evidence or to produce any document unless the necessary expenses of his attendance are paid or tendered to him.

Failure to comply with directions

23. (1) If a party has not complied with a direction to it under this Part of these Regulations within the time specified in the direction the tribunal may –

    (a) where the party in default is the parent, dismiss the appeal without a hearing;

    (b) where the party in default is the authority, determine the appeal without a hearing; or

    (c) hold a hearing (without notifying the party in default) at which the party in default is not represented or, where the parties have been notified of the hearing under regulation 24, direct that neither the party in default nor any person whom he intends should represent him be entitled to attend the hearing.

(2) In this regulation "the party in default" means the party which has

307

failed to comply with the direction.

Notice of place and time of hearing and adjournments

24. (1) subject to the provisions of regulation 25, the Secretary of the Tribunal shall, after consultation with the parties, fix the time and place of the hearing and, send to each party a notice that the hearing is to be at such time and place.

(2) The notice referred to in paragraph (1) above shall be sent –

    (a) not less than 5 working days before the date fixed for the hearing where the hearing is held under regulation 14, 31 or 36;

    (b) not less than 10 working days before the date fixed for the hearing in any other case

    or within such shorter period before the date fixed for the hearing as the parties may agree.

(3) The Secretary of the Tribunal shall include in or with the notice of hearing

    (a) information and guidance, in a form approved by the President, as to attendance at the hearing of the parties and witnesses, the bringing of documents, and the right of representation or assistance as provided by regulation 11(4) or 15(1); and

    (b) a statement explaining the possible consequences of non-attendance and of the right of –

    (i) a parent; and

    (ii) the authority, if it has presented a reply, who does not attend and is not represented, to make representations in writing.

(4) The tribunal may alter the time and place of any hearing and the Secretary of the Tribunal shall give the parties not less than 5 working days (or such shorter time as the parties agree) notice of the altered hearing date:

Provided that any altered hearing date shall not (unless the parties agree) be before the date notified under paragraph (1).

(5) The tribunal may from time to time adjourn the hearing and, if the time and place of the adjourned hearing are announced before the adjournment, no further notice shall be required.

(6) Nothing in paragraph (1) or (4) above shall oblige the Secretary of the Tribunal to consult, or send a notice to any party who by virtue of any provision of these Regulations is not entitled to be represented at the hearing.

(7) In this regulation "working day" means any day other than a Saturday,

a Sunday, Christmas Day, Good Friday or a day which is a bank holiday within the meaning of the Banking and Financial Dealings Act 1971(a).

PART 4

DETERMINATION OF APPEALS

Power to determine an appeal without a hearing

25. (1) The tribunal may –

(a) if the parties so agree in writing; or
(b) in the circumstances described in regulations 14 and 23;

– determine an appeal or any particular issue without a hearing.

(2) The provisions of regulation 27(2) shall apply in respect of the determination of an appeal, or any particular issue, under this regulation.

Hearings to be in private: exceptions

26. (1) A hearing by the tribunal shall be in private unless –

(a) both the parent and the authority request that the hearing be in public; or
(b) the President, at any time before the hearing, or the tribunal at the hearing, orders that the hearing should be in public.

(2) The following persons (as well as the parties and their representatives and witnesses) shall be entitled to attend the hearing of an appeal, even though it is in private –

(a) subject to the provisions of paragraph (8) below, any person named by the parent in response to the enquiry under regulation 17(b) unless the President has determined that any such person should not be entitled to attend the hearing and notified the parent accordingly;
(b) a parent of the child who is not a party to the appeal;
(c) the clerk to the tribunal and the Secretary of the Tribunal;
(d) the President and any member of the chairmen's or lay panel (when not sitting as members of the tribunal);
(e) a member of the Council on Tribunals;
(f) any person undergoing training as a member of the chairmen's or lay panel or as a clerk to the tribunal;
(g) any person acting on behalf of the President in the training or supervision of clerks to tribunals;
(h) an interpreter.

(a) 1971 c.80.

(3) The tribunal, with the consent of the parties or their representatives actually present, may permit any other person to attend the hearing of an appeal which is held in private.

(4) Without prejudice to any other powers it may have, the tribunal may exclude from the hearing, or part of it, any person whose conduct has disrupted or is likely, in the opinion of the tribunal, to disrupt the hearing.

(5) For the purposes of arriving at its decision a tribunal shall, and for the purposes of discussing any question of procedure may, notwithstanding anything contained in these Regulations, order all persons to withdraw from the sitting of the tribunal other than the members of the tribunal or any of the persons mentioned in paragraph (2)(c) to (f) above.

(6) Except as provided in paragraph (7) below none of the persons mentioned in paragraph (2) or (3) above shall, save in the case of the clerk to the tribunal or an interpreter as their respective duties require, take any part in the hearing or (where entitled or permitted to remain) in the deliberations of the tribunal.

(7) The tribunal may permit a parent of the child who is not a party to the appeal to address the tribunal on the subject matter of the appeal.

(8) Where the parent has named more than two persons in response to the enquiry under regulation 17(b) only two persons shall be entitled to attend the hearing unless the President has given permission before the hearing or the tribunal gives permission at the hearing for a greater number to attend.

Failure of parties to attend hearing

27. (1) If a party fails to attend or be represented at a hearing of which he has been duly notified, the tribunal may –

   (a) unless it is satisfied that there is sufficient reason for such absence, hear and determine the appeal in the party's absence; or
   (b) adjourn the hearing.

(2) Before disposing of an appeal in the absence of a party, the tribunal shall consider any representations in writing submitted by that party in response to the notice of hearing and, for the purpose of this regulation the notice of appeal, any reply by the authority under regulations 12 or 13 and any response by the parent under regulation 8 shall be treated as representations in writing.

Procedure at hearing

28. (1) At the beginning of the hearing the chairman shall explain the order of proceeding which the tribunal proposes to adopt.

(2) The tribunal shall conduct the hearing in such manner as it considers

most suitable to the clarification of the issues and generally to the just handling of the proceedings; it shall, so far as appears to it appropriate, seek to avoid formality in its proceedings.

(3) The tribunal shall determine the order in which the parties are heard and the issues determined.

(4) The tribunal may, if it is satisfied that it is just and reasonable to do so, permit a party to rely on grounds not stated in his notice of appeal or, as the case may be, his reply or response and to adduce any evidence not presented to the authority before or at the time it took the disputed decision.

(5) If at or after the commencement of any hearing a member of the tribunal other than the chairman is absent, the hearing may, with the consent of the parties, be conducted by the other two members and in that event the tribunal shall be deemed to be properly constituted and the decision of the tribunal shall be taken by those two members.

Evidence at hearing

29. (1) In the course of the hearing the parties shall be entitled to give evidence, to call witnesses, to question any witnesses and to address the tribunal both on the evidence and generally on the subject matter of the appeal:

Provided that neither party shall be entitled to call more than two witnesses to give evidence orally (in addition to any witnesses whose attendance is required pursuant to paragraph (2) below) unless the President has given permission before the hearing or the tribunal gives permission at the hearing.

(2) Evidence before the tribunal may be given orally or by written statement, but the tribunal may at any stage of the proceedings require the personal attendance of any maker of any written statement:

Provided that neither party shall be entitled to give evidence by written statement if such evidence was not submitted with the notice of appeal or submitted in accordance with regulation 8 or (as appropriate) regulations 12 or 13.

(3) The tribunal may receive evidence of any fact which appears to the tribunal to be relevant.

(4) The tribunal may require any witness to give evidence on oath or affirmation, and for that purpose there may be administered an oath or affirmation in due form, or may require any evidence given by written statement to be given by affidavit.

Decision of the tribunal

30. (1) A decision of the tribunal may be taken by a majority and where the tribunal is constituted by two members only under regulation 28(5) the chairman shall have a second or casting vote.

(2) The decision of the tribunal may be given orally at the end of the hearing or reserved and, in any event, whether there has been a hearing or not, shall be recorded forthwith in a document which, save in the case of a decision by consent, shall also contain, or have annexed to it, a statement of the reasons (in summary form) for the tribunal's decision, and each such document shall be signed and dated by the chairman.

(3) Neither a decision given orally nor the document referred to in paragraph (2) above shall contain any reference to the decision being by majority (if that be the case) or to any opinion of a minority.

(4) Every decision of the tribunal shall be entered in the records.

(5) As soon as may be the Secretary of the Tribunal shall send a copy of the document referred to in paragraph (2) above to each party, accompanied by guidance, in a form approved by the President, about the circumstances in which there is a right to appeal against a tribunal decision and the procedure to be followed.

(6) Where, under regulations 7(1)(c), or 11(1) or (2)(a) a parent has stated the name of a representative the Secretary of the Tribunal shall (notwithstanding regulation 42) send a copy of the documents referred to in paragraph (5) above to the parent as well as to the representative.

(7) Every decision shall be treated as having been made on the date on which a copy of the document recording it is sent to the parent (whether or not the decision has been previously announced at the end of the hearing).

Review of the tribunal's decision

31. (1) Any party may apply to the Secretary to the Tribunal for the decision of the Tribunal to be reviewed on the grounds that –

(a) its decision was wrongly made as a result of an error on the part of the tribunal staff;
(b) a party, who was entitled to be heard at a hearing but failed to appear or to be represented, had good and sufficient reason for failing to appear;
(c) there was an obvious error in the decision of the tribunal which decided the case; or
(d) the interests of justice require.

(2) An application for the purposes of paragraph (1) above shall be made not later than 10 working days after the date on which the decision was sent to the parties and shall be in writing stating the grounds in full.

(3) An application for the purposes of paragraph (1) above maybe refused by the President, or by the chairman of the tribunal which decided the case, if in his opinion it has no reasonable prospect of success, but if such an application is not refused –

(a) the parties shall have an opportunity to be heard on the application for review; and

(b) the review shall be determined by the tribunal which decided the case or, where it is not practicable for it to be heard by that tribunal, by a tribunal appointed by the President.

(4) The tribunal may of its own motion review its decision on any of the grounds referred to in sub-paragraphs (a) to (d) of paragraph (1) above, and if it proposes to do so –

(a) it shall serve notice on the parties not later than ten working days after the date on which the decision was sent to the parties; and

(b) the parties shall have an opportunity to be heard on the proposal for review.

(5) If, on the application of a party under paragraphs (1) to (3) above or of its own motion under paragraph (4) above the tribunal is satisfied as to any of the grounds referred to in sub-paragraphs (a) to (d) of paragraph (1) above, the tribunal may review and, by certificate under the chairman's hand, set aside or vary the relevant decision.

(6) If, having reviewed the decision, the decision is set aside, the tribunal shall substitute such decision as it thinks fit or order a rehearing before either the same or a differently constituted tribunal.

(7) If any decision is set aside or varied under this regulation or altered in any way by order of a superior court, the Secretary of the Tribunal shall alter the entry in the records to conform with the chairman's certificate or order of a superior court and shall notify the parties accordingly.

Review of the President's decision

32. (1) If, on the application of a party to the Secretary of the Tribunal or of his own motion the President is satisfied that –

(a) a decision by him was wrongly made as a result of an error on the part of the tribunal staff; or

(b) there was an obvious error in his decision; or

(c) the interests of justice require,

– the President may review and set aside or vary the relevant decision of his.

(2) An application for the purposes of paragraph (1) shall be made not

later than 10 working days after the date on which the party making the application was notified of the decision and shall be in writing stating the grounds in full. Where the President proposes to review his decision of his own motion he shall serve notice of that proposal on the parties within the same period.

(3) The parties shall have an opportunity to be heard on any application or proposal for review under this regulation and the review shall be determined by the President.

(4) If any decision is set aside or varied under this regulation the Secretary of the Tribunal shall alter the entry in the records and shall notify the parties accordingly.

Orders for costs and expenses

33. (1) The tribunal shall not normally make an order in respect of costs and expenses, but may, subject to paragraph (2) below, make such an order –

    (a) against a party (including any party who has withdrawn his appeal or reply) if it is of the opinion that that party has acted frivolously or vexatiously or that his conduct in making, pursuing or resisting an appeal was wholly unreasonable.

    (b) against a party which has failed to attend or be represented at a hearing of which he has been duly notified;

    (c) against an authority which has not delivered a written reply under regulation 12; or

    (d) against the authority, where it considers that the disputed decision was wholly unreasonable.

(2) Any order in respect of costs and expenses may be made –

    (a) as respects any costs or expenses incurred, or any allowances paid; or

    (b) as respects the whole, or any part, of any allowance (other than allowances paid to members of tribunals) paid by the Secretary of State under section 180(3) of the 1993 Act to any person for the purposes of, or in connection with, his attendance at the tribunal.

(3) No order shall be made under paragraph (1) above against a party without first giving that party an opportunity of making representations against the making of the order.

(4) An order under paragraph (1) above may require the party against whom it is made to pay the other party either a specified sum in respect of the costs and expenses incurred by that other party in connection with the proceedings or the whole or part of such costs as taxed (if not otherwise agreed).

(5) Any costs required by an order under this regulation to be taxed may be taxed in the county court according to such of the scales prescribed by the county court rules for proceedings in the county court as shall be directed in the order.

PART 5

ADDITIONAL POWERS OF AND PROVISIONS RELATING TO THE TRIBUNAL

Transfer of proceedings

34. Where it appears to the President that an appeal pending before a tribunal could be determined more conveniently in another tribunal he may at any time, upon the application of a party or of his own motion, direct that the said proceedings be transferred so as to be determined in that other tribunal:

Provided that no such direction shall be given unless notice has been sent to all parties concerned giving them an opportunity to show cause why such a direction should not be given.

Miscellaneous powers of the tribunal

35. (1) Subject to the provisions of the 1993 Act and these Regulations, a tribunal may regulate its own procedure.

(2) A tribunal may, if it thinks fit, if both parties agree in writing upon the terms of a decision to be made by the tribunal, decide accordingly.

Power to strike out

36. (1) The Secretary of the Tribunal shall, at any stage of the proceedings if the authority applies or the President so directs, serve a notice on the parent stating that it appears that the appeal should be struck out on one or both of the grounds specified in paragraph (2) below or for want of prosecution.

(2) The grounds referred to in paragraph (1) above are that –

    (a) the appeal is not, or is no longer, within the jurisdiction of the Special Educational Needs Tribunal;

    (b) the notice of the appeal is, or the appeal is or has become, scandalous, frivolous or vexatious.

(3) The notice under paragraph (1) above shall state that the parent may make representations in accordance with paragraph (8) below.

(4) The tribunal, after considering any representations duly made, may order that the appeal should be struck out on one or both of the grounds

specified in paragraph (2) above or for want of prosecution.

(5) The tribunal may make such an order without holding a hearing unless either party requests the opportunity to make oral representations, and if the tribunal holds a hearing it may be held at the beginning of the hearing of the substantive appeal.

(6) The President may, if he thinks fit, at any stage of the proceedings order that a reply, response or statement should be struck out or amended on the grounds that it is scandalous, frivolous or vexatious.

(7) Before making an order under paragraph (6) above, the President shall give to the party against whom he proposes to make the order a notice inviting representations and shall consider any representations duly made.

(8) For the purposes of this regulation –

- (a) a notice inviting representations must inform the recipient that he may, within a period (not being less than 5 working days) specified in the notice, either make written representations or request an opportunity to make oral representations;
- (b) representations are duly made if –
- (i) in the case of written representations, they are made within the period so specified; and
- (ii) in the case of oral representations the party proposing to make them has requested an opportunity to do so within the period so specified.

Power to exercise powers of President and Chairman

37. (1) An act required or authorised by these Regulations to be done by the President may be done by a member of the chairman's panel authorised by the President.

(2) Where, pursuant to paragraph (1) above, a member of the chairman's panel carries out the function under regulation 5(2) of selecting the chairman of a tribunal, he may select himself.

(3) Where, pursuant to paragraph (1) above a member of the chairman's panel makes a decision, regulation 32 shall apply in relation to that decision taking the reference in that regulation to the President as a reference to the member of the chairman's panel by whom the decision was taken.

(4) Subject to regulation 39(6) in the event of the death or incapacity of the chairman following the decision of the tribunal in any matter, the functions of the chairman for the completion of the proceedings, including any review of the decision, may be exercised by the President or any member of the chairman's panel.

The Secretary of the Tribunal

38. A function of the Secretary of the Tribunal may be performed by another member of the staff of the tribunal authorised for the purpose of carrying out that function by the President.

Irregularities

39. (1) An irregularity resulting from failure to comply with any provisions of these Regulations or of any direction of the tribunal before the tribunal has reached its decision shall not of itself render the proceedings void.

(2) Where any such irregularity comes to the attention of the tribunal, the tribunal may, and shall, if it considers that any person may have been prejudiced by the irregularity, give such directions as it thinks just before reaching its decision to cure or waive the irregularity.

(3) Clerical mistakes in any document recording a decision of the tribunal or a direction or decision of the President produced by or on behalf of the tribunal or errors arising in such documents from accidental slips or omissions may at any time be corrected by the chairman or the President (as the case may be) by certificate under his hand.

(4) The Secretary of the Tribunal shall as soon as may be send a copy of any corrected document containing reasons for the tribunal's decision, to each party.

(5) Where under regulations 7(1)(c) or 11(1) or (2)(a) a parent has stated the name of a representative the Secretary of the Tribunal shall (notwithstanding regulation 42) send a copy of the document referred to in paragraph (4) above to the parent as well as to the representative.

(6) Where by these Regulations a document is required to be signed by the chairman but by reason of death or incapacity the chairman is unable to sign such a document, it shall be signed by the other members of the tribunal, who shall certify that the chairman is unable to sign.

Method of sending, delivering or serving notices and documents

40. (1) A notice given under these Regulations shall be in writing and where under these Regulations provision is made for a party to notify the Secretary of the Tribunal of any matter he shall do so in writing.

(2) All notices and documents required by these Regulations to be sent or delivered to the Secretary of the Tribunal or the tribunal may be sent by post or by facsimile or delivered to or at the office of the Special Educational Needs Tribunal or such other office as may be notified by the Secretary of the Tribunal to the parties.

(3) All notices and documents required or authorised by these Regulations to be sent or given to any person mentioned in sub-paragraph (a) or (b) below may (subject to paragraph (5) below) either be sent by first class post or by facsimile or delivered to or at –

(a) in the case of a notice or document directed to a party –

(i) his address for service specified in the notice of appeal or in a written reply or in a notice under paragraph (4) below, or

(ii) if no address for service has been so specified, his last known address; and

(b) in the case of a notice or document directed to any person other than a party, his address or place of business or if such a person is a corporation, the corporation's registered or principal office and if sent or given to the authorised representative of a party shall be deemed to have been sent or given to that party.

(4) A party may at any time by notice to the Secretary of the Tribunal change his address for service under these Regulations.

(5) The recorded delivery service shall be used instead of the first class post for service of a summons issued under regulation 22 requiring the attendance of a witness.

(6) A notice or document sent by the Secretary of the Tribunal by post in accordance with these Regulations, and not returned, shall be taken to have been delivered to the addressee on the second working day after it was posted.

(7) A notice or document sent by facsimile shall be taken to have been delivered when it is received in legible form.

(8) Where for any sufficient reason service of any document or notice cannot be effected in the manner prescribed under this regulation, the President may dispense with service or make an order for substituted service in such manner as he may deem fit and such service shall have the same effect as service in the manner prescribed under this regulation.

Extensions of time

41. (1) Where, pursuant to any provision of these Regulations anything is required to be done by a party within a period of time the President may, on the application of the party in question or of his own motion, in exceptional circumstances extend any period of time.

(2) Where a period of time has been extended pursuant to paragraph (1) above any reference in these Regulations to that period of time shall be

construed as a reference to the period of time as so extended.

Parent's representative

42. (1) Subject to paragraph (2) below where, pursuant to regulation 7(1)(c) or 11(1) or (2)(a) a parent has stated the name of a representative, any reference in Parts 3, 4 or 5 of these Regulations (however expressed) to sending documents to, or giving notice to, the parent shall be construed as a reference to sending documents to or giving notice to the representative and any such reference to sending documents to or giving notice to a party or the parties shall in the context of the parent be likewise construed as a reference to sending documents to, or giving notice to, the representative.

(2) Paragraph (1) above does not apply if –

    (a) the parent has notified the Secretary of the Tribunal that he does not wish it to apply;

    (b) the parent has notified the Secretary of the Tribunal under regulation 11(2)(b) that no person is acting as a representative; or

    (c) the representative named has notified the Secretary of the Tribunal under regulation 11(3) that he is not prepared or no longer prepared to act in that capacity.

Revocation and transitional provisions

43. (1) The Special Educational Needs Tribunal Regulations 1994**(a)** (in this regulation referred to as "the 1994 Regulations") are hereby revoked.

(2) Notwithstanding paragraph (1) above –

    (a) any notice of appeal received before 1st March 1996 may comply either with regulation 7 of the 1994 Regulations or with regulation 7 of these Regulations; and

    (b) the 1994 Regulations shall continue to apply in relation to any appeal where the notice of appeal was entered in the records under regulation 17(2) of the 1994 Regulations before 1st January 1996.

(a) S.I. 1994/1910

Part 9

Glossary

GLOSSARY

Advice. This is the name given to the reports which professionals write when a child is being assessed for special education provision. The local education authority must get advice, or written reports, from a child's school (the educational advice), an educational psychologist (the psychological advice), a medical officer (the medical advice) and the social services department (social service advice).

When parents receive a copy of a proposed statement of special educational needs, they must also be sent copies of all the advice which the LEA has obtained.

Assessment. An assessment under the 1996 Education Act should take no more than ten weeks. This is what it involves: the local education authority asks for advice (see above) from a number of professionals, as well as a written contribution from the parent. Sometimes a child will be examined by a professional before a report is written. After reading all of the reports, the LEA decides whether or not to write a statement of special education needs. If they decide not to, they must write and tell the parents why not, and must inform them of their right to appeal to the Special Educational Needs Tribunal. If they decide to write a statement, they must send a proposed (or draft) version of the statement to the parents and ask them for their comments. An assessment under the 1996 Education Act is sometimes called a 'formal assessment' or a 'statutory assessment'.

Code of Practice. This is a book published by the Government. It advises schools on the arrangements they must make to provide for children with special educational needs who do not have a statement. The Code also advises local education authorities on how they should fulfil their legal duties towards children with special educational needs. Although the Code is not legally binding on an LEA or school, they must have a good reason to act contrary to its advice. You can get a free copy by ringing 0845-602 2260.

DfEE. The Department for Education and Employment. This is the government department which is responsible for ensuring that local education authorities fulfil their legal duties. If you believe that your LEA is not obeying the law on special education you can make a formal complaint to the DfEE (see Part 6 of the guide).

Individual education plan. This is drawn up when a child is on stage two or three of the school-based stages (see below). The plan is produced by the school's SENCO (see below) and should set out clearly a child's needs, the action to be taken to meet these needs and a date for a review of progress being made.

LEA (Local education authority). This is the part of the local authority which has the legal responsibility to ensure that children with special educational needs receive the provision they need. LEAs are named after the counties or boroughs they serve, e.g. Lancashire Local Education Authority; London Borough of Merton Local Education Authority. If you are not sure of the name of your LEA, ask in your local library.

Maintained schools. These are schools which are paid for out of public money, i.e. community, foundation or voluntary schools (e.g. church schools). Some are special schools, some are ordinary schools.

Named person. LEAs sometimes give parents the name of a person who can advise them on their child's needs. The named person should be independent of the LEA. It is important not to confuse this person with the 'named officer' or special educational needs officer – see below.

Note in lieu. Sometimes LEAs send parents a note in lieu of a statement after an assessment when they decide not to issue a statement. It should describe a child's needs and the provision necessary to meet them. It should also have attached to it all the professional advice collected as part of the assessment. The main difference between a note in lieu and a statement is that the note in lieu is not binding in law. This means that parents do not have a right of appeal against a note in lieu and that LEAs do not have to arrange the provision set out in them.

School-based stages. The Code of Practice advises schools to adopt a system which registers children who have special educational needs, but who do not have a statement, on one of three stages. Children on stage one will be helped by their class teacher. Children on stage two will be helped also by the special educational needs co-ordinator, who will draw up an individual education plan (see above) for them. Children on stage three will also receive support of some kind from an outside specialist. This may be in the form of teaching or therapy from a visiting specialist or advice and support for their teacher.

Secretary of State. The Secretary of State for Education and Employment is the government minister who is responsible for the Department for Education and Employment (see above).

Special educational needs. These are learning difficulties which cause a child to have significantly greater difficulty in learning than other children of the same age, and which call for different or additional provision. A disability which prevents or hinders a child from making use of the facilities generally available in an LEA school is also called a special educational need. If a child under 5 is likely to have a learning difficulty or a disability when they start school, they are also said to have special educational needs.

Special educational needs co-ordinator (SENCO). This is the teacher in a school who has responsibility for co-ordinating special educational provision. In a small school, the headteacher may take on this role.

Special educational needs officer. This is the officer who acts on behalf of the LEA when a child is assessed and when a statement is issued. He or she is sometimes called the 'named officer', which should not be confused with the 'named person' – see above.

Special educational needs register. This is a register kept by individual schools which lists the pupils with special educational needs and records which of the three school-based stages (see above) they are at.

Special Educational Needs Tribunal. This is an independent body set up under the 1996 Education Act to hear parents' appeals against decisions made by LEAs. The Tribunal can summons witnesses and place them on oath. Its decisions are binding. See part 3 of this guide for advice on appealing to the Tribunal.

Special educational provision. This is the provision required by a child who has special educational needs. It is provision which is additional to, or different from, provision which is made generally for children of the same age in the LEA.

Statement of special educational needs. This is a document issued by an LEA following an assessment when the LEA believes that a child needs provision over and above what is available in a school. Part 3 of a statement specifies the special education provisions to be made and an LEA is legally bound to arrange this provision.

Part 10

Index

Note: Page numbers in **bold** refer to the Glossary.

Index

Index

Index